Architecture and the Mimetic Self

Buildings shape our identity and sense of self in profound ways that are not always evident to architects and town planners, or even to those who think they are intimately familiar with the buildings they inhabit. *Architecture and the Mimetic Self* provides a theoretical guide to our unconscious behaviour in relation to buildings, and explains both how and why we are drawn to specific elements and features of architectural design. It reveals how even the most uninspiring of buildings can be modified to meet our unconscious expectations and requirements of them—and, by the same token, it explores the repercussions for our wellbeing when buildings fail to do so.

Criteria for effective architectural design have for a long time been grounded in utilitarian principles of function, efficiency, cost, and visual impact. Although these are important considerations, they often fail to meet the fundamental needs of those who inhabit and use buildings. Misconceptions are rife, not least because our responses to architecture are often difficult to measure, and are in large part unconscious. By bridging psychoanalytic thought and architectural theory, *Architecture and the Mimetic Self* frees the former from its preoccupations with interpersonal human relations to address the vital relationships that we establish with our nonhuman environments.

In addition to providing a guide to the unconscious behaviours that are most relevant for evaluating architectural design, this book explains how our relationships with the built environment inform a more expansive and useful psychoanalytic theory of human relationship and identity. It will appeal to psychoanalysts and analytical psychologists, architects, and all who are interested in the overlaps of psychology, architecture, and the built environment.

Lucy Huskinson, PhD, is Senior Lecturer in the School of History, Philosophy, and Social Science at Bangor University, UK. She is author and editor of various books and articles on philosophy, psychoanalysis, and the built environment. She is also co Editor-in-Chief of the *International Journal of Jungian Studies*. Her previous books include *The Urban Uncanny: A Collection of Interdisciplinary Studies* (Routledge).

"In the architectural theorizing of the past decades the psychoanalytic approach has not been very popular. Architectural writings have predominantly dealt with physical forms, focused vision and conscious perceptions and intentionality, instead of the pre-reflective ground of experience and consciousness. Now that the understanding of architecture as a mental and experiential reality rather than aestheticized objects is gaining strength, Lucy Huskinson's book brings the essential interactions of the self and the setting into the discussion. We are simply not mere observers of architecture, as our very sense of self is molded by our own constructions. Architecture creates the pre-reflective horizons for the experience and understanding of our being in the flesh of the world, to use the beautiful notion of Maurice Merleau-Ponty. This book is a thorough and perceptive survey of the role of the unconsciousness in our interactions with space, place and domicile."

–Juhani Pallasmaa, Architect SAFA, HonFAIA, IntFRIBA, Professor Emeritus at Aalto University, Finland, International Academy of Architecture; and author of several works on architectural theory, including *The Eyes of the Skin: Architecture and the Senses* (John Wiley & Sons, 1996)

"The intimate relationship between building and self is captured by the single word 'world' (old German 'wer') which means 'man'. Etymology can provide, however, only an insight. Its detailed unfolding calls for a scholar of philosophical perspicacity and psychoanalytic skill, a rare combination of virtues that very few have. Dr. Lucy Huskinson is one of the very few. For evidence, read *Architecture and the Mimetic Self*."

–Yi-Fu Tuan, J. K. Wright Emeritus Professor of Geography and the Vilas Professor Emeritus of Geography at the University of Wisconsin–Madison, USA; acclaimed author; and winner of the Vautrin-Lud International Geography Prize

"Much contemporary architecture is efficient, clean cut and clever but lacks responsiveness to real human needs, with consequences for our wellbeing. Lucy Huskinson in *Architecture and the Mimetic Self* encourages us to look at these needs, further for authentic sources of enrichment, renewal and integration.

In what she calls an Architectural blueprint of being, we become our buildings and they become us in a creative reciprocity balancing surety of containment with freedom to explore the uncertainties of ourselves and our environment. She suggests a place in this Architectural event for a loosening: a playfulness, ambiguity and surprise that can engage support and revivify us, setting in motion a new self-awareness to find the means to keep on recreating ourselves.

This is a scholarly and timely contribution to the understanding and possibilities of a more fully human architecture."

–Gregory Burgess (AM), award winning architect; recipient of the Sir Zelman Cowen Award for Public Buildings, the Victorian Architecture Medal for the best building of the year, the Australian Institute of Architects Gold Medal, the Robert Mathew Award for the development of architecture in the Commonwealth, and twice awarded the Kenneth F Brown Asia Pacific Culture and Architectural Design Award. He was appointed a Member of the Order of Australia (AM) in the Queen's Birthday 2011 Honours List, for service to architecture in the area of environmentally sensitive building design and community

"Arguably architecture has become increasingly commodified, drained as it is of any psychological intent and associated meaning. In *Architecture and the Mimetic Self* Lucy Huskinson addresses this issue comprehensively, by drawing on an extensive command of psychoanalytical theory, and applying it to our innate and personal experiences of the ways in which buildings affect us."

–Flora Samuel, Professor of Architecture in the Built Environment, University of Reading, UK

Architecture and the Mimetic Self

A Psychoanalytic Study of How Buildings Make and Break Our Lives

Lucy Huskinson

LONDON AND NEW YORK

First published 2018
by Routledge
2 Park Square, Milton Park, Abingdon, Oxon OX14 4RN

and by Routledge
711 Third Avenue, New York, NY 10017

Routledge is an imprint of the Taylor & Francis Group, an informa business

British Library Cataloguing in Publication Data
A catalogue record for this book is available from the British Library

Library of Congress Cataloging in Publication Data
Names: Huskinson, Lucy, 1976– author.
Title: Architecture and the mimetic self / Lucy Huskinson.
Description: New York : Routledge, 2018. | Includes bibliographical references.
Identifiers: LCCN 2017045716 (print) | LCCN 2017046372 (ebook) |
ISBN 9781351247320 (Master e-book) | ISBN 9780415693035 (hardback) |
ISBN 9780415693042 (pbk.)
Subjects: LCSH: Architecture–Psychological aspects.
Classification: LCC NA2540 (ebook) | LCC NA2540 .H87 2018 (print) |
DDC 720.1/9–dc23 LC record available at https://lccn.loc.gov/2017045716

ISBN: 978-0-415-69303-5 (hbk)
ISBN: 978-0-415-69304-2 (pbk)
ISBN: 978-1-351-24732-0 (ebk)

Typeset in Times New Roman
by Out of House Publishing

For Number 20, CB1 2HN

Contents

Acknowledgements

The contents of this book were conceived over a decade of research and have been inspired by many conversations, presentations, and discussions with a wide range of people and audiences. To that end, there are a great many people that I wish to thank who have contributed in one way or another to the shaping of my ideas.

In particular, I thank Martin Gledhill, Leslie Gardner, and Joseph Laredo; those who have contributed images for the book; and Susannah Frearson and Elliott Morsia at Routledge for their friendly advice and proficiency. I also thank the Opus Archives and Research Center in California for the grant support that allowed me to pursue my various ideas in relation to James Hillman's interpretation of the built environment.

Most importantly, I wish to give especial thanks to Eleanor Huskinson-Smith and David Sullivan, and to Arthur David Smith (in memoriam). This book is dedicated to them, and to the house at 20 Lyndewode Road, where I lived from the age of one until I left to go to university. Although I no longer live there, its every nook and cranny continue to live in me.

List of figures

Plates

Chapter 1

Introduction

Buildings design us as much as we them

This book argues that the more we understand the hidden motivations that underpin human behaviour, the better equipped we will be in designing buildings that satisfy our basic, existential, needs. The criteria for effective architectural design have for a long time been grounded in utilitarian principles of function, efficiency, cost, and visual impact. Although these are important considerations, they often fail to meet the fundamental needs of those who inhabit and use buildings. There is often a mismatch between the values endorsed by the architect and town planner, and the existential needs of the person who uses their designs. In this book I intend to establish how we engage with architecture on a day-to-day basis in ways that are not so obvious to those who design our built environments, and not always so evident, even, to their inhabitants and to those who believe they have mastered their neighbourhoods and familiarised themselves with all that the buildings of their home and workplace have to offer. I am concerned with the manner in which we identify with architecture and use its features unconsciously, and how this has fundamental repercussions for our wellbeing. A central thesis of this book is that buildings design us as much as we them, and our appreciation of architectural design is rooted in a fundamental need to establish an identity or sense of self that is coherent and abiding. In other words, I shall go to explain how we are attracted to the structural forms of architecture, and seek somehow to *mimic* their character, in order to acquire from them essential qualities and experiences that we desire for ourselves. We shall see that the characteristics of architecture can therefore impact on our wellbeing to positive or negative ends.

Architects and town planners are pressured by having to balance the changing demands of those who use and interact with their designs with constraints such as budgets, building codes and regulations, and the dictates of geography and engineering, to name just a few. If we consider as well the fact that buildings outlive the architectural styles and aesthetics of passing trends, we find that architecture is in a precarious position, one that inevitably disappoints, for its ambition is met with ever present pressures to compromise. There is a necessity, therefore, for architects to become acquainted with the fundamental needs of human beings, and to understand the innate desires that inform and shape our relationships with the built environment; in other words, to appreciate what our expectations and requirements of buildings are, how they impact on our sense of self and our general well-being, and, moreover, how architectural designs can be modified to meet these needs.

There is extensive scholarship on the relationship of human behaviour to architecture and urban planning, but most of it bypasses the important connection between architectural design and the construction of personal identity. One likely reason for this is the lack of clarity on what personal identity actually involves. What exactly constitutes the self, one's state of mind, and existential wellbeing is open to debate. With almost as many definitions and theories as there are philosophers, psychologists, and scientists to argue for them, how is the architect to choose between them? What are the salient features of this vital and complex phenomenon that will help the architect to design and construct buildings that are satisfying to those who will come to use them? This book addresses key aspects of the formation and construction of personal identity in relationship to the built environment, and provides a framework for considering our need of specific architectural design features and our expectations of them.

Disagreements likewise prevail over what constitutes successful architecture. These are perhaps most viscerally felt between architectural practitioners—the supposed experts—and public opinion. In recent decades it is not uncommon, for instance, for designs to win prestigious awards for architectural excellence while at the same time featuring on popular 'name-and-shame' lists of the 'ugliest' buildings. A case in point is Strata SE1, or the 'Electric Razor' or 'Knuckleduster', as it is commonly known (Fig. 1.1): a forty-three-storey residential high-rise building in Southwark, London (built 2007–2010; BFLS Architects).

'Successful architecture' is arguably something of a misnomer. Popular opinion of successful architecture is often skewed by the emphasis given to visual aesthetics, and, for the many who aren't regular users of a building, it is often only the aesthetics of the façade that is taken into account. Nevertheless, as I shall argue, measures can be taken to achieve the idealistic goal of 'successful' designs if architects and planners stay clear of common misperceptions about what it is that we seek in architecture and expect to find in it, and conversely, what we seek to avoid and find problematic about it.

Broadly conceived, problematic designs can be construed as failures to arrive at an appropriate compromise between utility on the one hand and artistic vision on the other. Architecture that accommodates the former at the expense of the latter is designed and constructed to maximise functionality and efficiency, often seeking maximum floor space with minimum cost, and often designed according to a generic template with minimal embellishments and ornamentation (see Fig. 1.2). But buildings designed to such

Figure 1.1 Strata SE1, Southwark, London (BFLS Architects, 2010)
Strata SE1 has won several awards, a number of which recognise its sustainability and efficiency, due in part to its onsite wind turbines and combined heat and power system.[1] Less appreciative, however, are the general public, who expressed their contempt for the building by nominating it for the Carbuncle Cup, an award given annually by *Building Design* magazine to the 'worst new building in the UK in the previous 12 months'—an award it went on to win in 2010 'for services to greenwash, urban impropriety and sheer breakfast-extracting ugliness'. *The Telegraph* newspaper ranks it number seven of the '30 ugliest buildings in the World'. Rival newspaper *The Guardian* ranks it number three of the '10 worst London skyscrapers', comparing it to Tolkein's fictional Dark Tower of Mordor (2014).[2]

utilitarian specifications often come at great existential cost to those who use them. Utilitarian principles alone cannot accommodate the complexities of our instinctual needs; they lead instead to sterile buildings that treat people as if they are predictable and machine-like, and reducible to the same rational precepts that inform their designs. Buildings of this nature tend to feel oppressive and alienating because they fail to accommodate our contrasting, non-rational nature—a nature expressed by artistic vision.

An architecture that promotes artistic vision at the expense of its utility is equally problematic. This can lead to an idiosyncratic or 'quirky' architecture that aims to make a provocative statement by circumventing our expectations of the built environment, and subverting the utilitarian principles upon which conventional architecture relies. Its distorted references to historical

Figure 1.2 Examples of sterile architecture: Manchester, UK
Examples of sterile architecture, designed according to utilitarian principles that tend towards repetition of features in the promotion of efficiency over creative vision. Superficial attempts to make uniform buildings appear distinctive may include the addition of different colours or textures. As Jane Jacobs notes in her study of American cities, these superficial attempts may be 'eye-catching' momentarily but ultimately fail to disguise their lack of character or distinction (1961: 292–4). The illustrations here are of buildings in Manchester, England, but could be from any town or city in the UK. Cities in other countries have their own monotonous styles. The last two buildings depicted here have colourful cladding. These images have been reproduced in colour in the plate section.

Figure 1.3 Example of 'quirky' architecture: M2 Tokyo, Aoyama Technical College (Makoto Sei Watanabe Architects, 1990)

Commonly known as 'the Robot' (specifically, the robot 'Optimus Prime' from the *Transformers*, in mid-transformation), this building is intended to exemplify 'a new order' through 'the tolerance of chaos' (www.makoto-architect.com).

style and their ironic social commentary often fail to establish a rapport with the people who use or encounter them. Instead of captivating our imagination or provoking us into fresh ways of thinking, their twisted shapes and complicated juxtapositions often appear to be a parody of themselves; more ridiculous, naff, or kitsch than genuinely intriguing (see Fig. 1.3).

Misconceptions about what we require from our built environment are rife, not least because our responses to architecture are often difficult to measure, and are in large part unconscious. It is therefore both unfair and unrealistic to expect architects and planners to have expertise in the complex workings of the unconscious and to factor this knowledge into their designs and constructions accordingly. It is hoped, therefore, that the chapters that follow will provide a useful theoretical guide in their explanation of the most salient aspects of our unconscious behaviour in our response to architecture, and will help us to understand our needs and uses of buildings, and both how and why we are drawn to specific elements and features within architectural designs.

The ideas of psychoanalysis and its related schools of thought are well placed to make sense of unconscious behaviour and its role in the construction of identity and relationship.[3] Traditionally, psychoanalysis as a field of study and therapeutic practice has been heavily preoccupied with interpersonal and intrapersonal relations, and has passed over in relative silence the vital relationships we inevitably have with nonhuman objects and environments. To assume that the built environment has little or no part to play in shaping our lives is nonsensical, and tantamount to assuming that human behaviour can be understood as if in a vacuum. Problems taken to psychotherapy are almost always attributed to interpersonal and intrapersonal conflict, but this is of little help in those cases where the underlying problem is, for instance, an aspect of the building in which the client or patient lives or works. The psychologist and cultural critic James Hillman briefly alludes to this conceptual problem by noting that 'psychological problems' that we experience at work—such as absenteeism, the need to take pills, sexual harassment'—are often 'architectural problems' (Hillman quoted in Kidel 1993: 1).

By developing psychoanalytical ideas to account for our intimate relationship with the built environment, I seek not to undermine them, but to extend their application to a vital dimension of our experience that has largely been ignored. Thus, in addition to providing a framework that emphasises the unconscious behaviours that are most relevant for architects, I explain the significance of architecture and the built environment for elaborating and extending psychoanalytic theories about human relationship and identity.

There have been few attempts to relate psychoanalytic theories to architecture, and the majority have sought to emphasise Freud's theories of sexuality and to make sense of our identifications with buildings in somewhat reductive terms as unresolved Oedipal issues. Although I am not denying the validity of such research, their discussions are often unhelpful to the practical needs and objectives of the architectural theorist, practitioner, and planner. This book, by contrast, considers psychoanalytic ideas of unconscious behaviour more broadly, and seeks to adapt them by grounding them in related ideas from other subjects and disciplinary practices, including other fields of psychology, aesthetics, and, of course, architecture.

Architectural blueprints of being

The importance of architecture for personal identity and wellbeing is far-reaching and demands an interdisciplinary response. The widespread interest in the intimate relationships between human self and architectural form is perhaps most vividly demonstrated in the centuries-old custom of characterising human nature through architectural metaphor and analogy. Examples of this custom, or the various 'architectural blueprints of being' as I shall refer to them, are discussed in an array of texts, scattered across the ages from antiquity to present day and spanning disparate fields, discourses, and traditions. Collectively, they identify an extensive catalogue of interpretations about human nature and behaviour. In order to introduce the arguments of this book, let us turn briefly to two of the more prominent types of 'blueprint of being': those that emphasise human bodily form as an architectural template, and those that arrive at similar templates by stressing the workings of the human mind. The purpose of these blueprints is not, as is often assumed, an arbitrary exercise of rendering ideas about human nature into abstract architectural imagery. Rather, as I shall demonstrate throughout my investigation, they reveal useful insights into the various ways in which we attempt, often unconsciously, to inscribe ourselves into the architectural fabric of our environments, in such a way as to experience their features as if incorporated into us as animate parts of ourselves. In the chapters that follow I explain the impressive consequences of this relationship with architecture for the cultivation of our sense of self and the quality of our relationship with the buildings we encounter on a daily basis.

Perhaps the most recognisable 'architectural blueprints of being', to architects especially, are those that identify correspondences between architectural features and the human body. This convention is often traced back to the Roman architectural engineer Marcus Vitruvius Pollio, who in his *Ten Books on Architecture* [*De architectura libri decem*], written c. 13–15 BC (1486), asserts that every architectural composition should have 'an exact system of correspondence to the likeness of a well-formed human being' (3:1.1).[4] This idea was elaborated upon in the Italian Renaissance by such architects as Leon Battista Alberti, who in *On the Art of Building* [*De re aedificatoria*] (written between 1443 and 1453, published 1485) refers to columns and the fortified areas of walls as the 'bones' of a building, the infill walls and panelling as its 'muscles and ligaments', and the finish of a building as its 'skin' (6:12:180, 3:7:71, 3:12:81). Filarete in *Treatise on Architecture* [*Trattato d'architettura*], written between 1461 and 1464 (1464) asserts that buildings should be designed according to the most beautiful part of human anatomy, the head and its constituent parts—with the doorway forming a mouth, and the windows above, eyes (Book 7, folio 49r: 85). Francesco di Giorgio Martini, in his *Treatises on Architecture, Engineering and Military Art* [*Trattati di Architettura, Ingegneria e Arte Militare*], the first written between 1478 and 1481 and the second in the 1490s (c. 1478–1490), illustrates his ideas with an array of drawings that superimpose the human face or body over building plans, elevations, columns, capitals, and cornices.[5] But it is the drawing known simply as *Vitruvian Man* or *L'Uomo Vitruviano* by Leonardo da Vinci (c. 1490) that has become the iconic emblem of this tradition.

The convention of equating body and building continues into the modern era with such initiatives as Le Corbusier's *Le Modulor* (1948), and so pervasive is the convention that it often seems to take on a life of its own, manifesting itself autonomously beyond the intentions and control of the architect. Many of us have recognised, for example, the resemblance of a building's façade to a human face, in a manner not dissimilar to Filarete's description cited above, with

Figure 1.4 Face. Detail of Whittle Building, Peterhouse College, Cambridge, UK (John Simpson Architects, 2014)

Detail of the back of the building showing its surprised-looking face—surprised, perhaps, upon hearing of its nomination in 2015 for the Carbuncle Cup, awarded to the 'ugliest' building in Britain of that year.[6]
© Lucy Huskinson

windows as eyes, and doorways as gaping mouths (see Figs. 1.4 and 1.5). Indeed, according to neuroscientific research, we are all predisposed to perceive simple, schematic, face-like patterns in our environments, with two points for eyes, and below this a different—usually vertical—shape for the nose, and a horizontal shape further below for the mouth (as indicated by the iron gate, Fig. 1.6).[7]

The tendency in scholarship has been to investigate the numerous metaphors and analogies that find resemblances between architecture and human body according to their abstract symbolism, with a focus on the mathematical measurements involved. But I wish to address their wider significance and value by investigating them in the light of the insights they impart into the manner of our identifications with buildings and how we employ our bodies and experiences of embodiment to do so. Furthermore, I wish to explore the implications of this bodily interaction with the built environment for understanding why we tend to be attracted to specific architectural designs over others.

At the heart of these depictions of the human body inscribed in architecture is, I shall argue, an innate human tendency to construct or seek out—albeit

Figure 1.5 Face. Detail of Grosvenor Museum, Chester, UK (Thomas Meakin Lockwood Architects, 1885–1886)
© Lucy Huskinson

unconsciously—appropriate architectural forms with which to furnish and facilitate meaningful bodily experiences. Each depiction is a rendering into abstract terms of a vital experience that we set in motion, often unawares, on a daily basis with the various buildings, streets, and other architectural structures we encounter.[8]

Architectural theorist Neil Leach suggests that the full significance of Vitruvius's comments on the proportional semblance of body and building has yet to be understood, given the scant consideration of 'how the use of these proportions might help human beings to relate to buildings at a psychical level' (2005a: 210–11). Although the focus of Leach's discussion is different from mine,[9] he alludes to an idea that is central to my argument; and that is the process of mimetic identification. Representations of the human figure inscribed into plans and other drawings of the Renaissance, he says, could be 'understood as emblematic of an attempt to relate to a building by a process of mimetic identification' (2005: 210). We shall explain how this important process of mimetic identification is set in motion when we experience architecture in such a way that we come to incorporate its forms and the various subjective meanings we ascribe to them as parts of ourselves, as though

Figure 1.6 Face. Detail of iron gate, Gaskell Memorial Tower, Knutsford, UK (Richard Harding Watt, 1907)
Although most likely unintended by its designer, the gate clearly presents within its railings a simple face with two points for eyes, a shape below for the nose, and horizontal mouth below that.
© Lucy Huskinson

body and building are merged into one composite form. A psychoanalytic approach provides a useful framework in which to make sense of this curious interaction, and in the chapters that follow I shall explain how it takes place and why it does; and, moreover, I shall give reasons why architectural designs have so vital an impact on how we experience ourselves.

The second prominent 'architectural blueprint of being' that provides useful context for our investigation is the kind that employs architectural imagery in order to encourage particular ideas. 'Memory buildings' or 'memory palaces', as they have come to be known, are a well-documented case in point. The origins of utilising architectural imagery as a mnemonic device is often attributed to ancient Roman and Greek rhetorical treatises, such as *Rhetorica ad Herennium* (anonymous author, written late 80s BC) (Anon. 1994), Cicero's *De Oratore* (55 BC) (1902), and Quintilian's *Institutio Oratoria* (AD 95) (1970).[10] The technique involved is principally an act of composition that involves one imagining an architectural layout of a number of discrete loci, such as a building or sequence of buildings on a street. One then imagines oneself walking around them, and placing within each locus a composite image of a particular feature of the locus and the idea that is to be recalled later. The recall of ideas is achieved when one again imagines oneself walking through the loci, whereupon the architectural features encountered there activate the sought-after ideas that were associated with them.

The convention of employing architectural imagery to encourage thinking extends far beyond their efficacy as 'storehouses' for ideas and mechanisms for establishing the effective arrangement of thoughts. Indeed, architecture has become synonymous with the act of theorising itself; such that, thinking *is* construction. Philosopher Martin Heidegger is famous for having made the literal identification of thinking with building in his late essay 'Building, Dwelling, Thinking' (1951), but his ideas were already part of a wider, pervasive tradition of thinking *through* architecture. René Descartes, with his philosophical 'edifice' constructed by a single architect upon 'secure foundations' (1641), is often cited as having popularised the convention in Western philosophy, whereas Immanuel Kant is thought to have institutionalised it, through his criticism of Descartes's hasty construction methods, and his own attempt to erect the definitive metaphysical building. Kant's supposedly more enduring edifice is built according to universal principles of pure reason—a method, he claims, that gives 'full guarantee for the completeness and certainty of all the components that comprise this edifice' (1781: 140). And architectural imagery is not limited to the rational constructs of philosophers; it is prevalent also within the contemplative discourses of religion. In the Christian tradition, for instance, architectural imagery is employed amongst other things as a teaching device, on matters related to the body and community of the Church, romantic love, and the virginal body, and also as a meditational aid for prayer and spiritual contemplation.[11] In the 17th century, the production of architectural imagery, often drawing on the rich array of architectural allusions in the Bible, reached industrial proportions, where it was churned out for an eager audience.[12]

Whereas those 'architectural blueprints of being' that emphasise the semblance[13] of architectural form with human bodily form allow us insight, I claim, into the way in which we use our bodies to identify with the built environment, I suggest that the second type of blueprints—those that emphasise a correlation between architectural structure and the construction of thought—give insights into another method or strategy we tend to employ to identify with the built environment. Thus, in addition to the mimetic identifications we establish via our experiences of embodiment, I shall explain how we unconsciously seek to mimic or 'merge' with buildings through the processes that underpin the very construction of our thoughts. The analogy of architecture as a storehouse of ideas is, I argue, illustrative of our unconscious tendency to utilise the various impressions of the built environment we acquire on a daily basis to help us to process ideas that we otherwise might not have had, had we not identified so intimately with their architectural features. Scholar Mary Carruthers convincingly argues that the goal of the 'art of memory' in ancient times was not simply, as Frances Yates had maintained, to recollect ideas and thus to furnish the student with a prodigious memory for the information they might be asked to repeat, but rather to provide them with 'the means and wherewithal to invent his material' (1998: 9). In this respect, the imagined building with its various loci enables both access to forgotten ideas—or *repressed* ideas, as psychoanalysts often understand them—and the discovery or construction of new lines of thought.

I shall argue that we are drawn to specific architectural features to facilitate various thought processes and to formulate ideas. Given the variety of disciplinary approaches that draw on the analogy of building and ideas, we can assume that we use architecture to arrive at a variety of kinds of thought and experiences of ourselves as thinking, reflective beings. We may, for instance, use architectural features to establish an abstract argument, composed of ideas arranged in a logical sequence; and, as we do so, we may lose ourselves in thought, or experience ourselves as integrated and in control. By contrast, an architectural structure may encourage our thoughts to wander through various associated ideas and unpredictable pathways, allowing us to entertain ideas that are inaccessible through a more direct and logical approach. Such thinking may well elicit insights into ourselves that we hadn't until that point in time realised.

Just as psychoanalysis is well placed to explain the process of mimetic identification in our bodily identifications with architecture, it also helps us to make sense of both why and how we utilise architectural imagery in creative thinking. For instance, in *The Interpretation of Dreams* (1900), Freud explains how, when we allow our thoughts to wander, we trigger a process (which he refers to as 'dream-work') that knits together various perceptions of our environment with memory-traces, feelings, and other experiences, according to associative links that are personally meaningful to us. By drawing on case studies—including Freud's own report of his visit to the Acropolis in Athens—I shall demonstrate how specific architectural features encourage us to access ideas that might otherwise have eluded us, and to engage with aspects of ourselves that, until we encountered those features, had gone largely unnoticed. Architecture provides material food for thought, and the quality of its design will have repercussions on the nutritional value of those thoughts. Successful architecture in this context is that which I shall describe as *evocative* architecture. Designs that embody extremes of utility or artistic vision do not constitute an evocative architecture because they tend to distract us in ways that are unhelpful and inhibiting to our creative thought processes and to the creative elaboration of ourselves.

I have described just a few 'architectural blueprints of being' from an expanding repository of examples. My decision to select the two types for this introduction was determined in part by their likely familiarity to the reader, given the abundance of their examples, and in part by the fact that, taken together, they represent the two halves of human identity as it is traditionally conceived in Western thought—as a dualistic composite of body and mind. In their focus on one or other, neither type seeks, however, to expunge body or mind from its considerations. For instance, architects who design buildings according to bodily proportions often do so with a view to inducing a harmonious state of mind and encouraging the contemplation of higher truths. Likewise, the efficacy of the 'art of memory' is greatly enhanced if the subject recalls to their imagination the tangible experience of their body in motion as they walked between the various imagined loci.

An obvious criticism of the various blueprints of being as illustrations of our tendency to identify with actual buildings in the elaboration of ourselves is the privilege they by and large grant to the visual aesthetics of architecture and human form, with little or no acknowledgement of the impressions we inevitably garner of both body and building through our other senses. It is difficult to argue against the importance assigned to the visual aesthetics of architectural design—popular opinion, we noted, would likely contest such arguments—but as this book seeks to demonstrate, there are also vital non-visible aspects to architectural design that have as much, if not more, of a role to play in making an impression and provoking a response in us. The effects of these non-visible components of architecture can lead a person either to cultivate an intimate and personally meaningful identification with a building, or to establish a problematic distance from it, resulting potentially in deep-seated feelings of alienation and disorientation. The successes and failures of architecture rest in great part on these non-visible, often intangible, elements of design. The failure of some architects and planners in their comprehensive investment in visual aesthetics with little consideration given to the impact of their designs on other senses is well documented, and is the impetus for many a petition for a more holistic approach to architectural design, one that takes into account a fuller range of sense experiences. Sight, traditionally regarded as the 'noblest' of the senses due to the detailed information it imparts without emotional interference from the body, establishes an instinctive distance between the subject and object. Sound is similar in this regard, but is deemed inferior due to the relative lack of detailed information it imparts. Taste, smell, and touch, by contrast, implicate the subjective experience of the body directly, and, although traditionally spurned on this basis, smell and taste in particular are thought to arouse the memory most vividly. Heidegger, for one, asserts that it is through a building's odour that we come to recall its design features most distinctly (1935: par. 25).[14] But unlike the visual image, impressions made by smells, tastes, and touch are more difficult to summon to the imagination. They are therefore less useful to the practitioner of the art of memory. An evocative architecture, I shall claim, is one that elicits a full range of sensuous experience.

Some ideas in the psychoanalytic tradition (notably those that go by the name of 'object relations') emphasise the vital role of bodily sensation in the development of personality, with especial importance ascribed to the self-reflexive nature of touch as a principal means through which a person establishes their sense of self and their relationships with other people and things. Research in this area is fertile ground for architectural theory, and by bringing these discourses into dialogue with each other, we can begin to identify the non-visible, evocative capabilities of architecture and how they can be harnessed.

Given my advocacy of the psychoanalytic approach and claims for its efficacy in gauging the impact of architectural designs on our identity and wellbeing, it is fitting to enquire into the extent to which psychoanalytic discourses have themselves appropriated architectural images in their theorising about human behaviour. I mentioned that psychoanalysis is principally concerned with relationships between people, and simply hasn't had the time, as one psychoanalyst puts it,[15] to investigate the nature of our relationships with the nonhuman environment. Nevertheless, as I shall argue, similar processes of identification underpin the two, making the built environment no less an affective feature of our lives. Allusions to architecture and the built environment within psychoanalytic literature are sparse and scattered across passages in various texts, but when collated and analysed together they provide a valuable commentary on our instinctual need for architecture and its integral role in the construction of self.

Especially relevant to our investigation are various descriptions of 'buildings of psyche', as I shall refer to them, which can be identified, and which together comprise a little-known group of architectural analogies that seek to explain the composition and dynamics of the psyche or mind as if it were a building of several storeys or parts. We find the most detailed descriptions in the writings of Karl Albert Scherner (1825–1889), Josef Breuer (1842–1925), Sigmund Freud (1856–1939), and Édouard Claparède (1873–1940), and in the writings and architectural designs of Carl Gustav Jung (1875–1961). Although rarely scrutinised, these buildings of psyche have influenced the ideas of other well-known figures whose work is widely discussed within architectural discourse. But because the ideas these analogies go on to influence are more recognisable than the buildings that inspired them, any inconsistencies between the two often go unacknowledged and unnoticed. For instance, in his celebrated work, *The Poetics of Space* (1957), Gaston Bachelard discusses the value of the oneiric house ('dream-house') for the integration of the self, and he acknowledges C.G. Jung as a source of his thinking on the matter. Unknown to most of his readers, however, Bachelard misinterprets the spatial layout of an architectural metaphor that he attributes to Jung, with comical consequences for architecture and psyche alike. By inadvertently placing rooms meant for the cellar at the top of the building and those intended for the attic in its basement, Bachelard arrives at something more akin to a disoriented, topsy-turvy house of psyche (see Huskinson 2013). Le Corbusier is another case in point. Thought by some also to have been directly influenced by Jungian ideas,[16] Le Corbusier's architecture has come to represent to those who are familiar with Jung's ideas what can only be described as a perverse misunderstanding of them. Indeed, as James Donald aptly remarks,

Le Corbusier's supposed 'therapeutic modernism' was most likely driven by a 'phobic reaction' against the messy dynamics of cities and the unpredictable nature of human behaviour (Donald 1999: 137–8; cf. Samuel 2002: 44). As a result, Le Corbusier's architecture is not so much aligned with the therapeutic endeavour Jung subscribed to, but is, in stark contrast, paranoid and oppressive, and cleansed of all disturbance and desire.

It is unfortunate that the various buildings of psyche have received such little attention, and are in large part dismissed in psychoanalytic circles as arbitrary metaphors.[17] Such ignorance is regrettable, given that, as this book seeks to demonstrate, their careful consideration leads us to a more grounded appreciation of the integral role of architecture in our lives. Gathered together and analysed here in detail for the first time, these metaphorical buildings reveal to us a framework for making sense of various behavioural strategies that we employ in our negotiation of our built environments, and the impulses that are activated in our response to specific architectural features and designs—whether they be the buildings we live and work in or the buildings we imagine, such as those that inform the multifarious architectural 'blueprints of being'.

The chapters

Following this introductory chapter, we begin Chapter 2 with a survey of the buildings of psyche that are employed in psychoanalytic discourse as architectural blueprints of being. The key features of their design will be elaborated throughout our investigation. The survey introduces us to the psychoanalytic notion of self and the aspects of mind or psyche that govern our relationships with architecture. Broadly conceived, the psychoanalytic self is governed by instincts that are rooted in the unconscious mind. Often at variance with the reasoned intentions of our conscious mind, the unconscious gives rise to instinctual tensions that can lead to problematic behaviours and creative achievements alike. The architectural layouts of the buildings of psyche disclose the dynamic interaction of its parts in response to the impressions the subject receives from 'outside' stimuli. As we shall see, the greatest emphasis is given to the contrast between the conscious and unconscious aspects of mind as different loci and their interactions.

We shall examine a range of buildings and architectural constructions that are employed in pioneering works of psychoanalysis in order to elaborate their central ideas about the instinctual motivations for human behaviour and the workings of the healthy and unhealthy mind. They include the 'house of hysteria' outlined by Josef Breuer (1893) to house the troubled memories of hysterics, and its architectural renovation by Freud into a castle-like fortress (1897), whose hand-drawn sketch to accompany his discussion is thought to replicate the turreted fortifications at Nuremberg in Bavaria. We examine Freud's analogies of ruined buildings and their archaeological excavation

(1896), and his presentation of the 'eternal city' of Rome as a city of memory (1930, 1937). The architectural furnishings of the body proposed by Karl Albert Scherner (1861) and Freud (1900) are considered, before we investigate Jung's architectural dreams alongside their real-life counterparts. The semblances between Jung's proposals for a house of psyche and the two houses he designed and constructed alongside Lake Zurich are curious and give invaluable insights into the manner in which his architectural constructions and psychological ideas directly inform each other.

In each example we find the unconscious aspect of mind placed below ground level, either as a series of darkened rooms that require special permission to enter, or as an assortment of fragments that are barely discernible as parts of a larger, more coherent architectural edifice. The conscious mind, by contrast, is a room above ground, well lit, and fully accessible, where nothing is hidden and all is revealed. The human body sustains the building at its foundations and, on occasion, various bodily organs feature as specific rooms within the building or appear as staircases, balconies, and windows.

In Chapter 3, I develop the idea of a building as a dynamic configuration of parts that negotiate the instinctual tensions and divisions of self, by considering the nature of architectural edifices as 'events'. Initially, this idea may sound odd, but the idea of architecture as a dynamic event rather than a passive object in our field of perception is prevalent and appears to be gaining in popularity in philosophical studies on architecture, especially those within the phenomenological tradition. I draw upon some of these, and relate their discussion to ideas within psychoanalysis and architectural theory to explain how architecture is defined by the manner in which it calls upon us to participate in its material features, and in which it draws attention to aspects of ourselves that we might otherwise be unaware of. I refer to this characteristic of architecture as the 'architectural event'. To help us to make sense of the 'event' and its implications for both architectural design and the experience of self, we elucidate the processes of identification that take place between subject and building as the event unfolds. The blueprints of psyche, with their depictions of the unconscious and conscious mind, give us clues into this, and specifically how each capacity of mind shapes and organises our perceptions of architectural design to establish the 'event'.

In Chapter 3 I explain an idea that is pivotal to our investigation, and that is the manner in which identity is shaped by a dynamic exchange between two contrasting tendencies or innate behaviours that are triggered in our response to the environment. These manifest themselves on the one hand as a desire to find ourselves securely held and contained by place, and, on the other, as a desire to find ourselves detached and free from place. If an environment is conducive to both, it facilitates an experience of self that is coherent and confident. By contrast, if it inhibits one or the other, the self is susceptible to anxiety and potential crises of identity. These anxieties are most appropriately understood as spatial anxieties, and can be categorised in the broadest of terms as either a claustrophobic or agoraphobic response to the environment. The former refers to an environment that is restricting and limiting, and threatens through its tight hold on the subject to merge with them, inducing within them suffocating feelings, while the latter describes an environment that is ill defined and lacks the structure and containing space required by the subject to make them feel securely in place, inducing instead feelings of isolation and alienation.[18]

The remaining chapters examine the architectural event in order to ascertain both why and how the event happens (Chapters 4 and 5), and what exactly is disclosed to a person in the event, in terms of the insights it reveals about their personality, and the value of particular architectural features and designs (Chapter 6). In the concluding chapter (Chapter 7) I explain how we can enhance and harness the architectural event, and make use of our experiences of architecture in order to build more effectively or evocatively. There we examine some common assumptions that architects and designers (and critics of architecture) adopt in their misguided approach to evocative architecture and their faulty judgements over what evocative architecture entails. In such cases, the architectural event, for one reason or other, most often fails.

In Chapter 4, I investigate the role of the body in the architectural event to explain how identity is constructed through a process of mimetic identification with the material features of the built environment. I mentioned earlier that there are schools of thought within the psychoanalytic tradition that emphasise the body as a decisive factor in the development of personality. Here I develop and extend these ideas to explain just how vital our identifications with architecture are for establishing a coherent and abiding sense of self. Architecture, I claim, heightens our experiences of embodiment, and can satisfy our need to feel contained, integrated, and securely in place. The quality of these experiences, however, is determined in large part by the particular features and designs of the architecture perceived. That is to say, while one room, building, or street may facilitate a reassuring sense of containment, another may trigger anxieties of too constricting or expansive a space. It is only when the subject feels sufficiently contained by their environment that they can start to use it to creative ends.

Chapter 5 examines a second process that underpins the architectural event. Here we investigate the role of memory in the event, and how buildings can be said to evoke traces of memories and inspire creative thoughts. We draw upon theories from cognitive psychology about the formulation of our creative thoughts, and Freud's established method of the 'dream-work', to explain how architecture facilitates thoughts, ideas, and experiences that have otherwise been inaccessible to us, made unconscious and repressed. By way of illustration and case study, we analyse a personal account of Freud's that describes a trip he took to the Acropolis in Athens to demonstrate how his perceptions of its architectural features led him to discover insights about himself that couldn't have been thought through by more logical or direct means.

Following our consideration of mimetic identification and dream-work as two interconnected processes that underpin the architectural event, Chapter 6 addresses the nature of the insights that are disclosed in the event, in terms of both the type of information it brings to light and the feelings it arouses. Here we concern ourselves with the aesthetic experience of architecture. In itself, this is a vast and complex topic that has engaged scholars for centuries. We are concerned, however, with two particular aesthetic categories of experience that have traditionally been assigned to architecture, and which, as I shall demonstrate, convey with striking clarity the architectural event as it unfolds. These are the uncanny and the sublime.

There continues to be, within Freudian psychoanalytic commentary especially, a desire to maintain a conceptual distance between the concerns of psychoanalysis and those of aesthetics, with attempts to downplay the value of the latter. I wish to undermine such assertions by demonstrating how the theories of the unconscious and its impact on the conscious mind as postulated by Freud and Jung are rooted in aesthetic concerns. We shall discover that the blueprints of psyche designed by Freud and Jung reveal significant differences in their basic plan, with Jung wishing to extend the basement rooms of the unconscious beyond the remit, or 'planning permission', granted by Freud. This point of divergence has implications for the kinds of insight disclosed in the architectural event, and leads to different kinds of experience. I argue that architecture, when perceived and interpreted through a Freudian lens, evokes experiences that are decidedly uncanny prior to the disclosure of insights that are by nature sublime. A Jungian lens, by contrast, perceives architecture as uncanny before arriving at insights that, although often confused with the sublime, are in fact distinctly numinous. That is to say, Jung's architectural extension to the unconscious points to his concern for an enlarged capacity for our creative thoughts, a capacity he characterises with a term that has religious connotations and that has traditionally been used to describe sacred architecture.

The many examples of architecture that have been and continue to be cited as distinctively uncanny, sublime, or numinous therefore denote in their features the dynamic components of the architectural event as it unfolds. Given that the unconscious processes of identification that underpin the event engage the full array of sense experiences, those investigations that seek to expose the 'uncanny', 'sublime', or 'numinous' characteristics of buildings by considering their visual appearance alone will inevitably arrive at insufficient conclusions. Arguably, it is partly due to the emphasis given to visual aesthetics that many investigations translate the feelings of elation and profundity that underpin the sublime and the numinous into images of vast geometric measurement or intense ornate detail, and thereby identify their effects with an architecture that impresses through sheer size or intricate ornamentation, with Gothic cathedrals, towering edifices, and huge domed palaces cited as favourite examples.

The reduction of the sublime and the numinous to a matter of sheer size is problematic, and indicative of the problems and failings of architecture and urban planning today. Chapter 7 offers a remedy to the situation. There I highlight principles for evocative architectural designs that are not the preserve of the few grand and iconic buildings that have preoccupied many a discourse on the sublime and numinous, but are present and prevalent within the otherwise ordinary and mundane buildings that line our streets and are encountered on a daily basis. In other words, I suggest that all buildings have the capacity to elicit the architectural event, but, as we shall see, only some do.

In Chapter 7 we also consider why some buildings seem more evocative than others, and how the architectural event can be harnessed and encouraged in even the most sterile and uninspiring of buildings. The impact of architecture is a two-way street between the building and the subject who perceives it. Thus, on the one hand, I explain how we can enhance our capacity to *notice* the unique features of our built environment in order to become more receptive to their evocative power and enable the most seemingly banal and lifeless of buildings to capture our imaginative attention. On the other hand, we explore basic principles that can be adopted to augment the designs and strategies of architects and planners, helping them to build more effectively for our existential needs. We also consider some common problems that occur when designers disregard these principles.

We shall see that the answers to designing evocative architecture lie not, as is traditionally thought, in designing more 'beautifully' or 'harmoniously'; nor are they found in a desire to shock and startle through radical designs that attempt to subvert commonly held assumptions about what a building ought to look like or how it should function. Rather, evocative architecture is cultivated in the creative tensions that are generated when both positions are considered at once: when the radical and convention collide. Architecture is most evocative when it responds to both aspects of our mind, without favouring one over the other, when it meets our competing needs for regularity *and* inconsistency, for certainty *and* obscurity, expectation *and* surprise, for beauty *and* ugliness. The result is an ambiguous design that creeps up on us unannounced and captivates us.

Notes

1 Including Considerate Constructors Scheme: Gold Award 2011; Overall winner of 2010 Concrete Society Award; Structural Steel Design Awards, 2010; London District Surveyors' Association: Best Sustainability Project, 2011; shortlisted for the London Civil Engineering Awards, 2011.

2 The quotation from *Building Design* is from its Executive Editor, Ellis Woodman (2010); see: www.bdonline.co.uk/strata-tower-wins-2010-carbuncle-cup/5004110.article (accessed 8/2016). For *The Telegraph* article, see: www.telegraph.co.uk/finance/property/pictures/9126031/The-worlds-30-ugliest-buildings.html?frame=2875028 (accessed 8/2016). For *The Guardian* article, see: https://www.theguardian.com/artanddesign/2014/apr/29/top-10-worst-london-skyscrapers-quill-odalisk-walkie-talkie (accessed 8/2016).

3 The term 'psychoanalysis' refers technically to the psychological ideas of Sigmund Freud, with other related theorists and schools of psychology adopting their own terms to differentiate their ideas from Freud's. The term 'depth psychology' is often employed in specialist fields to refer broadly to all related schools that recognise unconscious mental processes underpinning a person's behaviour. However, given that the term 'psychoanalysis' is more recognisable and widely used outside the field to refer more generally to a psychology of the unconscious, I shall continue to use this term throughout, while also making it clear to the reader when Freud's ideas diverge from those of other related thinkers.

4 Some trace back the equation of body and building further, such as R.A. Schwaller de Lubicz, who in *The Temple in Man: Sacred Architecture and the Perfect Man* (1949) seeks to demonstrate how the Temple complex at Luxor, Egypt, is designed to represent the bodily form of the Pharaoh—the Perfect Man—with importance given to the crown of the skull. *De re aedificatoria* is the first printed book on architectural theory.

5 For further discussion, see Rykwert 1996; Mallgrave 2010: 9–25.

6 The annual award is given by the magazine *Building Design* (bdonline.co.uk) to the 'ugliest building in the United Kingdom completed in the last 12 months'. It is intended as a humorous parallel to the prestigious *Stirling Prize* given by the *Royal Institute of British Architects*. The award was launched in 2006.

7 This phenomenon is known as *pareidolia*. See Hadjikhani et al. (2009); Sussman and Hollander (2015: 56–106). For the perception of faces in nonhuman objects, see Robert and Robert (2000). For the perception of faces in architecture and the emotions they convey see Chalup et. al. (2010).

8 We can trace examples of this more personable identification in some of the works alluded to above, with suggestions of our need to care for our buildings or be cared for by them, as we would a family member or own body. Alberti recommends that every house have a large and 'welcoming bosom' (5:17:146; 9:3:296), and for walls to be constructed without undue thickness, so as to avoid criticism 'for having excessively swollen limbs' (3:12:79,219). Filarete requests that buildings be nourished with regular maintenance so as to prevent them from falling sick with disease, as one might a child, and goes so far as to suggest that buildings are children conceived by the architect and his client, who together must give birth to the building and bear it as their child. He writes:

> As it [procreation] cannot be done without a woman, so he who wishes to build needs an architect. He conceives it with him and then the architect carries it out. When the architect has given birth, he becomes the mother of the building. Before the architect gives birth, he should dream about his conception, think about it, and turn it over in his mind in many ways for seven to nine months, just as a woman carries her child in her body for seven to nine months.
> (2, folio 7v-8r:15–16)

9 In this essay Leach examines the harmonious proportion of body and building within the context of Freud's ideas of the death drive and the myth of Narcissus.

10 Also described by Frances Yates (1966) and by Alexander R. Luria (1968). The efficacy of this technique has been well established (Ross and Lawrence 1968; Crovitz 1969, 1971; Briggs, Hawkins and Crovitz 1970; Lea 1975—all cited in O'Keefe and Nadal 1978: 389–90).

11 For a thorough examination of the evolution of the architectural metaphor from antiquity to the late Middle Ages, in relation to social, political, and religious contexts, see Whitehead (2003).

12 Perhaps the most striking devotional account for its detail is St Teresa of Ávila's *El Castillo Interior* or *Las Moradas* ('Interior Castle' or 'Many Mansions'), which describes her mystical vision of her soul as a diamond-shaped castle containing seven mansions, and the 'principal room' at the centre, 'where much secret intercourse is held between God and the soul' (Saint Teresa of Jesus 1577: 7).

13 I use the term 'semblance' throughout this investigation to denote more than a mere resemblance between architecture and self-experience. To say that an architectural structure resembles our bodily form suggests there are physical characteristics that are common to both. For instance, one might recognise how the spatial alignment of a building—with its arrangement of windows and door—resembles the eyes and nose of a face. I shall argue, however, that there are powerful affinities between a person and building that go beyond their visible properties. A building that doesn't resemble a person may nevertheless have a strong attraction to a person. For instance, a person may recognise, albeit unconsciously, that a building has certain functional properties that the person desires for themselves, or a person may feel drawn to a building by the memories he or she has attached to it. In such cases, I argue that there is a semblance between the person and the building.

14 Heidegger writes:

> One can, as it were, smell the Being of this building in your nostrils, and often after decades one still has the scent in one's nose. The smell communicates the Being of this building far more immediately and truly than any description or inspection could ever do.
>
> (Lecture given in 1935, published in 1953; see Heidegger 1935: par. 25)

For further discussion of the importance of smell in architecture see Barbara and Perliss (2006).

15 Searles (1960).

16 For instance, Richard A. Moore claims that Le Corbusier was directly acquainted with Jung's work (Moore 1980: 135, n. 3); and Tim Benton maintains that Le Corbusier made a study of Jungian texts during his wartime exile in Ozon (Benton 1987: 243). See also Richards (2003).

17 See, for instance, Andrew Samuels, who criticises the metaphor of the house of psyche. Why should the psyche be a house or any sort of building at all? Samuels asks (1989: 26); cf. Hauke 2000: 62, 104–105.

18 Interestingly, Freud himself confessed to having suffered from agoraphobia. Theodor Reik, a prominent psychoanalyst and one of Freud's first students, recounts how, while walking with Freud one evening in Vienna, Freud hesitated before crossing a street, and proceeded to take Reik's arm. He then confessed that he was afraid of his agoraphobic symptoms returning. Reik thought that Freud's experience of agoraphobia influenced Freud's choice of career (Reik 1948: 15–16).

Chapter 2

Architectural blueprints of psyche

So prevalent are architectural analogies of the mind or psyche that they have infiltrated common parlance. We often speak of the 'recesses of the mind', 'corridors of the mind', eyes as 'windows to the soul', feeling 'at home with oneself' or being 'out of place' or 'sitting on the fence', and so on. C.G. Jung notes, 'When someone is not quite right in the head, we say in German that he [...] "has cobwebs in the attic"' (1958: par. 671).

It is easy to see how the psychoanalytic conception of the psyche as a divisible and divided whole invites analogous comparison to architecture. The theoretical models of psyche outlined by Freud and his contemporaries often rely on spatial arrangements to delineate the mind's structure and its various processes and affects, and are sometimes referred to as their 'topographical' models of the mind.

The examples we consider here can be construed as continuing in the vein of those traditions that employ architectural imagery as a mnemonic device for the gathering and recall of ideas, and of those that incorporate impressions of the human body into architectural design. For the architectural blueprints of psyche include features of both traditions and combine them into a single image. Thus the mind is presented in connection with and subsumed within the body as an embodied psyche, and depicted as a receptacle for the storage and discharge of forgotten memories and other impulses.

Although the various terms employed by Freud to characterise the mind change in accordance with the evolution of his ideas, the spatial structure he assigns to it remains constant. Freud and his contemporaries were at pains to point out the limitations of spatial analogies of the mind, for the mind does not have anatomical locality and, unlike the brain or other material organ, cannot be mapped (see Freud 1900: 536; cf. Breuer 1893: 227–8). According to Josef Breuer, a colleague of Freud, we have become accustomed to thinking in spatial relations, so that any attempt to make sense of the mind will likely draw upon spatial metaphors, with architecture being a popular choice. Breuer writes:

> Thus when we speak of ideas which are found in the region of clear consciousness and of unconscious ones which never enter the full light of self-consciousness, we almost inevitably form pictures of a tree with its trunk in daylight and its roots in darkness, *or of a building with its dark underground cellars.*
>
> (Breuer 1893: 228; emphasis added)

While Breuer defines the conscious mind simply as ideas of which we are aware, the ideas of the unconscious mind are characterised by him in terms of their spatial relation to conscious awareness: as those that 'exist and are operative *beneath the threshold* of consciousness' (1893: 222; emphasis in original). The threshold that separates the two aspects of mind can be penetrated from the unconscious side if the unconscious ideas generate sufficient energy to do so. These 'highly charged' ideas will become conscious unless the conscious mind finds them too troublesome or irrelevant to its needs, in which case they are overpowered by the ego and subsequently repressed and kept below the threshold, where they inhabit the 'underground cellar' of the mind.

Breuer's analogy suggests a simple two-storey house of psyche, with consciousness presented as the well-lit upper storey, presumably including a number of rooms to accommodate its various ideas, and the unconscious, by contrast, as dark rooms situated in the basement. Although he doesn't explicitly mention which part of the building represents conscious ideas (mentioning only unconscious ideas as the dark rooms below ground level), we can deduce from his corresponding image of the tree that consciousness resides in the part of the building situated above the ground floor, which, like the trunk of the tree, is open to natural light.[1]

Breuer's simple architectural analogy raises questions about the values he ascribes to spatial arrangements and the suppositions both he and we make about spatial relations generally. By placing the unconscious *below* consciousness we might assume that a hierarchical structure is implied, with the unconscious presented as somehow inferior to consciousness (as is denoted in psychoanalytic discourse with its interchangeable term '*sub*-consciousness'). On the other hand, we might assume that the placement of the unconscious denotes a more important role as the foundation upon which consciousness and the whole edifice of psyche depends, and without which it would collapse. We can speculate also on the values ascribed to the aesthetic features of the divided spaces, by deliberating over whether the darkness of the underground rooms implies a sinister or mysterious quality to the unconscious, or whether it is simply the case that uninhabited rooms rarely require light fixtures.

Although this simple spatial layout invites different interpretations, the architects of the various buildings of psyche that we shall survey often insist on exact specifications for their designs, and intend to convey explicit and unwavering meanings by them. Freud somewhat comically asserts, for example, that staircases are representations of the vagina, and to walk up and down them is indicative of sexual intercourse, while James Hillman, as we shall see later, identifies towers as expressions of the neurotic ego and disembodied self. Although it is important to keep in mind the emphatic warnings by Freud and Breuer about the dangers of literalising analogies of the mind—or, as Freud puts it, of mistaking 'the scaffolding for the building' (Freud 1900: 536)—they do not make it easy for us to heed their advice. That is to say, they do not grant us the imaginative freedom to renovate or furnish their buildings of psyche as we like (and as the art of memory would have us do). On the contrary, their buildings are often rigid and stylized, and none more so than those that illustrate the relationship between the mind and the anatomical arrangements of the body, for in such cases the architecture is guided by the predesignated structural arrangements of distinct body parts.

On those occasions when our psychoanalytic thinkers establish a definitive correlation between an architectural feature and its psychological counterpart, we can assume that, for them at least, there is something in the phenomenological quality of the specific architectural feature in question that resonates strongly with a certain function or component of our psychological make-up. Read in this light, we can deduce that the vertical structure of Breuer's building resonates with the upright posture of the body and our experience of our muscular density and its movements required to hold up the skeletal frame, while the staircase can be said to elicit the sexually active vagina for Freud due to their comparable shapes (as passageways), functions (to connect), and experiential presentation (as a rhythmic organ or component).[2] The latter analogy especially may seem somewhat crude, but both demonstrate how these architectural analogies reveal more about our relationships with architecture than they are presumed to convey. They are not simply abstract devices used to illustrate and clarify complex ideas; they give insights into the evocative potential of architecture and the capacity of certain architectural features to encourage our intimate relationship and participation in them.

By this I certainly do not wish to claim (and neither would Freud) that our encounters with staircases are inevitably sexual, or that we are likely to orgasm each time we reach the top step! It is, rather, that our psychoanalytic theorists have important things to say about the way we identify with architecture and our experiences of the built environment—even more important, it would seem, than they themselves realised, or is at least made explicit in their writings. In the chapters that follow we shall explore how each of us can be said to experience architecture as if its features were extensions of our own body and mind, and subsequently how we use the architectural features of our built environments to negotiate the various experiences we unconsciously ascribe to these aspects of ourselves. Using psychoanalytic theory, I explain how we come to find ourselves psychologically embedded within architecture, in a comparable manner to the attempts of our theorists in this chapter to render abstract interpretations of body and mind into imagined blueprints of buildings.

Let us now survey some of the more prominent architectural blueprints and buildings of psyche. We begin with another house of Breuer's, designed to accommodate the troubled memories of hysterics, before visiting various buildings of Freud's, including a castle-like structure and the entire architectural fabric of Rome as Freud's city of 'eternal' memory. In these buildings we discover the unconscious variously depicted, as a secretive domain of dark and silent rooms below ground level, a room that requires special permission to enter and pass through, and an assortment of architectural fragments. The conscious mind, by contrast, is the well-lit storey or set of rooms above ground, fully accessible, where nothing is hidden and all is revealed. Following these, we examine the architectural furnishings of the body as it imprints itself within the buildings of psyche, as described by Freud and Karl Albert Scherner (who influenced Freud's designs), before moving on to consider Jung's attempt at a radical renovation of the conventional house of psyche as he saw it. We shall see that the differences between the original buildings of psyche designed by Freud and Breuer and the renovation insisted upon by Jung have important implications for our relationships with the built environment, including the manner in which we identify with architecture and its aesthetic impact on us. We address these implications in Chapter 6, and in Chapter 7, where we also consider their significance for the design of evocative architecture.

Breuer's house of hysteria (1893–1895)

Breuer develops the simple blueprint we considered earlier into a more complicated design, one that enables him to describe in greater detail the nature and dynamics of unconscious ideas within a context of emotional disturbance and bodily ailments, or 'hysterical' symptoms as they were formerly known. *Studies of Hysteria* (1893–1895), the collaborative work of Breuer and Freud, is most commonly known for its inclusion of Freud's famous case study of his hysterical patient Anna O., and the introduction of his technique of psychoanalysis as a cure for her ailments. But it is Breuer's chapter 'Theoretical' that concerns us, for it is there that we find both his simple two-storey house of psyche and its renovations into a building of '*several storeys*' (1893: 244; emphasis in original). This more complicated design emphasises the verticality of its structure and continues to convey the unconscious located below consciousness. One might think it reasonable to postulate a different architectural arrangement to illustrate Breuer's theory of hysteria, with a horizontal trajectory, such as a single-storey house comprising a series of interlocking rooms, placed side by side. But this simply won't do for Breuer.[3] He asserts,

> Just as it is only possible to understand the structure of such a building if we distinguish the plans of the different floors, it is, I think, necessary in order to understand hysteria for us to pay attention to the various kinds of complication in the causation of the symptoms. If we disregard them and try to carry through an explanation of hysteria by employing a single causal nexus, we shall always find a very large residue of unexplained phenomena left over. It is just as though we tried to insert the different rooms of a many-storeyed house into the plan of a single storey.
>
> (Breuer 1893: 244–5)

Breuer's description of hysteria is complex and covers several pages, but from it we can extract his plans for a building of approximately three storeys, with two located 'underground' (pertaining to two unconscious activities that underpin the formation of hysterical symptoms), and one placed above ground (consciousness). Let us now turn to this house of hysteria, beginning as Breuer does, at its foundations.

The foundations of the building are biological in nature, and include the nervous system (1893: 244). Built upon this and presumably still below ground level are storeys that comprise, he says, 'ideogenic symptoms' (false beliefs or delusions) and other phenomena that similarly 'owe their origin to suggestion' (1893: 246). In other words, the bottom storeys of the house convey what Breuer calls 'abnormal expressions' of emotional content, and they are abnormal because they have become dissociated or stripped from the ideas or experiences that gave rise to the emotions in the first place. These ideas or experiences—which for Breuer (and Freud) are usually sexual in content—remain 'repressed' and housed within the underground storeys of the building until they generate sufficient emotional affect to push 'up' through the ceiling and into the upper storey of consciousness and into waking awareness. Breuer's house depicts through its structure the procedures through which unhealthy symptoms are created, describing how the emotions are first detached from their original ideas or experiences in the rooms below ground, before being 'converted' into the 'purely somatic' symptoms, above ground, where they can be experienced consciously by the hysterical person.

Within the lowest storey of the building ideas are stripped of their emotional affects due to the overwhelming 'sexual excitation' they arouse (or in some cases, Breuer concedes, to excessive shock, 'fright, anxiety and anger'), and undergo a process (of 'conversion' or 'suggestion') that transforms the affect into somatic phenomena (1893: 247). On the next storey up, and still beneath ground level, is the floor that accommodates the absence or 'vacancy of consciousness'; it is a storey that is close to ground level but not conscious enough to be so. This storey denotes a 'special frame of mind' that resembles hypnosis or 'hallucinatory confusion' (1893: 214, 248). This 'hypnoid' state, as Breuer refers to it, is caused by the excitation and emotional shocks that originated in the storey below, and also by 'exhausting factors' such as 'sleeplessness' and 'hunger' (1893: 215–22), which can also be placed there. Because Breuer tells us that this state of mind is present in some, but not all, cases of hysteria, we should not regard this storey as a definitive design feature of his house of hysteria, but as an optional floor or extension. It is located between the lower basement of the 'conversions of effective excitations' that we have already described, and the uppermost storey of consciousness, where the somatic symptoms are experienced. Breuer tells us that the 'hypnoid' state 'facilitates in the greatest degree both conversion and suggestion'—and it is perhaps due to the close relationship between the two that Breuer positions their respective storeys close to each other, with the hypnoid state placed 'on the top', as a 'higher storey' (1893: 248–9). Interestingly, Breuer tells us that, when the hypnoid state of mind is active, it often alternates rapidly with normal, waking states (1893: 216) and establishes a barrier to the normal conscious mind, preventing the hysterical person from recalling to conscious awareness the experiences they have had when in the throes of their hypnoid state of mind (1893: 247). Although Breuer himself doesn't make an explicit connection between the hypnoid storey and an uppermost storey of the conscious mind, given the 'clear-cut alternation' that he describes between the two we can assume they are intended to be in spatial proximity to one another, thereby positioning the hypnoid storey close to ground level.

Finally comes the top storey of consciousness, which, although not explicitly identified in this analogy as a storey in its own right, is nevertheless implied as such. Consciousness, Breuer notes, is the place where hysterical phenomena finally 'emerge' as if brought, at last, into light (1893: 217); a place above ground—like the trunk of a tree—if we are to be guided by his earlier analogy. We further deduce from Breuer's description of the conscious mind of the hysteric that the aesthetics of its architectural counterpart is one of two extremes. It is either strongly lit, distinctive, and with a clearly delineated and organised structure, or it is disorganised, dull, and in part-shadow. That is because hysterical people, he asserts, either have 'the clearest intellect, strongest will, greatest character and highest critical power', or are, in stark contrast, 'feeble-minded', and prone to 'silliness, incompetence and weakness of will' (1893: 232–3).

Breuer's house of psyche can be furnished with the installation of much-needed staircases to enable access between its storeys and the facilitation of the processes that connect them. Of stairs, architect Christopher Alexander aptly notes that they are 'not just a way of getting from one floor to another. The stair is itself a space, a volume, a part of the building; and unless this space is made to live, it will be a dead spot, and work to disconnect the building and tear its processes apart' (Alexander et al. 1977: 638). Likewise, architect Juhani Pallasmaa asserts:

> The staircase is the most important organ of the house [...] Stairs are responsible for the vertical circulation of the house in the same way as the heart keeps pumping blood up and down the body'. Without stairs, 'our houses would be without floors, cellars and attics [...]. As our modern houses have lost their attics and their cellars, they have also lost their memory.
>
> (Pallasmaa 2000: 9–10)

The addition of stairs in Breuer's building is particularly fitting when we consider their Freudian connotations alongside Breuer's assertion that hysterical symptoms originate in sexual excitation. Although Breuer's descriptive account begins at the bottom of the building and works its way up to the top, it doesn't follow that we must only ever walk up the imagined staircase within this particular house, as if it were an escalator programmed to travel ever upwards.[4] Indeed, Breuer suggests, for instance, that the hypnoid storey encourages a two-way movement, both up and down, between it and the floor below it (for the hypnoid state, he tells us, both facilitates and is shaped by the activity housed below). Similarly, he concedes that hysteria originates from causes that reside both below ground, in rooms 'inadmissible to consciousness', and in conscious ideas that he places above ground level (1893: 229). Suggestive of a staircase that allows passage in either direction, up or down the building's different storeys, is Breuer's reference to the various causes of hysteria as 'an almost unbroken scale, passing through every gradation of vagueness and obscurity, between perfectly conscious ideas' and those that remain unconscious (1893: 229).

Freud's architecture of psyche

When scholars allude to Freud's architectural metaphors of psyche they tend to refer mistakenly to Breuer's house of hysteria. Although Breuer's metaphor of the house features in a book jointly authored with Freud, it appears in a section written only by Breuer, and contrary to common belief, Breuer's blueprint does not represent Freud's own architectural vision of the psyche. Indeed, in a letter of 1907 written by Freud to Jung, Freud distances himself from Breuer's architectural design: although 'the idea of the building of several storeys comes from Breuer (in the general section of the *Studies*), the building itself, I believe, ought to be described rather differently' (Freud and Jung 1974: Letter 55F; 102[5]). We shall see that Freud took it upon himself to redesign the house of hysteria using a variety of examples. And although the general layout in most cases remains faithful to Breuer's blueprint, Freud went on to modify specific features of the design. Freud's architectural imagery is scattered throughout his letters, essays and monographs, and so we shall consider their various designs from the period shortly after 1895, when his publication with Breuer was finalised, up to and including Freud's mature works.

We begin with a simple Freudian design that is radically different from Breuer's in its horizontal alignment. Here the unconscious is placed not below consciousness, as Breuer insists, but to its side to create two adjoining rooms. Freud's description is rarely cited and is largely unacknowledged by Freud scholars and commentators. It appears in one of his introductory lectures on psychoanalysis called 'Resistance and Repression' (1917a), and is introduced by Freud in a similar manner to Breuer's introduction to his own simple, two-storey building, with the caveat that spatial metaphors for the depiction of psyche are limited (1917a:2 95–6). The building Freud describes comprises a large entrance hall with an adjoining drawing room. This simple building is intended to illustrate how the mind censors its unconscious material, allowing only some aspects to pass into the realm of consciousness while preventing others. The unconscious is represented by the hall, within which mental impulses jostle together 'like separate individuals' competing for the opportunity to enter the adjoining room. This second room is decidedly 'narrower' than the hall; it is 'a kind of drawing-room—in which consciousness, too, resides' (1917a: 295). The drawing room does not represent consciousness alone, as consciousness is just one of its inhabitants. Rather, Freud implies, the room is divided into two areas that represent two contrasting functions. The area further from the hall is inhabited or used by consciousness, and the area closer to the hall is assigned to the 'preconscious'—a part of the mind that is neither conscious nor unconscious, from which material that has not been repressed can be recalled to consciousness relatively easily at the command of the ego.[6] In this building, unconscious impulses can become conscious only when they pass into the 'end' of the drawing room where consciousness resides 'as a spectator' (1917a: 296).

As with Breuer's design, Freud's emphasises the division of a building into at least two parts to accommodate the psyche's contrasting conscious and unconscious aspects. These parts, depicted here as rooms, are divided by a barrier such as a ceiling or wall. In Freud's example the barrier between hall and drawing room is inhabited by a 'watchman', who 'acts as a censor' by examining the different mental impulses and refusing admission to the drawing room to those who 'displease him' (1917a: 295). The watchman is akin to a 'bouncer' who checks a person's identification at the nightclub door before granting them admission or turning them away. Within Freud's building, the watchman is responsible, Freud says, for the repression of instincts (those who are refused entry), and the censorship of dreams (those allowed inside but with limited access). Dream-like experiences, we shall see, play a large role in our everyday encounters with buildings, and denote the admission of unconscious ideas to conscious awareness, albeit in codified or censored form.

This one-storey layout is unusual among Freud's buildings of psyche, and as such it is unlikely on its own to encapsulate all that he intends for his vision of a different architectural design of psyche from the one proposed by Breuer; it is simply one of several potential plans for renovation that he presents. Let us now consult Freud's other plans and consider how they illuminate his understanding of the relationships between the conscious and unconscious aspects of mind, and between memory and somatic experience. This will become useful in our later discussion of the nature of our relationships and identification with architecture.

Freud's buildings of hysteria

In May 1897, two years after the publication of Breuer's house of hysteria, Freud visited Nuremberg. Upon his return he sent four letters to physician and colleague Wilhelm Fliess, with a series of detailed notes entitled 'The Architecture of Hysteria'. In these notes Freud likens hysteria to architectural structures of defence and fortifications or outworks, designed to prevent access to the vulnerable interiors of towns and cities—or, in the case of hysteria, the traumatic memories of the subject's past. Scholar W.J. McGrath maintains that Freud was so impressed with the medieval buildings he saw on his trip to Nuremberg that he incorporated their image into this description of hysteria. McGrath goes so far as to suggest that the 'origin' of the very idea of 'the Architecture of Hysteria', and the reason Freud selected this title for his account of hysteria, is the strong impression made on him by 'the architecture he had seen' in Nuremberg (1986: 153). The fact that Breuer had described a similar house of hysteria just two years earlier within his major collaborative work with Freud, *Studies of Hysteria*, surprisingly eludes McGrath. Also escaping his attention is another pertinent and well-known architectural image that Freud published just one year before he wrote his letter to Fliess. This was Freud's description of an archaeological excavation of architectural remains, which he uses to illustrate psychoanalytic methods of interpretation in the light of his assertion that consciousness is dependent on the unconscious for its organisation and expression. It appears in his essay 'Heredity and the Aetiology of the Neuroses' (1896) as follows:

> Imagine that an explorer arrives in a little-known region where his interest is aroused by an expanse of ruins, with remains of walls, fragments of columns, and tablets with half-effaced and unreadable inscriptions. He may content himself with inspecting what lies exposed to view [...] and he may act differently. He may have brought picks, shovels and spades with him [...] [W]ith them he may start upon the ruins, clear away the rubbish, and beginning from the visible remains, uncover what is buried. If his work is crowned with success, the discoveries are self-explanatory: the ruined walls are part of the ramparts of a palace or a treasure-house; the fragments of columns can be filled out into a temple [...]
>
> (Freud 1896: 192)

While the analyst may readily observe the *conscious* expression of the psychological problem (which is represented here as the visible surface above ground where architectural fragments poke out, in similar manner to the upper storey of Breuer's house, where hysterical symptoms are perceived), the *unconscious* foundation or cause of the problem remains hidden and out of sight. The cause must therefore be unearthed and analysed carefully if it is to be understood. Just as the discovery of an architectural fragment or a wall or column will not lead one immediately to comprehend the entire complex, palace, or temple of which it is part, the conscious experience of a psychological illness, Freud claims, does not always lead one immediately to an accurate diagnosis and understanding of its cause and aetiology. Here the ruined building represents the psyche, and the architectural fragments the psychological conflicts of the troubled psyche. The metaphor suggests that we can learn more about the conflict and understand its cause if we examine the spatial arrangements of the fragmented, dissociated parts of the self in relation to the psyche as a whole.[7]

The archaeological theme of this analogy also addresses the degrees of effort it takes for a person to recall to consciousness events that happened in their recent and distant past. In other words, the layers of the architectural remains tend to increase in age the more deeply situated they are in the ground, and the same can be said of memories—memories of the distant past being less accessible and harder to recall than recent events: they are further from 'the surface' of consciousness. Freud is keen, however, to emphasise that traumatic experiences are difficult to unearth, irrespective of when they happened in a person's life, because their emotional, affective nature makes them difficult to recall, and therefore they have been banished from memory, repressed, or, we might say, 'stuck' underground. This is why, in the archaeological analogy, we may excavate a fragment of the base of a column before locating its pediment, or unearth a brick from the bottom of a wall before discovering one originally from the top.

Freud's archaeological metaphor parallels Breuer's house of several storeys, but with notable differences that contribute to Freud's overall vision of a different building of psyche. These include the fragmentary arrangement of its parts, the search for structure, and the direction of movement at the start of the analogy, with Freud excavating downwards from the ground surface, and Breuer at the foundations working his way upwards.

Returning now to Freud's letters to Fliess entitled 'Architecture of Hysteria', we can begin to appreciate how its architectural analogy is just one in an evolution of architectural analogies that Freud employs to make sense of the dynamics of psyche. Indeed, if the architectural sites of Nuremberg influenced the imagery in Freud's letters to Fliess, it was simply in order to furnish the architectural blueprints that had already begun to take shape in his mind. Let us turn to the second series of notes that Freud sent to Fliess, which includes a curious diagram of hysteria (Fig. 2.1), which several commentators have interpreted as a sketch of a building, and thus Freud's architectural design of hysteria.

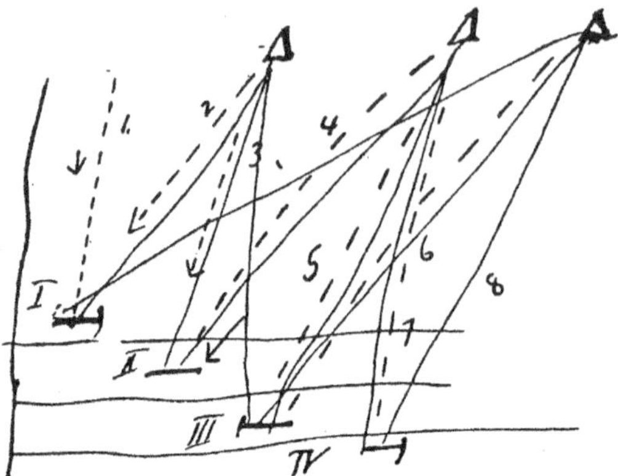

Figure 2.1 Freud, Diagram from 'House of Hysteria', 1897
In the original sketch, the dotted line, arrows, and numerals are in red ink, as is the word 'work' that appears to the right of the sketch.
Freud (1897: 248–51) ©Vintage/Random House

According to scholars William McGrath (1986) and Joan Resina (2003), the diagram is an image of a Nuremberg tower, complete with its traditional spires and roof tops. Whitney Davis regards it as a generic castle with turrets (1996: 295–6), while Laurence Simmons describes it as a 'fortress' (2006: 10). Jane Rendell interprets it more abstractly as an architectural blueprint or topographical model that emphasises spatial perspective generally (2012: 2).

As a diagram of hysteria, the sketch depicts as layers the memories, both recent and long-past, of the hysterical patient which have become attached to their current symptoms. The symptoms are represented by the little triangles, while the psychoanalyst's 'work' with the patient is depicted as a movement represented by broken lines. Freud describes the therapeutic work as having to make 'repeated loops through the background thoughts' that underpin each symptom, until at last the psychoanalyst and patient succeed in exposing these thoughts to consciousness, and thereby reveal, too, their connection to the deepest, repressed memories of the patient that otherwise manifest themselves through the patient's symptoms. In the diagram this breakthrough occurs with the eighth loop, where the line of the work comes to an end. The repeated visits to the background thoughts, represented by the looping orientation of the broken line, is reminiscent of the movement we envisaged within Breuer's house of hysteria, of going up and down the imagined staircases that connect the storeys of the building. If we regard Freud's diagram as a sketch of a building, we could well imagine each break of its looping lines as individual steps, and the lines themselves as staircases that connect the various background thoughts to the different layers—or storeys—of memory. Whitney Davis imagines the broken line of the therapeutic work differently, comparing it to the techniques of a 'restoration worker', who attends to a building by

Figure 2.2 Medieval fortifications, Nuremberg, Germany

'descending the façade of a building from above'. Similar to the work of psychoanalyst and patient, Davis notes that restoration workers 'climb down the memory system and climb out again' (1995: 81).

At a glance Freud's sketch is perhaps easier to comprehend as an architectural image than an aetiological account of hysteria. Its semblance to a castle is easily recognised, and both McGuire and Resina are keen to give the castle in question a specific identity by associating it with the façades of those medieval fortifications that Freud encountered in Nuremberg shortly before he drew the sketch (Fig. 2.2). Resina's rationale for equating the two is based on the notion that 'architecture as densely historical as that of Nuremberg is well suited' to Freud's theory of hysteria, which 'seeks to account for layers of experience concealed by symptoms' (2003: 229). McGrath supports his claim by alluding to the similarity of their specific design features, noting, for instance, how the diagram's solid lines 'form three pyramidal spires' that 'echo the pyramidal shape of the roofs atop the Nürnberg [Nuremberg] fortifications'. Furthermore, the hysterical symptoms, he says, are depicted as small triangles atop 'each spire', just like the 'small weather vanes in the shape of flags' that would have adorned the spires of the towers that Freud visited (McGrath 1986: 192).[8]

Architectural Rome as City of Memory

In Freud's Rome the excavation work of the archaeologist is abandoned as the architectural legacy of this city is already immediately and fully exposed to the eye. If an archaeologist were to feature in this analogy, they would very quickly find themselves out of a job and in the impossible position of being able to observe every historical layer of the city at once, with every building and architectural feature that has at one time or another been erected in Rome intact and in place. Freud's account appears in his major work *Civilization and Its Discontents* (1930) as an illustration of the manner in which the mind conserves its experiences within the unconscious. Given that, as Freud claims, 'nothing which has once been formed' in our minds can 'perish', every experience we have had that isn't of immediate relevance to our conscious concerns has to be stored within a different 'layer' of the mind. 'The Eternal City' of Rome represents for Freud the analogous architectural counterpart to the unconscious mind as a storage place, where nothing is lost and all is preserved. We can postulate Rome as a 'mental entity', he says, with a 'long and copious' past in which 'nothing that has once been constructed has perished' and all the 'stages' of its architectural 'development' have 'survived alongside the latest'.

Remains of ancient Rome are conspicuous in the modern-day city—'woven' into its 'fabric', as Freud put it—but in his analogy, Freud seeks to amplify their presence alongside every other architectural structure that has at one time or another been erected in the city, by resurrecting in mind every building no longer physically present and imagining each intact and in place alongside their modern-day counterparts. In doing so, we observe the memory of the city. Freud writes:

> [T]he palaces of the Caesars and the Septizonium of Septimius Severus would still be rising to their old height on the Palatine and the castle of S.Angelo would still be carrying on its battlements the beautiful statues which graced it until the siege by the Goths [...] In the place occupied by the Palazzo Caffarelli would once more stand—without the Palazzo having to be removed—the Temple of Jupiter Capitolinus; and this not only in its latest shape, as the Romans of the Empire saw it, but also in its earliest one, when it showed Etruscan forms and was ornamented with terracotta antefixes. Where the Coliseum now stands we could at the same time admire Nero's vanished Golden House. On the Piazza of the Pantheon we should find not only the Pantheon of today, as it was bequeathed to us by Hadrian, but, on the same site, the original edifice erected by Agrippa; indeed, the same piece of ground would be supporting the church of Santa Maria sopra Minerva and the ancient temple over which it was built. And the observer would perhaps only have to change the direction of his glance or his position in order to call up the one view or the other.
>
> (Freud 1930: 70)

Plate 1 Two examples of 'sterile' architecture, as discussed in Chapter 1 (see *Figure 1.2*)

Plate 2.3 The Professor's Dream (C.R. Cockerell, 1848). This painting, with its buildings from around the world, superimposed on to each other, resembles what Freud had in mind for his eternal city of Rome

Freud's composition of Rome contrasts starkly with the philosophical constructions of Descartes and Kant, who, as we noted in Chapter 1, require the architectural blueprint of being to be designed and built by a single architect according to precepts of certainty and reasoning so as to ensure the structure's overall unity, coherence, and reliability. Freud wildly flouts such principles in this blueprint by assigning the construction work to a great number of architects, spanning centuries, each with their different styles and methods of construction. In so doing, he establishes an incoherent and incongruous cityscape that collectively appears as if designed and built according to precepts of 'phantasy'[9] and 'imagination'. These contrasting approaches will become significant in our investigation in terms of the manner in which they convey the two principal strategies that each of us employs in our interactions with architecture and in the elaboration of our selves. In the next chapter we explain how certainty and reason, on the one hand, and phantasy and imagination, on the other, describe the instinctual divisions of self and the manner of their expression or manifestation within our behaviour. On the one hand, ego-consciousness, with its rational disposition, seeks to appropriate the environment, to order and stabilize it, so as to find it familiar and predictable; the unconscious, on the other hand, engages with the environment haphazardly, in unpredictable and unfathomable ways that can destabilise the ego, surprise it, and dislodge it from the comforts of its dwelling.

Freud decided to abandon his Rome analogy due to the implausible nature of its spatial relations, with several buildings positioned in one and the same location. It was as if his rational sensibilities caught up with him, encouraging him to yield to the inescapable fact that buildings are not 'eternal'; they eventually fall apart, or are demolished, and replaced by others. The city of Rome became for him an inappropriate metaphor for the timeless preservation of the unconscious. Freud's decision may seem abrupt given the detail he invests in his description of the analogy, and his criticism of his description is rooted in a fact that is glaringly obvious from the outset. However, we find him arriving at similar conclusions elsewhere in his writings, which suggest that he had been mulling over the validity of this analogy for some time both before and after its appearance as the city of Rome within *Civilization and Its Discontents*. For instance, in an essay that precedes the Rome analogy by fifteen years, Freud describes the following:

> When a village grows into a town or a child into a man, the village and the child become lost in the town and the man. Memory alone can trace the old features in the new picture; and in fact the old materials or forms have been got rid of and replaced by new ones.
>
> (Freud 1915a: 285)

And seven years after the Rome analogy, in the essay 'Constructions in Analysis' (1937), Freud highlights some of the discrepancies between the methods and objectives of psychoanalysis and those of archaeological excavation and the building of houses. While archaeology merely *reconstructs* the past, psychoanalysis, he says, *constructs* it, and in a manner different from the construction of a house. That is to say, architects plan their construction in advance; they know immediately 'where all the walls must be erected and all the windows inserted before the internal decoration of the rooms can be taken in hand'. But 'things happen differently in an analytic treatment', because the unconscious material out of which the psychoanalyst and patient construct their work is volatile and unpredictable. Freud's castle-like diagram illustrates the therapeutic work as a broken, looping pathway, and here its indirect, non-linear progression is described as bits of work carried out 'side by side', and 'alternating' between different focal points or features (1937: 260). To illustrate Freud's point, we might imagine the builder, who in attempting to construct a building using psychoanalytic methods, finds he is having to decorate its internal rooms before or at the same time as constructing the external walls that will determine the position of each room.

Freud's criticism of his Rome analogy harks back to his warning about the limitations of spatial metaphors for elucidating the dynamic nature of the mind. Just as the builder who employs psychoanalytic construction methods to construct his house will inevitably fail, the Rome analogy collapses on the ground that no two buildings can be in the same place at one and the same time. However, Freud's criticism isn't altogether persuasive. Scholar and Freudian analyst Christopher Bollas notes:

> Perhaps if Freud had sustained the metaphor a bit longer its dialectic would have worked. For obliterations are indeed part of the unconscious, so much so that depending on how one wished to look at the Rome of one's unconscious life, we could see both the preserved and the destroyed.
> (Bollas 2000: 28)

Scholar E.V. Walter finds Freud's criticism similarly unconvincing, and suggests that the Rome analogy is sustainable if we focus on the evocative nature of Rome's buildings rather than their geographical location. He writes:

> [A] city like Rome does hold in storage the entire contents of past experience—as the individual mind conserves its own experience in the unconscious. In Freud's metaphor, Rome is a physical reality—a set of buildings and streets. But a place is more than its physique, and the ruins of an historic city are the expressive spaces holding the experience of its past.
> (Walter 1988: 109)

Walter's point here touches upon central themes of our investigation, which will be examined in the chapters that follow, such as the usefulness of architectural analogies of psyche for their insights into the evocative nature of architecture, and the relationship of actual buildings to the unconscious impulses that manage our experiences and cultivate our sense of self.

Freud himself certainly recognised the evocative power of architecture. For instance, I suggested that the correspondence he makes between the staircase and the vagina is determined in part by the rhythmic sensations one has when walking upstairs; but this is just one example of many that Freud makes in his allusion to the affective nature of architecture. Others are his discussion in his introductory *Lectures on Psychoanalysis* (1910) of stone monuments and their semblance to psychological symptoms by virtue of their 'mnemonic', symbolic nature. Stone monuments do not simply commemorate the past but express, and often relieve, traumatic experiences (1910: 16–17[10]). But perhaps the most striking example is his intriguing description of his experience of the Acropolis in Athens. Reminiscent of his invitation to have us imagine Rome's buildings, both past and present, in their original placement and condition, we find Freud unintentionally undertaking a similar exercise when observing the architectural ruins of the Acropolis. We examine this case in detail in Chapter 5 to demonstrate how the impressions of the fragmented building compel him to imagine how it would once have appeared in its pristine condition, and, following this, how the juxtaposition of these contrasting images led Freud to recall to mind other fragmentary information of a more personal nature—including memory traces of experiences that had until that point in time lain dormant, forgotten, unconscious, and repressed within him. Although causally unrelated, Freud's experience of the Acropolis also reveals, on closer inspection, that its architectural features and unconscious material converge in Freud's mind via a sequence of associated meanings that are personally evocative and poignant to him. Freud's anecdotal account provides us with a useful case study that helps to clarify how we can engage with architecture in such a way that it impresses upon us various meanings and experiences that are otherwise unconscious and inaccessible to us, and that can as a consequence be incorporated into our conscious ego-personality as a psychological reconstruction of ourselves.

Psychosomatic houses of Freud and Scherner

While Freud warns us of the dangers of literalising spatial metaphors, he comes treacherously close to flouting his own instruction by ascribing hard and fast psychological meanings to architecture. But, as I have suggested, this tendency may in fact express a deeper concern at work—an attempt on Freud's part (whether or not deliberate) to indicate how particular forms and features of architecture give rise to or resonate with specific experiences we have of ourselves. Freud tends to focus on bodily experiences, and so the architectural features of his buildings of psyche are most often assigned specific body parts. Indeed, we could interpret the Freudian building of psyche as a map of the human body and its various bodily sensations. Freud develops the tradition of designing buildings according to bodily form and measurement with the inclusion of the psychological experiences, as he interprets them, of the various body parts in question. Freud's architectural representations of the human body are most apparent in his iconic work, *The Interpretation of Dreams* (1900), where he discusses them as 'dream symbols', by which he means the motifs and images that are generated by the unconscious mind as we sleep, imagine, or daydream.

According to Freud, the unconscious uses architectural images, among others, to depict and convey its material to us. This imagery, he says, more often than not seeks to convey important information about the condition of our body, and our genitals in particular. He writes: 'The frequency with which buildings, localities, and landscapes are employed as symbolic representations of the body, and in particular (with constant reiteration) of the genitals, would certainly deserve a comprehensive study, illustrated by numerous examples' (1900: 484, n.1). Although he implies that there hasn't yet been such a study, Freud refers at length to a study that could certainly be interpreted as one. This is the work of the physiologist K.A. Scherner (1861).

Freud's motive for citing Scherner's study is not altogether clear. Some thirty years before Breuer published his house of hysteria, Scherner sought to demonstrate, Freud tells us, the precision by which the 'human body as a whole is pictured by the dream-imagination as a house and the separate organs of the body by portions of a house' (Freud 1900: 225). On the one hand, Freud applauds Scherner for demonstrating how the unconscious generates dream-symbols, and architectural ones in particular: 'It is perfectly true,' Freud says of Scherner's hypothesis, that 'dreams contain symbolizations of bodily organs and functions', so that, for instance, 'the male genitals can be represented by an upright stick or a pillar, and so on' (1900: 322). But on the other hand, Freud is keen to dismiss Scherner's hypothesis for being 'over-fantastic' and 'extravagant'.

A closer reading reveals, however, that Freud's qualm isn't with the strict equation Scherner establishes between architectural image and body part, but with Scherner's insistence that dream-images are caused by physical bodily sensations that occur when we sleep, and not, as Freud wishes to argue, by unconscious conflicts that seek conscious expression. In other words, while Scherner arrives at something that could be construed as a 'house of body', Freud postulates a 'psycho-somatic house'—one that both represents and evokes the tensions between body and mind and thereby includes the 'psychical residues', 'memory-traces', and other features of hysteria that appear in the houses of Breuer and Freud.

An important implication of their diverging views on this matter is that for Freud, images or 'symbols' of the unconscious arise at all times of the day, not simply when we are asleep; they are, he says, 'habitually present' in all our thoughts and behaviours, not merely in our dreams. This means that architectural imagery is enlisted by the unconscious to express its material at any given time.[11] Later we shall develop this idea and explain how Freud's theories of unconscious thinking can be applied to our everyday experiences of architecture, and how buildings enable the transition of unconscious ideas to conscious awareness.

Freud refers to several examples from Scherner's study of occasions when bodily sensations are said to shape architectural dream-imagery. Dreams that are stimulated by sensations originating in the teeth, for instance, will feature large entrance-halls, with high, vaulted roods (which correspond to the oral cavity) and staircases (which denote here not the vagina but the descent from throat to oesophagus). And dreams 'with an intestinal stimulus may lead the dreamer along muddy streets' (1900: 157). Most comical is the description of dreams caused by headaches, for these will likely present 'the top of the head' as the 'ceiling of a room covered with disgusting, toad-like spiders' (1900: 320, 157[12]). Freud furnishes his discussion with several examples of his own. Given Freud's attribution of dream-imagery to repressed experiences, and his insistence that these experiences are usually sexual in nature, Freud tends to describe architectural imagery as representations of male and female genitalia. If one were to perceive the built environment through a Freudian lens, one might well survey a landscape of sexualised body parts. Thus for Freud, 'narrow spaces', 'steep passages', 'locked and opened doors', 'cupboards', 'hollow objects', and 'vessels of all kinds', describe the vagina or uterus (1900: 124,471); while 'steps', 'ladders', and 'staircases', as we noted, are 'unquestionably, symbols of copulation', for 'we come to the top' of them 'in a series of rhythmical movements and with increasing breathlessness and then, with a few rapid leaps, we can get to the bottom again. Thus the rhythmical pattern of copulation is reproduced in going upstairs' (1900: 472 n.2, 489).[13] 'Smooth walls over which [one] climbs and, the facades of houses', he says, correspond to 'erect human bodies' (1900: 472), and window-sills and balconies on houses are projected female breasts (1900: 492). 'Two rooms which were originally one' or 'a familiar room divided into two' denote an infantile conception of the female genitals and anus. Pillars and columns represent the legs, and 'every gateway stands for one of the bodily orifices (a "hole")' and 'every water-pipe is a reminder of the urinary apparatus' (1900: 462). Freud concludes his discussion by asserting that it is only when the correlation between the architectural form and bodily representation is known that 'dreams become intelligible' and can be interpreted adequately (1900: 474).

The meanings Freud imparts to architectural imagery can seem reductive, despite his suggestion that the interpretation of each dream-image ought to be considered within the particularity of its context, including the disposition of the subject who creates it. He further concedes that the house, although a 'favourite symbol' of the body for Scherner (and clearly for him too), is not the only one (1900: 462). The impact of this latter point is somewhat lessened, however, when we consider that the various examples Freud gives to convey these other possibilities depart from the house-motif only partially and continue to present variations on its architectural theme. He suggests, for instance, the kitchen, passageways, courtyards, city streets, and rows of houses.[14] Freud writes:

> Fortunately, however, [the dream-imagination] does not seem to be restricted to this one method of representation [the house]. On the other hand, it may make use of a whole row of houses to indicate a single organ; for instance, a very long street of houses may represent a stimulus from the intestines. Again, separate portions of a house may stand for separate portions of the body [...] [T]he narrow space where the thighs come together may be represented by a courtyard surrounded by houses, while the vagina may be symbolized by a soft, slippery and very narrow foot-path leading across the yard.
>
> (1900: 156–7, 462)

Freud is often accused of reductionism in his interpretation of symbols, whether dream-images or physical symptoms.[15] Such reductionism has important implications for our investigation, as it makes certain assumptions and value claims about the way we perceive our bodies and, by extension, the quality of architectural designs. For instance, if a headache corresponds, as Freud claims, to a ceiling covered with 'disgusting' creatures, we are led to assume that a broken window, a faulty door, a cracked ceiling, or any other faulty or misaligned feature also denotes a physical ailment or mental disorder. If we were to adopt such an approach, we would likely question whether postmodern or deconstructivist architectural designs, with their disembodied features and twisted, fragmentary structures, are conveying a pathological message, revealing themselves, or those who use or appreciate their constructions, to be somehow defective, sick, and in need of a cure. We shall explore these issues throughout our investigation.

Next, however, we turn to the architectural blueprints of psyche proposed by C.G. Jung, whose ideas about the unconscious depart significantly from Freud's. Jung believed that his approach to the unconscious and its symbolic imagery was more flexible and realistic than Freud's. This is reflected in the designs of his buildings of psyche, and is suggested too in his comments about the meaning of the house-motif as it appears in dreams: 'The house recurs very often as a symbol in dreams', he says, 'and it generally means the habitual or inherited attitude, the habitual way of living, or something acquired like a house, or perhaps the way one lives with the whole family' (1928b: 39). We shall see later, however, that his architectural analogies do not escape charges of reductionism by those who claim that they, too, fail to convey the evocative nature of the psyche as realistically as they might.[16]

The houses that Jung built

Given that Jung's general conception of the psyche as a divisible and divided whole is similar to that of Freud and Breuer, it is not surprising that the general structure of his architectural blueprints of psyche is also like theirs. Indeed, Breuer's house of psyche (which, as we noted, is often incorrectly attributed to Freud) is regarded by some as having had a direct influence on Jung's own.[17] Certainly Jung appears to replicate Breuer's simple house of psyche when describing his own early views of the unconscious, at a time when Jung hadn't developed his own distinctive psychology. 'In those times', he writes, 'I thought of the conscious as a room above, with the unconscious as a cellar underneath and then the earth wellspring, that is, the body, sending up the instincts' (Jung 1925: 23; cf. 1935: 371[18]; 1955: 266[19]). When Jung establishes his own ideas about the mind, the structural layout of his buildings of psyche likewise changes. The contrast between Jung's own architectural blueprint of psyche and those of Freud or Breuer highlights their key theoretical disagreements and expose the major points of contention between their respective schools of thought. But, as we shall see in Chapter 6, their different structural layouts also have practical implications in terms of the nature of our identifications with architecture and the extent to which the built environment shapes us.

If we regard the houses of Freud and Breuer at their most basic as two-storey buildings with a storey above ground (consciousness) and one below it (the unconscious), Jung renovates the design with the addition of a third storey, situated beneath the basement rooms of the unconscious.[20] Jung thereby divides the unconscious into two: the *personal* unconscious (which loosely corresponds to the unconscious postulated by Freud and Breuer), which is placed immediately below ground level, and a deeper, more archaic realm that he names the *collective* unconscious. If the personal unconscious comprises those ideas and experiences that have been forgotten or repressed by a person, the collective unconscious is an instinctual realm of human experience comprising universal or 'archetypal' patterns of behaviour that affect us all.[21]

The most iconic of Jung's architectural descriptions is an account of a dream he claims to have had in 1909, when travelling with Freud to Massachusetts. The dream, he says, brought to his attention the existence of the collective unconscious, and thereby heralded his theoretical departure from Freud's model of mind, and the traumatic breakdown of their relationship that occurred as a result. Interestingly, two years earlier, in 1907, when Jung first met Freud in Vienna, Jung reportedly dreamt of another architectural edifice, the details of which, I suggest, can be interpreted as an earlier warning of the differences between their ideas and the disaster that would befall their personal relationship. Early in their relationship, Jung came to regard Freud's approach as reductive and restrictive in its interpretations of psychological experience—a problem that imprints itself in a dream of a claustrophobic architectural structure that Jung had while staying with Freud. Jung reported the dream to his friend E.A. Bennet, who recounts it thus: 'He was in a ghetto in Prague and it was narrow, twisted and low-ceilinged with staircases hanging down. He thought: "How in hell can people live in such a place?"' (Bennet 1985: 65). But it would seem that Jung had to wait until the dream-house of 1909 before he was able more fully to articulate his differences with Freud, and to convey this disagreement in more detailed architectural terms, while at the same time realising more generally that buildings are veritable 'images of the psyche' (Jung 1961b: 184, 185).

Jung's dream-house of psyche (1909)

Jung describes one dream but four slightly different versions of the dream-house that appears within it. These are described in four publications, written between 1925 and 1964.[22] In the dream Jung finds himself inspecting 'a big complicated house with many rooms, passages and stairways' (1925: 23), the design features of which become progressively older as he descends through its several storeys. He begins on the upper storey of the building in a room of eighteenth-century, European rococo design—an ornate design of frilly surfaces and elegant ornamentation that boasts, he says, an 'inhabited atmosphere' (1961b: 184), and thereby expresses the much lived-in domain of ego-consciousness. Jung asserts that 'we live on the upper storey'; just as 'the building rises freely above the earth, so our consciousness stands as if above the earth in space, with a wide prospect before it' (1927: par. 55). He leaves this part of the building and finds himself walking down steps and into rooms of fifteenth- or sixteenth-century construction with a medieval red brick ground floor (1961b: 182). A 'careful examination of the masonry reveals' the floor to have been 'reconstructed from a tower built in the eleventh century'. The ground floor of the building represents, Jung says, the 'first level of the unconscious': the personal unconscious (1961b: 184). Jung discovers additional floors beneath ground level, which denote 'deeper', 'darker' levels of the unconscious: the collective unconscious. In the dream these floors incorporate an ancient vaulted room, deduced by Jung to be Roman, and a still more ancient room at the lowest level of the house that appears as a tomb-like cave cut into rock, thick with dust, skulls, bones, and broken shards of pottery (1961b: 182–3; 1961a: par. 484), and 'Neolithic tools' and 'remnants of fauna' (1927: par. 54). It is in the basement of the collective unconscious that Jung says he discovered 'the world of the primitive man within myself' (1961b: 184; 1935: par. 197).

By exploring the building's several storeys Jung is investigating the different realms of psyche, traversing the boundaries between consciousness and personal and collective unconsciousness. Jung attributes the creation of this dream-image to the depths of the collective unconscious, but one could also argue that its imagery reflects in its design features the residues or imprints of other buildings that were of personal significance for Jung, buildings that had been preserved within his personal unconscious mind and had subsequently been woven into the dream-image via a sequence of unconscious processes that we consider later (in Chapter 5). Certainly, Jung believed that the dream-house was his own; it was, he says, 'my house' (1961b: 182; Bennet 1966: 73); 'my home' (Jung 1964: 42; Jung 1961a: par. 484); 'where [I] lived' (Bennet 1985: 118).[23]

228 Seestrasse in Küsnacht and the upper storey of the dream-house

Of the many houses that made an impression on Jung there are several that resemble in one way or other the architectural configuration of the 1909 dream-house.[24] We could point to a number of houses of similar design and décor to the eighteenth-century upper storey of the dream-house that featured prominently in his life prior to this dream. More remarkable, however, is its resemblance to the house at Küsnacht by Lake Zurich, which Jung designed (in collaboration with his cousin, architect Ernst Fiechter) as his family home and therapeutic practice, and a place to entertain acquaintances (Figs 2.4, 2.5).

Figure 2.4 C.G. Jung's house, 228 Seestrasse, Küsnacht: façade (built 1907–1909)
© Martin Gledhill

Figure 2.5 C.G. Jung's house, 228 Seestrasse, Küsnacht: detail of tower
© Martin Gledhill

The Küsnacht house was designed and built within two years, allowing Jung to move in on 25 May 1909—four months before he dreamt his house of psyche into being.[25] Andreas Jung, architect and grandson of Jung (and current resident of the Küsnacht house), finds the correspondence between the original design of the Küsnacht house and Jung's description of the dream-house 'astonishing': they 'coincided exactly' (A. Jung 2009: 23, 25). A working sketch for the Küsnacht house, drafted by Jung in or around 1906, depicts, as A. Jung puts it, a 'baroque upper storey' with 'lavish volute gables' which 'sits on a simple, rustic semi-basement with narrow slits for windows, which may date from the early fifteenth century' (A. Jung 2009: 23). Andreas Jung underscores the point I wish to make in his assertion that, once built, the house 'would only reflect the conventional—that is, "conscious"—layers of the image of the human psyche outlined in the dream (namely the "upper storey [...] in rococo style")' (2009: 25). For Andreas Jung, it is 'the core of the house', which is to say, its 'enormous 3.6-meter high dining room on the ground floor' that most appropriately exemplifies the upper storey of the dream-house and 'Jung's fondness for the eighteenth century' (A. Jung 2009: 75): 'whitewashed, with its deep window recesses, its doors, built-in glass cabinets, [its] panelling in walnut wood, and its ceiling decorated with a curved stucco frame', this house 'breathes the spirit of the eighteenth century' (A. Jung 2009: 67). According to Bennet, Jung's confidant, for Jung himself the study room resonated most strongly with the rococo décor of the dream-house's upper storey (Bennet 1985: 35). Although Andreas Jung makes the connection between the architectural resemblance of the Küsnacht house to Jung's dream-house of 1909, he, somewhat curiously, seems unaware of the significance of his own description of the hall of the Küsnacht house. The hall is an impressive room situated on the ground floor of the building and includes, as Andreas Jung explains, a 'floor covering of red clay tiles and [a] spacious staircase' (2009: 67). In other words, the floor at ground level resembles the medieval red brick ground floor of Jung's dream-building.

We know from his letters to his cousin and to Freud that Jung was intensely preoccupied with the design and construction of the Küsnacht building. Indeed, if we accept, as Jung did, Freud's hypothesis that the events of the day shape the imagery of dreams at night, we can suppose that the plans for the Küsnacht house influenced his dreams around the time of its construction and also on the occasion of his first trip away from his new home, when he dreamt of the house, whose upper storey resembled the house he invested so much of his waking attention in.

The rectory at Basle, the 'tower' at Bollingen, and the lower storeys of the dream-house

If the house at Küsnacht corresponds to the 'conscious' storeys above ground level of the 1909 dream-house of psyche, both the rectory at Basle Cathedral, where Jung's uncle lived,[26] and the house Jung designed and built at Bollingen by Lake Zurich exemplify its lower storeys and the unconscious aspects of psyche.[27] Together, these two buildings represent the entire dream-house of psyche in concrete form—though, as we shall see, the Bollingen building on its own achieved this, according to Jung (Fig. 2.6).

Bennet recalls Jung's interest in the similarities between his dream-house and his uncle's rectory. The dream-house was, as Jung recounted to Bennet, 'a big complicated house, vaguely like my uncle's very old house built upon the ancient city walls at Basle' (Bennet 1966: 73), and 'in the old moat of the town' (Bennet 1985: 118). The significant feature of the rectory was its two cellars, arranged one above the other, the 'lower one' of the two being 'very dark and like a cave' (Bennet 1985: 118). In 1960—half a decade after Jung purportedly dreamt of his multi-storeyed house—the rectory was excavated so that alterations could be made to it. During these excavations it was discovered not only that the building had been 'built on Roman remains', but also that underneath this Roman layer were remains of 'a cellar'—an architectural arrangement that matched Jung's own 'discoveries' in his dream-house. Bennet recalls how this uncanny coincidence was of great interest to Jung, and consolidated his feeling that the dream-house 'was in the family' (Bennet 1985: 124).

Figure 2.6 C.G. Jung's 'Tower' house, Bollingen (built c. 1923–1956)
© Ruth Ammann, Zurich

Jung's house, or 'tower' as he refers to it, is no less striking in its associations with the unconscious aspect of psyche. It was regarded by Jung as a concrete embodiment of his personality, 'innermost thoughts', and 'knowledge' (1961b: 250). This may account for why he dedicates an entire chapter to it in his autobiography. Despite its significance to Jung, the building has attracted little scholarly attention and so has an air of mystery to it, acquiring something akin to mythical status (see Gledhill 2014).[28] The tower is interpreted by Jung scholars as a representation of Jung's unconscious personality and, according to Jung himself, it symbolises the whole psyche, not simply in its method and elements of design, but also in its evocative effect. Jung describes how the tower helped him to engage with his unconscious mind, and feel at one within himself. The Bollingen tower is a house of psyche because it contains Jung, enabling him to negotiate the conflicts and divisions within himself, and to feel integrated as a result.[29]

The building was constructed in five stages between c. 1923 and c. 1956 (see Figs. 2.7–2.11). Its final design and arrangement of parts was not fixed from the start. It was not built to a prescribed blueprint, but gradually grew, as if organically, in response to Jung's psychological needs at the time.[30] Jung describes the building as 'a place of maturation – a maternal womb or maternal figure in which I could become what I was, what I am and will be. It gave

Figure 2.7 C.G. Jung's 'Tower' house, Bollingen: stages of construction: Stage 1: the 'round house'
© Martin Gledhill

Figure 2.8 Stage 2: the tower-like annex
© Martin Gledhill

me a feeling as if I were being reborn in stone' (1961b: 252). Each developmental phase of its construction was elicited by a symbolic 'death' and subsequent desire for 'rebirth' within Jung's personality, and both its initial and final phases of construction were initiated in part by the actual deaths of his mother and his wife.[31] Jung himself describes how the start of each stage of the building's construction gave him intense feelings of 'renewal', and following their completion he would become increasingly aware that 'something was still lacking' in himself, such that he felt 'incomplete' (1961b: 251).

The first phase of construction saw the completion of a 'primitive one-storey dwelling', a 'round structure with a hearth in the centre and bunks on

Figure 2.9 Stage 3: the round room for 'spiritual concentration'

Figure 2.10 Stage 4: the courtyard and loggia

Figure 2.11 Stage 5: the upper storey

the walls' (1961b: 250). According to architectural historian Joseph Rykwert (1972), after the Renaissance the primitive hut became a popular image of the quest for 'architectural purity'; and Jung's intentions for his own one-storey dwelling certainly chime with such a quest, for by this structure, he tells us, he sought to 'concretise an idea of wholeness' (1961b: 250). Jung, however, soon found this structure to be 'too primitive' for his needs. A 'mere hut crouched on the ground', as Jung refers to it, could not express for him the dynamic quality of the unconscious; and so in c. 1927 he made the first of several additions to it by constructing something akin, he says, to a 'regular two-storey house' or 'dwelling tower' with a 'maternal hearth'.

Just as the initial one-storey hut was unsatisfactory for Jung, the two-storey building that replaced it did 'not yet express everything that needed saying [...] something was still lacking' (1961b: 251). And so, another four years later, in c. 1927, he added a central structure with a second short, square tower as an annex. When the foundations for it were being dug, a human skeleton was discovered seven feet underground—a feature that relates to the skulls and bones situated below ground level of the dream-house.[32] Following the completion of this extension, he began to find his building still 'too primitive', and so, after another four-year span, he extended it again in c. 1931, this time by adding a room in the tower similar to those he had seen in Indian houses, where, he says, 'I could exist for myself alone'; a space for 'spiritual concentration' and solitude.[33] The addition of this room elevated the tower and gave it a rounder shape. Four years later still, in c. 1935, Jung fenced in a portion of land and built a courtyard and logia to satisfy his desire for an open and more expansive space, one in contrast to the isolated space of his previous renovation that could connect him to the vastness of the sky and to nature. Jung felt he had completed his building with its four different parts. However, twenty years later, in c. 1956, following the death of his wife, Jung, now in his eightieth year, experienced another push to become, as he puts it, 'what I myself am'. This resulted in an extension to the area between his 'maternal' and 'spiritual' towers, with the construction of a third tower. This tower, the tallest of the three, was to become the central tower of his home. He recalls this final architectural phase of his personal development as follows:

> To put it into the language of the Bollingen house, I suddenly realised that the small central section which crouched so low, so hidden, was myself! I could no longer hide myself behind the 'maternal' and 'spiritual' towers. So, in that same year, I added an upper storey to this section, which represents myself, or my ego-personality. Earlier, I would not have been able to do this; I would have regarded it as presumptuous self-emphasis. Now it signified an extension of consciousness achieved in old age. With that the building was complete.
>
> (1961b: 252)

Compared with the heavy stone of the other parts of the building, this storey of ego-consciousness, located at the top of the third tower, was built in part from wood with large windows that overlook the lake, giving this tower a lighter feel. Jung was at last satisfied with the overall building following this final phase of construction. It was for him, the 'meaningful whole: a symbol of psychic wholeness'—a description he had applied to the primitive hut of its original design (1961b: 251–2). Jung came to know himself through the construction of the Bollingen building, and its design became apparent to him and took gradual shape as and when aspects of himself were disclosed to him through his interactions with it. Once he had constructed this final storey and came to realise that it represented his ego-consciousness, he felt he had become 'his own person'.

Given the gradual—one might say, 'organic'—architectural development of the building in its alignment with Jung's realisation of self, the Bollingen tower could be construed as an unusual construction using unconventional methods of design and engineering. Its blueprint could not have been drawn up in advance; it had to be discovered. Jung's methods of construction were akin to those of the impractical architect we cited earlier in relation to an analogy of Freud's. Such an architect employs psychoanalytic methods of construction, and designs haphazardly to the dictates of the unconscious. Although Jung didn't achieve the feat implied by Freud's analogy of decorating the internal rooms of a building at the same time as erecting its external walls, there is a sense in which the unconscious led him to decorate the 'internal rooms' of his mind at the same time as establishing the outer, material fabric of the walls of the house. Given that the construction of the building was prolonged and in several stages, which were infused with emotional tension and conflict, it is perhaps unsurprising that its spatial arrangements are awkward, with some spaces blocked off, and it featured a juxtaposition of forms irregular and complex.[34] The 'tower' at Bollingen is a design that few, if any, would probably have commissioned.

The identification of the Bollingen building with the unconscious aspect of mind is accentuated when its rustic simplicity is compared with the busy elegance of the building at Küsnacht. The Küsnacht house, with its imposing baroque features, set out to impress (indeed, it is said that Freud for one was envious of its design[35]). Its similarity to the upper storey of the dream-house suggests its association with the realm of ego-consciousness—a point underscored by the intended function of the building as a place to accommodate Jung's busy schedule and his commitments to others. Jung's Bollingen building contrasts starkly with that of Küsnacht in its aesthetics and function. Its minimalist design and sparse furnishings, with small windows and rooms that largely face inwards, and its situation within a relatively remote and secluded setting, contribute to its interpretation as a structure for all time. Given its associations with the unconscious and its function as something more akin to a Heideggerian *dwelling* than a professional or familial domicile, the Bollingen building doesn't invite ornamentation or a stylised design, and the only furnishings that are required are those provided by the imagination and the contemplative thoughts of its inhabitant.[36]

Buildings gaze back

Through their associations with the unconscious and conscious aspects of mind, Jung's interactions with the buildings at Küsnacht and Bollingen enabled him to negotiate these aspects within himself and integrate them accordingly. The scholar Robert Mugerauer asserts: 'Together the houses strengthened each dimension of Jung's personality and made an opening for the integration that they now memorialize' (1995: 26). In the process of their design and construction, and in the experience of living in them, the two houses provided the containment required for the conscious and unconscious exploration of his self. It is as if Jung had found himself inscribed and embedded within the building, thereby bringing the architectural blueprint of being to life. If we examine Jung's biographical accounts, we soon discover that he had in fact been interacting with architecture in this manner throughout his life.[37] Thus from the age of seven to nine, Jung recounts a fun but poignant game he would play with a large stone (he described it as 'my stone', just as the 1909 dream-house was, he reports, 'my house') that jutted out of a wall in the garden of his childhood home in Klein-Hüningen. He describes the game as follows:

> 'I am sitting on top of this stone and it is underneath.' But the stone also could say 'I' and think: 'I am lying here on this slope and he is sitting on top of me.' The question then arose: 'Am I the one who is sitting on the stone, or am I the one on which *he* is sitting?' This question always perplexed me, and I would stand up, wondering who was what now [...] there was no doubt whatsoever that this stone stood in some secret relationship to me. I could sit on it for hours, fascinated by the puzzle it set me.
>
> (1961b: 35–6)

Engaging with the stone in this way eased Jung's troubled mind. 'It was', he says, 'strangely reassuring and calming to sit on my stone. Somehow it would free me of all my doubts. Whenever I thought that I was the stone, the conflict ceased (1961b: 59). On another occasion, at a similar age, Jung kept a 'smooth, oblong blackish stone' from the Rhine in a pencil tin with a small manikin figure that he had carved out of wood. He regarded the stone as the 'life force' of the manikin (1961b: 39)—and, we can assume (of the life force), of Jung himself too, since he notes that 'I had a vague sense of relationship between the "stone soul" and the stone which was also myself' (1961b: 43).[38]

Jung's intimate interactions with stone continued in the design and construction of buildings. Such activity was for Jung a 'rite of passage', one that enabled him to reconnect with memories of his youth, and other feelings and ideas that had been dormant and unconscious within him (1961b: 198–9).

It is well known that Jung embarked in midlife on an extraordinary exploration of his unconscious mind between 1913 and 1916 (which he referred to as his 'confrontation with the unconscious'[39]). The imaginative and visionary experiences that he experienced at this time (recorded in his legendary *Red Book* or *Liber Novus*, published in 2009) were thought to be direct expressions of the unconscious, disclosing to Jung various psychological conflicts that couldn't have been contemplated and negotiated through more rational means. His visions have been discussed at length, but what interests us here is the overlooked concession by Jung that his 'confrontation with the unconscious' began with the construction of model buildings. He recounts in his autobiography that, whenever he felt harassed by inexplicable feelings, he found himself building 'cottages', 'castles', and 'whole villages' out of 'ordinary stones, with mud for mortar' (1961b: 198): an activity he started in childhood, when he would construct 'little houses and castles' from stones, and 'gates and vaults' from bottles (1961b: 197). Jung describes how he became immersed in this construction work: 'I went on with my building game after the noon meal every day, whenever the weather permitted [as] soon as I was through eating [...] and [I] continued to do so until the patients arrived; and if I was finished with my work early enough in the evening, I went back to building' (1961b: 198). His architectural play inspired immense creativity—not simply by preparing the way for his larger architectural projects at Küsnacht and Bollingen, but in the development of his personality, the integration of his feelings and memories, and the theoretical ideas that he came to be known for. Although he doesn't expand upon the significance of his interactions with architecture, he concedes that they helped to clarify his thoughts and to 'grasp the fantasies whose presence in myself I dimly felt' (1961b: 197–8).

We can continue to trace the correspondence between architecture and Jung's self within the accounts of various dreams he describes as having led him to significant understandings about himself and the workings of the human mind more generally. Jung's dream-house of 1909 was, he says, 'in fact a short summary of my life—the life of my mind' (1961a: par. 484); and it 'pointed out that there were further reaches to the state of consciousness [than I had hitherto realised]' (1961b: 184). But this is just one architectural dream among many. Others include a dream-city (which he calls 'Liverpool') with 'dirty' streets that form a radial network of interconnected parts around the city's square, at the centre of which he discovers the 'healing function of the psyche' (1961b: 223–4). Jung also recounts a recurring dream of an unfamiliar 'guest wing' or annex of his house: 'an ancient historical building, long forgotten, yet my inherited property', with 'interesting antique furniture' (1964: 40). The recurring nature of this final dream allowed Jung to progress through the building a little more each time. Just before the series of dreams came to an end, he discovered in the building an old library containing several unknown books, including a book of symbols. 'The house, of course, was', he asserts, 'a symbol of my personality and its conscious field of interests; and the unknown annex represented the anticipation of a new field of interest and research of which my conscious mind was at that time unaware' (1961a: par. 478–9, 1964: 53–4).[40] The frequency with which buildings of an evocative nature appear in dreams led Jung to deduce from their common features certain characteristics about the dreamer's personality. In other words, given, as Jung claims, that buildings are symbolic representations of the psyche, then to dream of a building with unfamiliar, 'hidden or unexplored areas' is to engage with concealed aspects of one's personality—or, as Jung puts it, one's 'potential ego-structure', new attitude or orientation, of which the waking mind isn't yet aware (Jung 1961a: par. 479, 1961b: 228, 1964: 53–4). Likewise, to dream of a part of a building that is inaccessible and off-limits, or to dream of becoming lost or disoriented within a built environment suggests that the dreamer is resistant to the changes that are beginning to take shape within them.[41]

According to Jung, it is not simply those buildings—imagined or actual—that we ourselves bring into being that shape and transform us, but the buildings and cities that we interact with on a daily basis. Within the built environments of our cities there is, Jung asserts, a 'spirit that broods'. The architecture of cities can be enjoyed aesthetically, he says, but they can also affect you 'to the depths of your being at every step'. In similar vein to the stone within Jung's childhood garden, he says (with especial reference to the cities of Rome, London, Paris, and Pompeii) that 'a remnant of a wall here and a column there gaze upon you with a face instantly recognised' (1961b: 319).[42] In so doing, buildings 'open unforeseen vistas' and allow 'unexpected things [to become] conscious' (1961b: 319).

Conclusion: building the self and the self within buildings

I shall continue throughout our investigation to elaborate on my survey of the architectural blueprints of psyche proposed by Breuer, Freud, and Jung, and the buildings and architectural designs they used to convey the workings of the mind. The key feature for our argument is their portrayal of the unconscious and conscious as the two principal factions of mind that drive behaviour and shape identity. The aesthetic design of each feature of the building of psyche is intended to convey the dynamic quality of the specific component of mind that it represents, and the sorts of sensations it commonly elicits when activated. Thus, the architecture of consciousness is situated above ground level to invite natural light into its rooms, in order to emphasise the accessibility of our waking state of mind, and the need for it to negotiate outside influences. We do not have to move far into the building to encounter consciousness; it is immediately evident. Furthermore, well-lit rooms reveal whatever is inside and ready-to-hand, and, as Jung's 1909-dream-house suggests, consciousness is full of furniture and other possessions and rooms of elaborate decoration to delight the eye, all of which preoccupy and comfort the ego. The architecture of the unconscious by contrast is hidden away and difficult to access; it resides in rooms we rarely frequent, and contains possessions we have forgotten we own. If objects can be discerned within (such as the bones and prehistorical fauna of Jung's cave), they indicate a life once lived. These rooms are dark, ambiguous, and expansive because the unconscious is full of hidden potentials.

The contrasting aesthetics of each part of the building exaggerate the distinctive ways we experience our environments when we engage with them through a conscious or unconscious mindset. For the purpose of their intended function—as teaching aids that seek to clarify the divisions of the mind—the contrast between the two aspects of mind is exaggerated to present each in its pure form. Later, however, we shall see that, when we negotiate our environments, we utilise both aspects of mind, and to varying degrees, so our actual experience involves a combination of the two. When awake and fully conscious, our impressions are shaped by our powers of cognitive reasoning, and presented to us as a coherent sequence of thoughts. Our conscious mindset seeks meaning through order and certainty; and it is most comfortable in environments that facilitate and provide for its needs, such as those that are conventional, familiar, and predictable. The unconscious is not under the jurisdiction of conscious control. Occasionally the ego is able to prevent unconscious material from entering consciousness, but unconscious material is itself compelled in ways that elude the ego with its conscious scrutiny. From the perspective of ego-consciousness, the material and activity of the unconscious are nonsensical, irrational, unpredictable, chaotic, and mysterious. The unconscious manifests itself through aesthetics that are ambiguous, surprising, confusing, and unsettling. It can often appear threatening to the ego, but this threat cannot be fully discerned, only intuited or felt, as an apprehensive awareness that something is out of place, not quite right, without knowing exactly where or what.

The divided nature of the self is such that a person is under continual pressure to reconcile their conscious agendas and the strategies of their ego with the excitations of the unconscious. This is no easy feat. Whilst we are compelled by our conscious concerns to establish a secure sense of self, one that is self-contained with a coherent ego-identity, the unconscious seeks to loosen it and disrupt it by pressuring the ego to refashion itself anew. The volatile nature of the unconscious threatens to usurp the ego's best laid plans, rocking the foundations upon which it sits, and threatening to evict it from the home it believes it has created for itself.

By mapping the human mind and body onto architectural imagery, the blueprints of psyche give insights into the evocative potential of specific features of our built environments and the relationship of these features with the various needs of the psyche, and the manner in which they express themselves to us. We will draw upon their insights in the chapters that follow in order to explain how we come to identify with the built environment in a way that allows us to negotiate the competing instinctual demands within ourselves. In this chapter we began to see how the resemblance between architecture, body, and mind can lead a person to experience themselves as somehow embodied within the material fabric of a building. Furthermore, as we saw in relation to Jung's interactions with architecture and to the motivations that underpin Freud's equation of specific architectural features to specific body parts, this experience can be deeply evocative; it can set in motion a new self-awareness, one that can unlock the subject's creative potential. I call this evocative experience the 'architectural event', and in the following chapters I attempt to explain how it happens, why it happens, and why architecture is particularly good at disclosing to us latent, hidden, and unconscious aspects of ourselves. My argument has important repercussions for architectural design, and in the course of our investigation I shall begin to establish guidelines or a framework for the design and construction of evocative buildings, and conversely for approaches and designs that ought to be avoided. I shall explain, for instance, why stylized, idiosyncratic designs that seek to impress are often much less evocative than one might presume, whilst conventional, seemingly mundane and nondescript designs, by contrast, have the potential to be much more impressionable—for good or ill—than is often realised.

We will find that the basic differences between the blueprints of psyche put forward by Freud and Jung have significant implications for the 'architectural event', both in terms of the nature or depth of experience that is involved in our identification with architecture and in terms of the kinds of feelings that architecture can be said to elicit. Given the significance of these implications, I shall end this chapter by highlighting the key differences between Jung and Freud.

Jung regarded Freud's interpretation of the psyche as rigid, oppressive, and 'small minded'; it was tantamount to a 'narrow, twisted and low-ceilinged' 'ghetto', as in Jung's dream. It lacked, Jung claimed, an essential 'depth'. To accommodate this essential depth, we find Jung undertaking radical renovations to Freud's basic blueprint of psyche, with an extension situated below the underground storey. The addition of this part of the building and its aesthetic design emphasises the greater flexibility and wider expanse that Jung wishes to assign to the unconscious part of the psyche. Named the 'collective unconscious', this new storey situated at the building's foundations grounds the edifice within an all-encompassing terrain, one that includes within it all possibilities for human experience, including, as Jung is keen to assert, our relationship with God Himself. In this respect, Jung's blueprint of psyche can be interpreted as continuing in the tradition of those architectural metaphors and allegories of religious discourse mentioned earlier that characterise and seek to explain our spiritual nature. While Freud's architectural blueprints emphasise the relationship between body and mind, Jung's bring these aspects of our identity into relationship with the expansive nature of 'spirit'.

Jung's building accommodates a personality with far-reaching possibilities and concerns that are more objective and wide-ranging than those that preoccupy the inhabitant of Freud's building. While Jung's building opens itself up to new and unknown vistas, Freud's building looks inward and upon itself as a storehouse for unexpressed past experiences. Whether or not Jung succeeded in designing a more expansive building of psyche than Freud is a question we shall consider. The influential psychologist and cultural critic James Hillman, whose approach to architecture will become especially important to our investigation in Chapters 6 and 7, is (for one) adamant that Jung's tower at Bollingen, far from allowing Jung to engage productively with his unconscious, accomplishes the inverse, and sets about alienating him from the outside world by consolidating his current ego-identity and imprisoning it within its walls. Rather than allowing the free expression of unconscious contents, the Bollingen tower, according to Hillman, maintains their repression through an oppressive architectural design that prevents Jung from engaging meaningfully with the world outside it. In so doing, the tower, Hillman asserts, symbolises not the unconscious, but the pathological ego that draws its identity merely from its own resources (1993a: §6). As Hillman notes, 'We are really in a strange place inside [Jung's] tower'; as its architect and inhabitant, Jung identifies himself with a 'self-enclosed stone-walled personality'. The Bollingen building is for Hillman a 'monument in stone to the self-enclosed ego' (1993a: §6).[43] Hillman would probably situate Jung's building of psyche within an oppressive ghetto of the kind that Jung assigns to Freud. In this reading, the stones of Jung's building do not gaze *into* Jung's whole being, as Jung suggests; they simply look back *at* him, not in order to call ego-consciousness into question, but to affirm what the ego already thinks it sees.

We shall investigate why and how a building's design is vital to the shaping of our identity, and sense of self, and discuss some of the fundamental, existential problems we face when we find ourselves interacting with buildings that for one reason or another impede our use of them. Most evidently problematic are those architectural constructions that are overtly stylized or those with nondescript features that fail to impress us at all, both of which often lead their users to feel disoriented and out of place. Often not immediately detected or ascribed to the architecture itself, these experiences can have a detrimental effect on a person's wellbeing by inhibiting their capacity for self-expression and the negotiation of unconscious conflict, problems that can manifest themselves in a variety of symptoms.

In the next chapter we examine more closely how we come to establish intimate relationships with the material forms of architecture through the competing instinctive strategies of ego and unconscious that drive our sense of self. I shall explain how personal identity is established through the tensions and conflicts that arise in response to our environments. Identity is forged out of our desire on the one hand to consolidate experiences of order, structure, and security, and on the other to loosen and disrupt these so as to experience a freedom of detachment and unboundedness. This happens against the backdrop of our built environments, with our corresponding desire both to merge with their material features so as to feel enclosed by them and securely attached to their structural form, and to separate ourselves from them so as to feel autonomous and self-contained.

Notes

1 In this respect, Breuer's building is not dissimilar to Descartes's. Descartes describes a 'very dark cellar' that accommodates falsities and errors of reasoning. His description implies that there is a room above the cellar that has windows that are well lit to allow into the building the clarity and certainty of truths that are commensurate with the 'light of day' (Descartes 1637: 147).
2 See also Juhani Pallasmaa (2000).
3 Gaston Bachelard would later echo Breuer in this insistence (though Bachelard cites Jung as his psychoanalytic influence for the design of his own building of psyche, or 'oneiric house', as he refers to it). Bachelard writes:

> A house is imagined as a vertical being. It rises upward. It differentiates itself in terms of its verticality [...] Verticality is ensured by the polarity of the cellar and attic, the marks of which are so deep that, in a way, they open up two very different perspectives for a phenomenology of the imagination. Indeed, it is possible, almost without commentary, to oppose the rationality of the roof to the irrationality of the cellar [...] Up near the roof all our thoughts are clear. [The cellar is] first and foremost the dark entity of the house, the one that partakes of subterranean forces.
>
> (Bachelard 1957: 17–18)

4 Given this, it is ironic that Gaston Bachelard insists that the staircase in his oneiric house of psyche that connects the cellar rooms to the storey above 'always *go[es] down*'. But, 'we go both up and down the stairway that leads to the bed-chamber' because, he cryptically says, it is more commonly used, and 'we are familiar with it'. Likewise, 'we always *go up* the attic stairs' because 'they bear the mark of ascension to a more tranquil solitude' (Bachelard 1957: 25–6).
5 Letter written 8 December 1907. Freud mentions this in his criticism of a house of hysteria described by Édouard Claparède, psychologist and contemporary of Freud and Breuer. Claparède regards Breuer's house of hysteria as jointly authored by Breuer and Freud. He writes:

> *They* have quite rightly compared hysteria to a building of many storeys, each storey having its own symptoms. To be sure we are still far from being able to reconstruct this building. But it is perhaps worthwhile to try and sketch out the plan, hypothetical though it may be.
>
> (Claparède 1908: 185; my emphasis)

In response to this, Freud remarks to Jung that 'Claparède's article on the definition of hysteria amounts to a very intelligent judgement on our efforts; the idea of the building of several storeys comes from Breuer (in the general section of the *Studies*), the building itself, I believe, ought to be described rather differently' (Freud/Jung 1974: 55F, 102). Claparède's house of psyche is a building of five storeys. The uppermost storey is consciousness. Below this is a storey that accommodates the hypnoid state and the complexes. The storey beneath this is biological in nature, and includes the nervous system and the capacity for auto-suggestion. It is not clear what the storey immediately below this comprises. The basement storey is 'primitive disorder' with phylogenetic material of the collective unconscious.

6 The difference between the repression of material in the preconscious and unconscious is equivalent to the ease with which one can recall a friend's telephone number compared with the reliving of a trauma that has been repressed in order to protect oneself.

7 In the later essay, 'Constructions in Analysis' (1937), Freud alludes again to the archaeological analogy as follows. The 'reconstruction' work of the psychoanalyst

> resembles to a great extent an archaeologist's excavation of some dwelling-place that has been destroyed and buried or of some ancient edifice. The two processes are in fact identical, except that the analyst works under better conditions and has more material at his command to assist him, since what he is dealing with is not something destroyed but something that is still alive [...] But just as the archaeologist builds up the walls of the building from the foundations that have remained standing, determines the number and position of the columns from depressions in the floor and reconstructs the mural decorations and paintings from the remains found in the debris, so does the analyst proceed when he draws his inferences from the fragments of memories, from the associations and from the behaviour of the subject of the analysis.
>
> (Freud 1937: 259)

8 McGrath further notes the close analogy between the dynamics and psychological tensions of hysteria and the intense political and social tensions endured in Nuremberg that led to the construction of its defensive fortifications (1986: 193–4). Likewise, Resina draws attention to the peaked roofs that are apparent in Freud's diagram, as representations of 'the hysterical fantasy, an apparently static structure arising out of a dynamic power struggle'—which is to say, the struggle and conflict that arises from the unconscious memories and the symptoms they give rise to. Both 'psychic conflict' and 'historical clash' appear together, 'congealed in architectural form' (2003: 30).

9 The term 'phantasy' is employed here in order to denote the unconscious dimension of the experience, whilst 'fantasy' would denote an imaginative narrative that one consciously entertains. We shall come across the term 'phantasy' again later.

10 After describing two monuments one can encounter on 'a walk through the streets of London'—the Victorian replica of a 'richly carved Gothic column' in front of Charing Cross railway station (known as an 'Eleanor cross', which marked the final stopping place of Queen Eleanor of Castile's funeral cortège en route to Westminster Abbey in 1290), and the fluted Doric column called 'The Monument' that marks the site where the Great fire of London began in 1666—he describes how these affective mnemic symbols come to resemble hysterical symptoms:

> But what should we think of a Londoner who paused to-day in deep melancholy before the memorial of Queen Eleanor's funeral instead of going about his business in the hurry that modern working conditions demand [...]? Or again what should we think of a Londoner who shed tears before the Monument that commemorates the reduction of his beloved metropolis to ashes although it has long since risen again in far greater brilliance? Yet every single hysteric and neurotic behaves like these two unpractical Londoners. Not only do they remember painful experiences of the remote past, but they still cling to them emotionally; they cannot get free of the past and for its sake they neglect what is real and immediate.
>
> (Freud 1910: 16–17)

11 Speaking of the neurotic disposition, Freud writes: 'My analyses have shown me that it is habitually present in the unconscious thoughts of neurotics [...] It is true that I know patients who have retained an architectural symbolism for the body and genitals' (1900: 462). Given that neuroses for Freud are symptoms of frustrated instincts and their corresponding feelings of anxiety, he states that 'Everybody has some slight neurotic nuance or other, and as a matter of fact, a certain degree of neurosis is of inestimable value as a drive' (Joseph Wortis attributes this quotation to Freud during his personal analysis with Freud; see Wortis 1954: 154).

12 Recall, too, Jung's remark, 'When someone is not quite right in the head, we say in German that he [...] "has cobwebs in the attic"' (1958: par. 671)—a point he illustrates with a real life case study of a patient who dreamt of spiders in the attic while suffering from ego-inflation.

13 In order to elucidate the sexual connotations of the staircase, Freud describes a dream he had:

> One day I was trying to understand the significance of the sensation of being inhibited, of not being able to move from the spot, of not being able to get something done, etc., which occurs so frequently in dreams, and is so closely allied to anxiety. That night I had the following dream: I am very incompletely dressed, and I go from a flat on the ground-floor up a flight of stairs to an upper storey. In doing this I jump up three stairs at a time, and I am glad to find that I can mount the stairs so quickly. Suddenly I notice that a servant-maid is coming down the stairs – that is, towards me. I am ashamed, and try to hurry away, and now comes this feeling of being inhibited; I am glued to the stairs, and cannot move from the spot.
>
> (1900: 78–9)

14 Admittedly, these city streets provide the dream-setting for the discovery of other non-architectural artefacts (such as a clarinet and piece of fur), and it is these that supposedly refer to sexualised parts of the body. Nevertheless, their context of discovery on the street is difficult to ignore.

15 Physical symptoms are often regarded as 'mnemic symbols' for Freud. He writes, '*Our hysterical patients suffer from reminiscences.* Their symptoms are residues and mnemic symbols of particular (traumatic) experiences' (Freud 1910: 16).

16 Some commentators on Jung ascribe to him a reductive interpretation of architectural imagery that he himself is unlikely to have endorsed. See for instance Cooper (1974) and Hall (1983). Jungian analyst James A. Hall has written a dictionary of dream symbols, which he presents as a repository of Jungian dream symbols. It is improbable that Jung himself would have approved of such a venture, because it involves reducing dream symbolism to the level of mere sign, by giving these dream images definitive meanings. Hall has an entry for the symbolism of a house, and presents the following description as a Jungian reading of the house:

> Distinctions between parts of the house may be symbolically important: the cellar, the attic, the roof, balconies, bedrooms etc. Kitchens, for instance, are a place of transformation of raw food into cooked dishes; in dreams they sometimes have the character of the alchemical laboratory, a place of more profound transformations. Bathrooms in dreams may refer to 'elimination' or the difficulty in 'letting go'. Sometimes the mere setting of the dream action in a certain house from the past allows inferences as to the origin of the complexes involved.
>
> (Hall 1983: 82)

17 Steve Myers (2009) goes so far as to claim that Jung unwittingly stole Breuer's idea and passed it off as his own: that Jung's 'house of psyche' was the product of Jung's cryptomnesia. (Cryptomnesia, according to Jung, is when an idea or 'image vanishes without trace from the memory' and 'reappears' at a later time, to 'mislead' the subject, who believes his idea or image to be new and original (Jung 1902: 81, 1946: 110). Myers's hypothesis is improbable given the wealth of architectural metaphors with which Jung would have been familiar. Indeed, Myers undermines his claim when he himself concedes that 'at the start of the 20th century, building metaphors were aplenty' (Myers 2009: 520).

18 'Man's unconscious psychology decides, and not what we think and talk in the brain-chamber up in the attic' (Jung 1935: 371).

19 Jung writes:

> The building of the great cathedrals has gone flat. It is not lost, because it is a law that energy cannot be lost. Then what has become of it? Where has it gone? The answer is that it is in man's unconscious. It may be said to have fallen down into a lower storey.
>
> (Jung 1955: 266)

20 Some refer to Freud's house as having three storeys, in which case Jung's would have four. See, for example, George Steiner, who speaks of 'The Freudian tripartite scenario of the psyche (itself so beautifully a simile of the cellarage, living quarters and memory-thronged attic in the bourgeois house)' (Steiner 1991: 109).

21 On one occasion Jung indicates the sheer expanse of the collective unconscious through an architectural comparison. The personal unconscious denotes an oppressive architectural structure, and the collective unconscious denotes a lack of structure and absence of architectural form. Thus, he notes that if one conceived the personal unconscious (or, as he writes here, 'the shadow', which is his name for the personification of the personal unconscious and all those aspects of the personality that have been neglected and have not been integrated into conscious awareness) as 'a tight passage, a narrow door, whose painful constriction no one is spared who goes down to the deep well', what is encountered when one has successfully passed through the passage and doorway (and thereby has begun to 'learn to know oneself') is

> a boundless expanse full of unprecedented uncertainty, with apparently no inside and no outside, no above and no below, no here and no there, no mine and no thine, no good and no bad. It is a world of water, where all life floats in suspension; where the realm of the sympathetic system, the soul of everything living, begins; where I am indivisibly this *and* that; where I experience the other in myself and the other-than-myself experiences me.
>
> (Jung 1954c: par. 45)

The imagery of the juxtaposition of architecture and water here can be read in the light of Andreas Jung's comment that C.G. Jung wanted always to live near water (A. Jung 2009: 21).

22 It appears in his 1925 seminars (Jung 1925), in his essay 'Mind and Earth' (1927; Although 'Mind and Earth' does not allude to the house as having been dreamt, it is clear that Jung is referring to the same dream-house of 1909), in his pseudo-autobiographical work *Memories, Dreams, Reflections* (1961b), and in the essay 'Symbols and the Interpretation of Dreams' (1961a), which was later adapted with minor editorial changes into the chapter, 'Approaching the Unconscious', within

his introductory co-authored work *Man and His Symbols* (1964). One must bear in mind that *Memories, Dreams, Reflections* was not written by Jung directly; it comprises notes written by Jung and edited by others. Its content, however, was agreed upon by Jung.

23 Bennet notes, however, that Jung added the clause 'my house' in the later account of his dream, as it appears in *Memories, Dreams, Reflections* (1961b). Jung recalls how, in the original dream, the interior of the house was *not* familiar, but he nevertheless felt himself identifying with the house as 'it represented the external aspect of his personality, the side seen by others' (Bennet 1966: 73, n.)

24 Vaughan Hart (1994) offers an interesting discussion on the alchemical motifs of towers and the possible influence on these on the design features of Jung's 1909 dream-house. Of particular interest is the image of the primitive dwelling of the cave (as a repository for the secrets of nature) that is often depicted in alchemical manuscripts as a foundation to a tower (or knowledge).

25 For a helpful account of the house and its development, see A. Jung (2009) and Gledhill (2014).

26 It was also the childhood home of Jung's mother. The house can be seen in the illustration entitled 'Basle Broadsheet, 1566' in Jung's essay, *Flying Saucers: A Modern Myth of Things Seen in the Skies* (Jung 1958: par. 128). The house appears in the illustration to the right of Basle Cathedral.

27 Jung didn't build the construction at Bollingen himself, though it is often said that he did. He most likely laid its foundations and some of the walls of the first small tower of the building. In an interview with Stephen Black for the BBC radio series *Personal Call* (July 1955), Jung states, 'I have built with my own hands; I learned the work of a mason. I went to a quarry to learn how to split stones – big rocks'. Jung continues, 'I did actually lay stones and built *part* of my house up in Bollingen' (Jung 1955: 266–7). For detailed discussion of Jung's likely practical involvement in its construction, see Gledhill 2014.

28 For commentary on the building see: Lym (1980: 36–40), Hart (1994), Mugerauer (1995), Ziolkowski (1999: 131–48), Barrie (2010: 61–79), Richards (2003: 158–70), and Larson and Savage (2004).

29 Further affinities between the Bollingen tower and Jung's 1909 dream-house of psyche can be drawn from Hart's (1994) discussion of the symbolic events around its construction. Hart reports that Jung's tower at Bollingen was prefigured by dreams of caves, and the tower itself was apparently built upon a grave, thereby suggesting a link between the tower and the cave of the dream-house, which contained within it skulls and other bones.

30 One might argue, however, that the blueprint for the Bollingen building was already present in Jung's mind. This is suggested by similar architectural compositions that had made an impression on Jung prior to the construction of the Bollingen building. For instance, in 1913 Jung illustrated the chapter 'Liber Secundus', in his *Red Book* (2009), with an image of a castle in a forest, the elements of which are strikingly similar to the final composition of the Bollingen building. Gledhill also makes this connection, and suggests, furthermore, that the Bollingen building mimics on a smaller scale the castle at Laufen that formed part of the same complex as the rectory in which Jung had lived as a child (2014: 26).

31 Given this, one might interpret the building's construction as an attempt on Jung's part to reconstruct his identity and re-orientate his sense of self following the destabilising experiences brought about by his grieving.

32 Jung presumed the skeleton to be that of a French soldier, one of many who had drowned in the Linth in 1799, whose body had been washed up on the lake, coming to reside on the ground upon which Jung's tower was built (1961b: 259).
33 In a passage in *The Red Book*, Jung alludes to the *solitary* man who inhabits a house as one who has 'a cave within himself. Stones speak his thoughts.' Jung continues to note that this man 'became stone and cave' (Jung 2009: 273). Through this reading, we could tie this room in the Bollingen tower with the cave of the collective unconscious in the 1909 dream-house.
34 See: Larson and Savage (2004).
35 See: Pamela Cooper-White (2014: 8)
36 Jung associates the building at Bollingen with his unconscious 'number two' personality, as he refers to it. 'Number two', he says, is 'the son of the maternal unconscious' (1961b: 252), which is to say the one who dwells in the 'maternal womb' or hearth of the tower. Of the 'Tower at Bollingen', he writes that

> it is as if one lived in many centuries simultaneously [...] If a man of the sixteenth century were to move into the house, only the kerosene lamp and the matches would be new to him; otherwise he would know his way about without difficulty [...] There I live in my second personality and see life in the round, as something forever coming into being and passing on.
>
> (1961b: 264–5)

See also Giegerich (2004), who describes the compensatory nature of the two houses in terms that reflect characteristics of Jung's respective personalities. He notes that, whereas at Küsnacht Jung was 'the scientist who dug up facts' at his desk, at Bollingen he became 'the fish swimming in the waters' of the primordial unconscious' (2004: 47–8). On one occasion Jung describes his number two personality in architectural terms: 'in him light reigned, as in the spacious halls of a royal palace whose high casements open upon a landscape flooded with sunlight' (Jung 1961b: 107). His number two personality also experienced several architectural reveries, one of which recurred for several months while he was a schoolboy, during his walks from Klein-Hüningen into Basle. He would imagine an island of rock rising out of the lake, with a medieval city built on its slopes: 'On the rock', Jung recalls, 'stood a well-fortified castle with a tall keep, a watch-tower.' Again, as with the 1909 dream-house, Jung claims that this castle 'was my house' (1961b: 100). Jung, under the direction of his number one personality (his conscious, rational disposition), eventually found this daydream 'silly and ridiculous', and he abandoned it.
37 His interactions with architecture no doubt led to his interest in alchemy, with its notion of stone infused with dynamic affect or spirit.
38 Interestingly, Jung had a vision of a black stone temple when very sick and in great need of life force. Later, in 1944, again upon his sick bed, Jung had a vision of a large rock that he entered through its antechamber. He recalls that it was a 'tremendous dark block of stone, like a meteorite. It was about the size of my house, or even bigger' (1961b: 321).
39 A prolonged episode that has been variously interpreted as a sustained period of introspection, a creative illness, or even a psychotic breakdown.
40 Other dream-buildings of note include a Verona house (1961b: 229); another new annex to his house, this time containing a laboratory (1961b: 239–41); a 'very

roomy' eighteenth-century country house with several outbuildings that were looked after by Jung's dead father (1961b: 244); a castle in the middle of a swamp in a forest, home to a rigidly rational scholar (1951: pars. 360–1); a castle tower that Jung guards, keeping watch for intruders from the battlements (2009: 259); and a tower of smooth walls, embedded within a mountain and containing within it a labyrinth (2009: 320).

41 Of the many examples of this type of dream described either by Jung or by his colleagues that we could cite to illustrate this point, the following dream of one of Jung's pupils, reported by Jung, is perhaps the most poignant. Jung describes how he felt uneasy about his pupil, but couldn't work out why, until at last his pupil reported to Jung a recent dream. The man had dreamt that he had arrived at an unknown city. In the city centre he discovers a medieval building with 'handsome rooms' and 'long corridors'. Suddenly it becomes dark, and he loses his orientation and bearings. Unable to find his way out of the building, he becomes increasingly alarmed at the prospect of being lost and alone in the building. Now in a panic, he stumbles upon a dark and 'gigantic room', and discovers to his horror in the middle of the room an 'idiot child of about two years old' sitting on 'a chamber pot', having 'smeared itself with faeces' (1961b: 156–8). The dream-house, for Jung, explains why he was right to feel apprehensive about his pupil. For the building, Jung tells us, reveals the secret of a repressed aspect or split-off 'personality' of the dreamer, which in this case is a 'sinister', 'latent psychosis' that was just about to break out and manifest itself in the waking, conscious mind of the dreamer.

42 Jung elsewhere alludes to the open door that 'frees the gaze', so that it is no longer constrained by forethought (2009: 565).

43 Andreas Jung describes how Jung had desire for safety and security that was expressed not so much in his Bollingen house, but the house at Küsnacht, which he describes as a defensive fortress with its use of small barred windows and heavy locked doors (2009:66–7).

Chapter 3

The architectural event

Buildings as events that disclose our being

According to psychoanalytic theory identity or personality is not fixed, but develops through the interaction of the ego and the unconscious. The ego depends on unconscious instincts for its continual renewal, and the unconscious requires ego-consciousness as a vehicle for its expression. These contrasting aspects of the mind are co-dependent. If one were expressed to the detriment of the other, the personality would suffer as a result.[1] Broadly speaking, if unconscious material were denied its expression, and couldn't therefore replenish the ego or keep it in check, the ego would become stultified and rigidly self-contained, so as to be 'narrow-minded', prejudiced, and resistant to new experiences. A person in this situation is alienated from their environment, finding it persecutory. Likewise, if the unconscious were given full reign, the ego would be severely weakened and vulnerable to fragmentation by an onslaught of impulses that seek to rupture its bounded identity. A person in this situation would find it difficult to distinguish themselves from their environment, experiencing themselves as if merged with it. These are extreme cases that we would most likely attribute to mental illness. However, I claim that it is the dynamic interaction between these two positions, experienced in relation to the environment one finds oneself in, that underpins the healthy development of personality.

I am certainly not the first to make such a claim. The architect Neil Leach, for example, describes identity as a 'continual shuttling' between two contrasting human tendencies: to feel 'connected' to one's environment and 'distinct' from it (2007: 39). These operate, he says, as a 'figure/ground relationship' so that identity is 'ultimately a question of foreground and background. It is a matter of defining the self' through these oscillating movements 'against a given environment'. The environment is a crucial factor in the formation of identity, as it 'consists of a reservoir of impulses that condition human existence'. Furthermore, Leach contends,

> if we were to highlight the role of the physical environment within that regime, we could perhaps point to a range of iconic buildings and geographic formations that feature prominently in the national psyche [and]

> to those of less significance that nonetheless structure our everyday lives. It is here that we can recognize the potential of 'place' as a register of indexical markers that condition personal identity.
>
> (Leach 2007: 39)

Although the ordinary buildings that structure our personal lives may seem less significant than the iconic buildings that shape the cultural identity of nations, I shall go on to argue that they are no less vital from a psychological perspective. Indeed, any given building, and especially those we encounter regularly, shapes our identity.

Humanist geographer Yi-Fu Tuan describes human identity as a compelling paradox, one that develops out of competing desires that establish either our attraction to place (described by Tuan as 'topophilia') or our aversion to it ('topophobia') (Tuan 1974; Ruan and Hogben 2007). In a way that is similar to our description of the concerns of ego and unconscious, Tuan refers to place as the locus of 'security', and to space as 'freedom'; we require both, he claims, since we are 'attached to the one and long for the other' (1977: 3). The early twentieth-century sociologist Georg Simmel maintains that 'all our activity' is guided by our contrasting tendencies to 'separate' from and to 'connect' to things. These tendencies are demonstrated in our use of two architectural structures, the bridge and the door. Whilst the bridge, Simmel says, emphasises connectedness, the door has a 'richer and livelier significance' by reminding us that 'separating and connecting are only two sides of precisely the same act', for 'the bounded and boundaryless adjoin one another' (1909: 5–10). Jane Jacobs, in her influential study of American cities, alludes to our perception of the environment as guided by one of 'two conflicting sets of impressions'. On the one hand, we are compelled to identify with the 'intensity' of its 'details' and its 'activity', and on the other, its 'endless', 'amorphous' 'anonymity of distance'; the former inspires 'intimacy', and the latter 'detachment' (1961: 493, 494). According to Jacobs, if both impressions are present to a similar degree, the environment appears chaotic, incoherent, and disturbing; the subject is subsequently compelled to supress one impression to allow the other to take precedence. Interestingly, Jacobs maintains that architects and planners tend to supress the intimacy of details in favour of an aesthetics of detachment, distance, and repetition, which is in contrast to the majority of people, who are inclined to take the opposite approach.

Another altogether different kind of thinker, the nineteenth-century philosopher Friedrich Nietzsche, proposes two opposing traits—the Apollonian and Dionysian—that are discernible in the world as both creative impulses in people and aesthetic characteristics of works of art, including architecture (1872). Apollonian denotes traits that appeal to ego-consciousness, such as individuality, clarity, particularity, contrast, and convention, whereas Dionysian denotes those that resonate with the unconscious, such as chaos, uncertainty, frenzy, contradiction, and limitlessness. If ego-conscious has an Apollonian disposition, the unconscious is distinctly Dionysian in character, for Apollonian denotes an awareness of oneself as a distinctive, self-contained being that is distinguishable from one's environment; and Dionysian denotes the loss of individuality, and describes a self that is torn apart, and dissolved into its environment.[2] The most creative experiences, Nietzsche asserts, are those that involve the antagonistic tensions that arise when both aspects are present—with, he says, as much Dionysian energy as Apollonian consciousness can contain. We shall return to this idea in Chapter 7, where I underscore the significance of incorporating contradictions within architectural designs as a way of encouraging our identification with them.

Buildings, we shall see, are particularly good at helping us to reconcile our conflicting desires, by providing us with a fundamental orientation and containment. They are, thereby, instrumental in the cultivation of identity and self. Earlier I mentioned that psychological problems occur if either ego or unconscious material is denied expression, and this is equally true of the competing instincts we have in response to our environments: to seek either to merge with it or to separate ourselves from it. If either instinct is emphasised to the detriment of the other, the situation leads to spatial anxiety. The symptoms of this anxiety, broadly conceived as 'claustrophobia' and 'agoraphobia', alert us to the dangers of promoting one impulse to the neglect of the other, and are likewise indicative of problematic environments that fail to meet our existential needs.

Much has been written about agoraphobia and claustrophobia in the disciplines of psychology, urbanism, and architecture alike. Although there seems to be little consensus on the aetiology of these conditions, they tend to be presented as different phases of a single anxiety, expressed as an oscillation between, on the one hand, a desire for contact and relationship triggered by a fear of isolation and alienation and, on the other, a desire for withdrawal and distance triggered by a fear that contact and relationship will suffocate and annihilate.[3] These anxieties are usually regarded as problems that call for treatment and cure. But there is a sense, too, in which they reflect the dynamic interplay between the contrasting tendencies of the personality more generally, and express, albeit in extreme form, the different fundamental dispositions or impulses of the self that I have been describing. I suggest that these two anxiety types are the spatial or architectural correlates of the intra-psychic breakdown in relations that can occur when the needs of either the ego or the unconscious are denied their expression. In other words, claustrophobia and agoraphobia denote at one and the same time a breakdown in healthy spatial relations between self and environment, *and* an intra-psychic breakdown in relations between the ego and the unconscious. Read in this way, claustrophobia describes the ego that is too rigidly contained within its self-imposed confines,[4] and agoraphobia depicts the ego that is out of place and lost within expansive, unbounded space. The needs of both aspects of personality require adequate 'space' for their expression, if it is to avoid these anxieties and allow the healthy development of self to continue relatively unimpeded. As Leach puts it, 'it is between these two states, the horror of the undifferentiated self and the horror of the alienated self, that identity is formed' (2007: 32).

As I shall explain in detail later, the built environment provides opportunities for us to engage more productively with ourselves and to find ourselves better oriented and integrated within our environments. In the present chapter we shall see why buildings are particularly good at catering to the needs of both facets of our personality, and at encouraging their mediation or dialogue. I shall explain this first in terms of the ego, by describing the manner in which architecture imparts to the ego experiences of abiding structure, form, and containment that the ego is all too keen to acquire for itself. I shall argue that buildings fortify the ego, providing it with a robust and enduring impression of itself—one that helps it to feel more adequately equipped in its defence to ward off agoraphobic anxieties of self-doubt, lack of distinction, and potential dissolution or annihilation. Following this, we shall see how buildings accommodate the unconscious in their capacity to evoke a seemingly 'infinite' surplus of meanings and an expansive quality that cannot be appropriated or reduced to the rationalisations of the ego. This infinite quality furnishes the experience of structure and containment with a vital flexibility, one that grants a person an important experience of freedom and the impression that there are possibilities and uncharted potentials within them. It is an experience that enriches the ego with an enlarged and more objective disposition, helping it to defend itself against claustrophobic anxieties of isolation, constraint, and inertia. I shall conclude that buildings are profoundly evocative, and therefore are most appropriately construed as *symbols* of human identity.

I claim that when we perceive buildings we do not perceive them literally, as passive objects that submit fully and completely to our expectation and understanding. Rather, we perceive them as dynamic objects, or better still, as *events* that involve us as participants in their structural form and, by the same token, involve them in our bodily experiences and in the cognitive process that underpin our creative thoughts. Furthermore, I argue that this intimate relationship compels us to use the material features of the building both to orientate and to integrate ourselves, and in the process to acquire an enriched and more objective attitude. Buildings are *symbolic* of our being, and thus they evoke both facets of the divided self, affording us greater opportunities to experience aspects of ourselves that were previously hidden from our conscious awareness. From a Freudian perspective, the self-disclosure that can be evoked in one's perception of architecture amounts to an experience of material that had been forgotten and repressed; it discloses meanings of personal value and relevance. From a Jungian perspective, by contrast, the disclosure includes material of an 'archetypal' nature, material that has universal or collective meaning, and is thus applicable to every person. Buildings, I shall argue, are active participants in the creation and development of personality; they mediate between our instincts and desires and help to reconcile their conflicts. Buildings can be said, therefore, to design and construct or reconstruct us, as much as we them.

Building enduring structures for ourselves

Few would dispute that life itself is confusing. There are no self-evident truths about the meaning or purpose of life to which all subscribe. The pre-Socratic philosopher Heraclitus famously declared that life is a state of flux, of coming-to-be and passing away,[5] such that all structures that appear permanent and enduring are actually gradually dissolving and eroding away. The only certainty to life is that we, too, in our physical form at least, will eventually come to pass away in death. And yet the majority of us would find it difficult to live with this fact as our only guide, or to act in the belief that our personal experiences are ultimately meaningless and irrelevant in the grand scheme of things. To this end, many a philosopher has suggested that we are compelled to create our own truths and values, and that, by imposing these on the world, we make it coherent and meaningful. In other words, that we make life meaningful because we project our need for meaning onto it.

It is this trait of the human condition that the philosopher Nietzsche famously sought to expose. According to Nietzsche, the vast majority of us are motivated by a 'will to truth', which, he says, deludes us into thinking that the truths we invent to empower ourselves and make us feel secure in life are engrained in the universe as abiding, eternal realities. These fabricated truth-systems, he says, can severely impede our lives by dictating how we should live and preventing us from entertaining alternative, competing perspectives. Nietzsche (1872) offers a number of ways out of this dilemma, one of which is particularly relevant to our investigation: and that is to adopt an *aesthetic* approach to life. This can enable us, he claims, to find the containment we seek without surrendering ourselves to inhibiting delusions. Apollonian art forms—of which, architecture is the purest—help us, Nietzsche says, to overcome anxieties brought about by the flux of life, by evoking within us a 'dream-like' attitude to our experiences, one that cultivates the illusion that there is a deeper, hidden reality or higher truth that underpins the art forms we perceive. This hidden dimension is of our own creation and provides us with a flexible framework to help us to create and recreate our own values and sense of self. The important thing for Nietzsche is that we find the means to keep on recreating ourselves, and are never fooled into believing that our identities and values are fixed. Unlike those delusional narratives that are motivated by the 'will to truth', architecture as an Apollonian art form frees us from unhelpful delusions that enslave us to prescriptive ways of being. In this Nietzschean reading, the form of the building provides us with an illusory sense of the structure and continuity that we desire for our lives: a creative illusion that helps us to construct a coherent narrative for ourselves about life's value and meaning, in a way that doesn't constrain us or blind us to the possibility of discovering other ideas and ways of being that are latent within the chaotic flux of life that otherwise envelopes us.

Nietzsche suggests that architecture as an Apollonian art form can lead us through the 'dream-like' attitude it induces to a position that allows us to affirm the flux of life to creative ends. We shall examine the significance of the 'dream-like' effects of architecture later in this chapter and more extensively in Chapter 5; but what I want to emphasise here is the importance of the structural form of architecture for impressing upon us the illusion that we ourselves have abiding structural integrity. I am not the first to make such a claim. A handful of philosophers, architects, and psychoanalysts have implied a similar view, albeit less explicitly than I shall. For instance, an idea often suggested is that buildings help us to come to terms with our mortality and impending death. Here buildings are depicted as a kind of existential shelter that either defends against or helps to lessen anxieties brought about by agoraphobic fears of the dissolution of self. Psychoanalyst F. Robert Rodman, for example, asserts:

> The built environment is distinguished by its structural presence, its quality of survivability. [... buildings] give us a sense of abiding value. We cherish such buildings partly because they have *survived*; they speak of relative permanence in the flux of time. This much seems obvious. As human beings, made of flesh and blood, subject to the vagaries of the body and ultimately unable to escape from death itself, we value that which can be relied upon to continue, that which can protect us by its intrinsic strength. We value people above all, but we also value what is built, particularly the place we live in. [...] the ongoing non-destruction of the built environment reassures us [...] We cherish buildings in part because of their survival [...] This survival adds to the reassuring nature of the built world that surrounds our disorderly lives.
>
> (Rodman 2005: 62–3)

He goes on to suggest the position I wish to argue for:

> The built environment provides the illusion of order in which the work of creating order out of disorder is relieved [...] Here I am juxtaposing the internal disorder of the mind with the abiding and structural integrity of the built environment in which we largely dwell.
>
> (2005: 64)

Architect Yi-Fu Tuan makes a similar point by suggesting that buildings convey the vital sense of abiding containment through their solidity, size, and shape. 'If architecture has prestige', he says, 'one reason lies in the edifice's air of permanence', and this is achieved through

> solid building materials and sheer size. If the edifice is also symmetrical, built in the form of a circle, square, or polygon, it is making a claim to being atemporal—eternal. Not having a front or back in itself suggests that the building is beyond the human need for orientation and movement, that it transcends the pettier human divisions of time and their projects.
>
> (Tuan 2007: 27)

By somehow participating in or becoming integrated within the enduring structure of a building, we imagine ourselves preserved, and thereby find the means to manage our spatial anxieties. Peter Buchanan, an architect and cultural critic, explains that our experience of ourselves as inscribed within a building is an unconscious projection of the self into another material form:

> [O]ne of the very [*sic*] most fundamental purposes of architecture, one underestimated by most architects, is as a means by which we create ourselves. Arguably, only language plays as important a role as architecture in driving the cultural evolution by which we have created ourselves. But it goes much further than this: by projecting our psyches into space in this manner we not only create ourselves but also [create our] surroundings[,] to which we sense a strong relationship, so we feel at home in a world from which self-consciousness and awareness of death somewhat displaces us.
>
> (Buchanan 2012: 5)

Whereas Buchanan describes our tendency to project ourselves into space as a response to the uncomfortable feelings of displacement that accompany our awareness of death, I claim that we seek to project ourselves outside of our mortal bodies and into the enduring structure of buildings in order to

feel that we have acquired additional fortification and protection against the anxiety of death. Just as we make life meaningful and coherent by projecting onto or into it our desire for certainty and orientation, our perception of architecture involves us projecting onto or into its structure and solidity the experience of stabilising containment that we seek for ourselves. In the next chapter I shall explain the dynamics of projection and the important role it plays in our identifications with architecture, compelling us, for instance, to perceive buildings as extensions of ourselves.

Of course, buildings do not remain in pristine condition; they 'come to be and pass away', as Heraclitus maintains. Their material features are subject to renovation, deterioration, and demolition. But changes to their material fabric do not diminish their power to impress upon us the character of their—and our own—structural integrity. Indeed, it is often upon the occasion of a sudden and unanticipated change to a familiar building that our identifications with it are most viscerally felt. Reports suggest that the collapse or destruction of familiar buildings or the erection of new-fangled ones[6] within a well-established urban environment incite powerful feelings in people, causing them to feel disoriented, irrespective of whether they actually liked or disliked the building in question. If the solidity and structure of a building imparts a degree of existential fortification to a person, it is reasonable to assume that the demolition of its material form will convey to the person at some level the reality of their mortality and fragility. The 'work of the architect', as psychoanalyst Christopher Bollas aptly notes, 'involves important symbolic issues of life and death', for the act of '[d]emolishing the existent structure to make way for a new one plays upon our own sense of limited existence and foretells our ending' (2000: 29). Disorientation caused by the demolition of a familiar building is an anxious response to our sudden exposure to our mortality and the realisation that we aren't as enduring as we had imagined. The existential fortification lent by the building has gone and, at one and the same time, our sense of our own abiding order is substantially weakened and threatened. This reaction has agoraphobic characteristics, for it suggests a heightened desire to feel securely contained by one's environment in order to defend ourselves against exposure and dissolution. The construction of a new building in a familiar environment can evoke a similar threat to the comforts of self-containment that a person had up until then been cultivating. The presence of the new building calls into question their habitual approach to life, causing them to re-orientate themselves to the unfamiliar landmark. As scholar Juliet MacCannell asserts, 'It is as if innovative architecture disturbed some deep layer of existence that puts the fundamental structure of the world (or our fantasy place within it) in danger – or at least in doubt' (2005: 102). The new building threatens to invade and violate our experience of self-containment and thereby instigates something akin to a stifling claustrophobic reaction.

Sudden changes to the built environment provide invaluable opportunities to explore the identifications people had made with its features, and its impact on their sense of self and wellbeing. Although the ego often experiences unconscious activity as a threat to its self-containment, this threat may have a positive outcome for the ego. By loosening the ego's attachments, the unconscious can encourage it to explore beyond them, and rediscover itself as newly situated. The disorientation experienced upon the destruction of the familiar building or the imposition of an unfamiliar one, although unsettling and often unpleasant, could be the prelude to a new ego-orientation; it provides an opportunity for a person to reassess themselves and their attachments, and thereby to overcome outmoded preconceptions of themselves and their environments.

A familiar building that is suddenly absent can activate a need to find oneself securely contained elsewhere in the built environment; but its capacity to impart containment to the ego will often outlast its physical demise through a person's memory of its material forms. We preserve the structural integrity of the building in mind. In this respect, it is we who impart to the building its abiding nature through our mental reconstructions of it. In Chapter 2, I discussed the interchangeable preservation of self and building within Freud's analogy of the mind as the 'eternal city' of Rome; but for a more practical illustration we need simply to recall what it is like to move home.

We continue to occupy our former homes even though we are not physically present within them; likewise our former homes continue to occupy us. As Bachelard suggests, 'dwelling-places of the past remain in us for all time'. 'Over and beyond our memories, the house we were born in is physically inscribed in us'; even 'the feel of the tiniest latch has remained in our hands [...] In short, the house we were born in has engraved within us the hierarchy of the various functions of inhabiting' (1957: 6, 14–15). In an interesting move, Bachelard inverts the conventional architectural blueprint of psyche with its representations of the various functions of psyche as architectural imagery, to assert that 'we are the diagram of the functions of inhabiting that particular house [our first home]' (1957: 15). Bachelard maintains that the 'house we were born in becomes imbued with dream values that remain after the house is gone' and these values constitute, as both he and I have claimed, 'a body of images that give mankind proofs or illusions of stability' (1957: 17).[7]

Bollas, in terms strikingly similar to Bachelard's, equates the building we call home with the 'nooks and crannies of parts of ourselves' and the 'nesting places for our imagination';[8] and from there he goes on to consider the uncanny repercussions of the intimate identification we have with our former homes:

> Our belief in ghosts will always be at least unconsciously authorised by the fact that we shall always linger on in our former houses, just as we assume that upon moving into a new dwelling, its former inhabitants will also still be there.
>
> (Bollas 2000: 29)

Further opportunities for exploring identifications between self and building arise in those cases where a familiar building appears fragile and on the verge of collapse. The correspondence between the perceived instability of the building and feelings of self-doubt and insecurity in the perceiver is evident, for instance, in reported cases of burglary and accounts of 'uninhabitable' or ruined buildings. We explore the evocative nature of ruins in Chapter 5 with especial focus given to Freud's account of his uncanny experience of the ruins of the Acropolis. Suffice to say here that images of ruinous buildings play on our anxieties of dissolution and draw attention to the effects of the unconscious as it stirs within us, threatening to rupture the ego and the stabile identity it has established with streams of repressed feelings and thoughts. In reports of burglary, the victim (usually the homeowner) often describes the ordeal of having had their house invaded and ransacked as a violation to their personhood, comparing it to a physical attack on their body,[9] some going so far as to describe the ordeal in terms of a rape or sexual assault (Maguire 1980: 265–6; Shover 1991: 94). In cases where the security of a building has been breached, those who have identified themselves with the building will often feel that they too have been violated. A person's identification with the burgled building continues as it had prior to the burglary; all that changes is its character. As the building changes from a place of security and containment to one that is insecure, exposed, and vulnerable, the person likewise incorporates these changes into their sense of self.

According to MacCannell, buildings incite more 'emotional commotion' than any other object, causing us to react in 'such highly affective and extremely personal ways' (2005: 102). A reason for this, I suggest, is the intimate relationships we have with them, and the fundamental identifications we establish with them in order to make sense of ourselves. We relate to buildings with the unconscious expectation that they will contain us, orientate and fortify us through their own abiding structures, to the extent that when something unexpected happens to the building to make us question its abiding nature, we experience a shock to our system, as it were, with the unexpected disclosure or realisation that our lives aren't as stable and abiding as we led ourselves to believe. It was, as Nietzsche would say, an illusion after all. Buildings are the architects of us; they furnish us with a vital structural integrity that enables us to experience ourselves as coherent, stable, and securely in place. If we feel uncomfortable in relation to our built environments, it is no trivial matter; it is not simply a matter of aesthetic taste—of whether we dislike a building—but a matter of existential concern. That is to say, the dissonance a person feels between themselves and a building signifies a potential threat to their identity, a threat that can manifest itself in feelings of anxiety, alienation, and exposure. But such a scenario, as I have claimed, is not altogether disastrous, as it provides opportunity for self-discovery and personal growth.

Architecture that inhibits

Identity, I have claimed, is achieved through the dynamic exchange between two competing impulses that are stimulated when we interact with our environments. On the one hand, we are compelled to unify or merge with our environment in order to discover ourselves securely contained by it. To this end, we unconsciously seek out objects that impress upon us their abiding solidity and structural form, in such a way that we feel more integrated, strengthened, and fortified. On the other hand, we are compelled to withdraw from our environment and to loosen any attachments we made with it in order to experience ourselves as free, without constraint. We also noted that a counterbalance or oscillation between the two is required if the ego is to avoid problematic spatial anxieties that result from being too rigidly fixated in its attachments or isolated and uprooted without them. Architecture invites us to participate in the solidity of its forms and to find ourselves contained within them and integrated by them. But it also provides the vital counterbalance to this, by encouraging us to separate from it and experience ourselves as distinct and free. We shall address this shortly, but before we do, I want briefly to consider a group of thinkers who regard buildings and other architectural structures not as containers for the self or mediators of its development, but, on the contrary, its prison, restraint, and suffocation. For these thinkers architecture is nothing short of a symptom of our own pathology that alienates us from the natural world without opportunity for self-discovery and personal growth.

Many of these thinkers are associated with popular 'green' movements known by several names, such as eco-psychology, green psychology, and deep ecology. Such thinkers regard architecture as ego-centric edifices that isolate us from the unconscious impulses that enrich us by encouraging our engagement with the wider world beyond our own immediate interests. Buildings are described in terms befitting the neurotic ego, which is steeped in prejudice and sickness, with little hope of a cure.[10] The natural world as the antithesis to the built environment is revered as a place of health, a place which will revive us only if we are able to escape the oppressive city. The natural world is presented as a place under threat by the encroaching building site, which seeks to devour it with unruly urban sprawl. In a widely acclaimed work of eco-psychology, Theodore Roszak diagnoses the built environment as a *disease* of the ego that infects our relationships with our bodies and the natural world. Buildings have, he asserts, a muscular disorder that contorts their bodily mass and, in our identification with them, distorts our own capacity for 'sensuous intimacy' with others. This neurotic body-image and dysfunctional experience of embodiment, Roszak maintains, 'cuts us off from spontaneous vitality' and alienates us from the natural world (2002: 220).[11] Urbanization—or the infectious spread of 'city pox', as he refers to it—is interpreted by him as a pathological symptom of our ego's delusions of grandeur, omnipotence, and megalomania, which infect the world with 'mighty structures' that 'declare to the heavens, "See, we are here. Take notice of us!"' (2002: 216, 217).[12]

Psychologist James Hillman appears equally keen to equate architecture with the neurotic ego, and its desire to fortify itself in order to magnify its deluded magnificence.[13] Hillman's criticism of Jung's 'tower' at Bollingen as a 'monument in stone to the self-enclosed ego' that imprisons Jung within its walls can be interpreted in the wider context of his criticism of tower-structures more generally. Towers for Hillman are symbolic (or symptomatic) of the modern mindset and its failure to engage with life beyond its superficial appearance. They represent for him a problematic defensive structure that magnifies our need for stability and containment by seeking to enclose us within an impenetrable and paranoid architecture, one that isolates us from all that lies beyond its boundaries, as if life outside were a threat to the safety within. Hillman associates Jung's tower with the problematic 'towering sky-scrapers of Chicago and NYC [New York City]'; all of which express 'walled off individualism, the disease of [...] the twentieth century'; '[i]nstead of *connecting*, they are now *excluding*' (1993a: §5–6).

For Hillman, buildings generally—and towers especially—create in their inhabitants feelings of 'disdain' for the world (1993a: §2). In an undated, unpublished note, Hillman equates 'paranoia' with the perception one has at the top of a tall building: our 'looking far out' from it, 'looking down from it', 'looking up to it'—in other words, vistas of great distance that accentuate our separation from the world rather our participation in it.[14] In another unpublished note Hillman describes buildings as places of 'control', and towers as 'heroic' structures that place you 'at the top, above everyone' else (1993a: §3). Specific architectural features such as windows and doors are similarly targeted for criticism by Hillman. The window is emphasised, not as the old adage would have us believe, as an opening 'to the soul', but as a short-cut to social isolation and to the 'paranoid fantasy' that anything can enter and invade our private space.[15] The door is likewise a defensive mechanism, described by Hillman as an emblem of 'repression'. According to this idea, a door doesn't open us to a world of possibility, but closes upon us, to seal us off from whatever lies on the other side.[16]

If Roszak and Hillman were to explore the blueprints of psyche described in Chapter 2, they would find themselves stuck in the upper storeys, oblivious to the staircases that allow movement throughout the building and to the dark and expansive basement rooms at the other end of the building. Both thinkers appear to identify buildings with ego-consciousness alone and its corresponding aesthetic concerns for orderliness, stability, appropriation, and attachment to place. They appear to identify architecture with its capacity to structure and enclose us, and fail to acknowledge its capacity also to arouse those unconscious impulses that seek to loosen and detach us from its confines; in so doing, their architecture inevitably induces an unhealthy claustrophobia.

In contradistinction to the claims of Roszak and Hillman cited here, I suggest that buildings do not house ego alone; nor do they respond to its needs alone, but—as the blueprints of psyche suggest—they house and symbolise the interaction between ego-consciousness and the unconscious in the development of identity as a whole, not in part. Buildings lend themselves to the ego to satisfy its needs for abiding structure, but they are also well disposed to the contrasting concerns of the unconscious. Any compulsion we may have to find ourselves securely housed is matched by a desire to plunge ourselves into the mysteries of the unknown; and this dynamic interplay, I shall argue, underpins our perception of architecture, and determines the extent to which we identify ourselves with specific architectural designs.

Let us now turn our attention to the manner in which buildings cater to the needs of the unconscious by their capacity to impress upon us their expansive character and their 'infinite' surplus of meaning, which thwarts our attempts fully to comprehend and literalise our perceptions of them. The expansive quality of a building furnishes the experience of containment it provides with a vital flexibility that encourages us unconsciously to explore and re-evaluate our preconceptions of ourselves, and also the functional properties of the building. Here the *dynamic* nature of the building is disclosed, revealing itself to be an *event* that invites the subject to participate in the act of its disclosure, rather than a passive object for us to appropriate at will.

Architecture as event and container of infinite surplus

There is a definition of architecture that is gaining momentum in related disciplines, which at a glance seems radical or somewhat bizarre, but is less so when examined a little more closely. This definition is not so much concerned with the material fabric of a building as it is with the evocative experiences this fabric gives rise to, especially those that lead us to a heightened experience of ourselves or to an enhanced self-understanding. Theorists from disparate fields of study have come to define architecture as some sort of event. I shall argue that this 'event' of architecture imparts to the perceiver of the building insights about themselves that couldn't have been arrived at through the efforts of rational deliberation alone. Buildings, I claim, invite us to engage with them in order to explore uncharted, unconscious aspects of ourselves. In the following chapters I explain how this happens, and why it is important to conceptualise architecture not only in terms of its material features but also in terms of its dynamic potential.

The dynamism that underpins a building is regarded by many as its defining characteristic. In this respect, the value of architectural design isn't within its geometric features or the quality of its workmanship; nor can it be reduced to the mind of the perceiver. It is, rather, as scholar Lindsay Jones asserts, 'in the negotiation or the interactive relation that subsumes both building and beholder—in *the ritual-architectural event* in which buildings and human participants alike are involved' (2000: 41; emphasis in original). This dynamic event substantiates the ontological ground of the building; it is its defining characteristic, that which establishes it as a building and not something else. According to Jones, 'countless studies continue to perpetuate the fiction that buildings do have inherent, stable meanings—which [...] they certainly do not' (2000: xxviii). Consequently, if we wish to make use of a building and understand its properties, we should not waste time, he says, 'deciphering definitively the codes' that aren't within it, but approach it as we would a work of art, as 'a movement of history, a *process* or sequence of occasions in which neither the interpreter nor the work of art can be thought of as autonomous parts' (2000: 41). For Jones, architecture is 'an event that allures' (2000: xii); it is a 'dynamic occasion' or 'ceremonial situation' that brings 'people and buildings into active interaction' (2000: xxviii). Other theorists define architecture similarly. To mention just a few: Aldo Rossi regards architecture as 'ritual' (1981: 37); for Jane Jacobs, the streets perform a 'place ballet' (1961: 50); architecture is also a 'performance' for David Maclagan (2001: 131); Bernard Tschumi defines architecture as 'action' and 'event' (1996: 3); for Neil Leach it is a 'dynamic process' (2005a: 220); for Henri Lefebvre architecture is a 'project' embedded within 'qualitative, fluid, and dynamic' spaces (1974: 42).

The inherent dynamism of the building is often associated with its capacity to elicit a superabundance or 'surplus' of meaning (see Jones 2000: 21–37).[17] In psychoanalytic terms this would suggest that buildings invite a response at a different level or register of experience from the rational deliberations of our conscious mind. The building's surplus of meaning surpasses the limits and resources of ego-consciousness, and articulates an undifferentiated flux of meanings akin to those processed and expressed by the unconscious mind. Unconscious material, although incomprehensible and elusive, makes itself known through its effects, just as the superabundance of meanings evoked by the building brings us into relationship with it. Architect Henri Lefebvre's description of the dynamic nature of architecture in his celebrated work *The Production of Space* (1974) would sit comfortably in a psychoanalytic description of the nature of unconscious meaning: for architecture, he says,

> does not have a 'signified' (or 'signifieds'); rather, it has a *horizon of meaning*: a specific or indefinite multiplicity of meanings, a shifting hierarchy in which now one, now another meaning comes momentarily to the fore, by means of—and for the sake of—a particular action.
>
> (Lefebvre 1974: 222)

The same could be said of the following passage by Heidegger about a high-school building, the nature or 'Being' of which cannot be ascertained by its geometric structure, but by its affective textures:

> Over there, on the other side of the street stands the high school building. A being. We can scour every side of the building from the outside road through the inside from basement to attic, and note everything that can be found there: hallways, stairs, classrooms, and their furnishings. Everywhere we find beings, and in a very definite order. Where now is the Being of this high school? It *is*, after all. The building *is*. The Being of this being belongs to it if anything does, and nevertheless we do not find this Being within the being.
>
> (Heidegger 1935: 35–6)

The meaning of a building to these thinkers cannot be deciphered or decoded and put into rational terms, because a building continually generates meanings in its dynamic exchange with the person who perceives it. The person, as we have noted, engages with their environment both consciously and unconsciously, and the building, it would seem, has much to convey through our unconscious engagement with it. As Jones notes,

> once [their buildings are] erected, for better or worse, architects and builders almost immediately lose control of the significance and meanings of their projects. And consequently, as devotees (and scholars) use, reflect upon, and 'play with' the built structures in their environment, they endlessly disrupt old meanings and awaken fresh ones.
>
> (Jones 2000: 22)

To this I would simply add that any given person—not simply devotees or scholars—awakens meanings in the buildings they interact with. Heinrich Klotz, historian of postmodern architecture, similarly asserts that, 'whether architects like it or not, a building acts as a vehicle of meaning even if it is supposed to be meaningless' (1984: 3).[18] It is the building as a dynamic surplus of meanings that suggests its utility as a veritable container for the elusive, unconscious aspect of the self—that vital aspect that cannot be appropriated or fully comprehended by the ego.

The symbolic nature of buildings

Many thinkers have tried to pinpoint and explain the kinds of experiences that buildings evoke, and thereby try to make some sense out of the unthinkable surplus of meanings they elicit. Psychoanalysis and its related schools name this surplus the 'unconscious', and they take it upon themselves to investigate its nature and effects, and the role it plays in shaping our behaviour. While aesthetics as a field of enquiry doesn't have a specific name for this unknowable aspect, it too attempts as one of its principal objectives to make sense of it. The philosopher Susanne Langer, for instance, defines aesthetics as 'the comprehension of an unspoken idea' (1941: 259); and scholar Murielle Gagnebin defines it as 'a discourse about the unrepresentable', which has the 'impossible task of explaining the ineffable' (1994: 31; cited in Maclagan 2001: 39).[19] As Maclagan notes: 'In other words, both aesthetics and psychoanalysis have to deal with effects that are subliminal or unconscious, that depend upon various kinds of leakage between subjective and objective realities, and that are often almost beyond the reach of language' (2001: 40).

In the course of this investigation I shall adopt the useful and encompassing idea of the 'symbol' to elucidate the nature of that which eludes comprehension, but which nevertheless conveys through its image important meanings, effects, or, as Maclagan suggests, 'leakages'. The notion of the symbol is adopted by aestheticians and psychoanalysts alike to describe a 'surplus' of meaning, or that which evokes more than can be rationally discerned. In psychoanalysis and its related schools of thought, the symbol describes the ego's experience of unconscious affects, and is therefore regarded as a register of experience that mediates between and incorporates both the ego and the unconscious. The symbol pertains therefore to the known and unknown, the disclosed and concealed. The building in this context can be said to be a symbolic object, one that symbolises both aspects of the self, and facilitates the relationship between the two.

What then do we mean by this notion of the symbol, which, I claim, unites aesthetics and psychoanalysis[20] in their common endeavour to shed light on the dynamics that underpin our experience of architecture? Symbolism is a contested area of study that concerns a myriad of disciplines including, for instance, linguistics and theology. It should come as no surprise, therefore, that there is no definitive definition of the symbol. Indeed, even within psychoanalysis and its related schools there are competing theories about its nature and the power of its affects. In Chapter 6, I examine two of the most prominent theories, proffered by Freud and Jung, in order to explain how their contrasting views on symbolism have significant repercussions for our understanding of the architectural event, in terms of both the nature of our identifications with architecture, and the kinds of insights architecture is able to disclose about itself and about us.

In terms of its etymological meaning, 'symbol' derives from the Greek *symbolon*, and amalgamates the terms *syn*, meaning 'together', and *bolē* meaning 'throwing', 'casting', or the 'stroke of a beam or bolt', thereby suggesting its dynamic nature as a 'throwing together' of contrasting elements in order to extend outwards. Since the late sixteenth century[21] this 'throwing-together' has been interpreted as a relationship of one thing 'standing in for' or 'representing' another, so that symbols are generally thought to comprise a signifier that stands in for a signified. The signified in this case represents a value, truth, or meaning, which is not immediately discernible in the signifier itself, but is implied by it. The notion of the symbol that is adopted by aestheticians and psychoanalysts, however, has a greater evocative power and creative potential than this general definition suggests. These two disciplines lay stress on the fact that the signifier cannot encapsulate the meaning of the signified; both disciplines regard the signifier simply as the best available representation of the signified, and the signified unknowable in itself. Thus, when we allude to a symbol in aesthetic or psychoanalytic terms, we allude to a signifier *and* the 'surplus' of meaning that cannot be rationally discerned by the signifier but is nevertheless evoked by it.

The symbol comprises the known signifier and unknown signified as two contrasting aspects brought together in one and the same image. When we perceive something with symbolic status, we are compelled to employ a register of experience that is different from that which is involved in our literal perception of things, for our attention to the symbolic object does not rest on the object itself, but is directed beyond it, to meanings that are not immediately evident or discernible in the object. To reiterate Lefebvre's remarks about the architectural object, it 'does not have a "signified" ("signifieds")', but rather, directs us to an 'indefinite' '*horizon of meaning*'. Of course we can still perceive the building in literal terms and thereby register the geometry of its form and the solidity of its structure and so on. Indeed, I have claimed that such impressions as these provide vitality to the ego, feeding its desire for experiences of self-containment and coherent structure. But just as important is our capacity to perceive the symbolic nature of the building, and thereby engage with its non-literal or unconscious characteristics, through the superabundance of meanings and possibilities that it is said to evoke. Somehow architecture invites us to perceive its material form in a non-literal manner, and to bypass our cognitive understanding of its features so as to draw upon the unconscious reservoir of undifferentiated meanings that it elicits.

Descriptions of the symbolic nature of architecture—as with any discussion that attempts to elucidate that which extends beyond rational thought—will inevitably be tricky, and err towards the poetic and nonsensical. However, it is an important idea that finds support and some clarity in the influential ideas of others. The philosopher Roger Scruton, for instance, in his important yet often overlooked work *Aesthetics of Architecture* (1979), elaborates on the non-rational register of experience that we employ in our perception of buildings, to which he gives the name 'imaginative perception' (1979: 74). To his discussion we briefly turn.

Imaginative perception

Scruton draws upon the epistemology of Immanuel Kant to explain the difference between 'imaginative perception' and 'ordinary perception', as he refers to them. According to Scruton, Kant was most likely the first philosopher to give a proper account of imaginative perception, and to postulate 'imagination' as a faculty of our minds through which our sensations and concepts are united. For Kant, when we perceive something, such as a building, we inevitably and immediately postulate a concept of it. Simply put, we apply our understanding to the sense-data we receive to organise it into a unified whole and thereby understand the data as an impression of some particular thing: for instance, a 'building'. The difference between ordinary perception and imaginative perception, for Scruton and his reading of Kant, rests on the extent to which the imagination is bound by the rules of understanding that are enforced in the experience. In ordinary perception the imagination is constrained by rules of understanding, so that a building perceived ordinarily or literally will conform to the rational concept of 'building' to which the perceiver is accustomed. But if the building is perceived imaginatively—or 'aesthetically', in Kant's terms—the imagination is no longer constrained by rules of the understanding, but is 'free' to contemplate the object of the building beyond the bounds of reason. Imaginative perception, Scruton says, is bound instead to 'patterns of thought and attention that we are in no way compelled by what we see to engage in' (1979: 84). In other words, our imaginative perception of a building can lead us to entertain ideas that are not immediately and rationally discernible in the material form of the building itself. According to Scruton, buildings call forth this imaginative register of experience, and in so doing they present themselves not as 'an object of our attention' but as 'a mode of attention to other things' (1979: 77). He illustrates the point with the example of a cathedral. Seeing a cathedral through imaginative perception, he says, is not a matter of engaging with its material design features, but seeing it 'as we know it not to be'. That is to say, we gaze through it rather than at it and, as a result, find ourselves entertaining a stream of imaginative thoughts about things that are not visible in the cathedral itself. Scruton therefore claims that our perception of the cathedral 'is imbued with the thought of something absent' (1979: 84). Imaginative perception, I suggest, is equivalent to an unconscious register of experience.

Scruton distinguishes between the building that is perceived imaginatively and its material properties that are discoverable through ordinary perception. To perceive the building ordinarily as a 'mass of masonry' is to attend to it with a 'special intellectual aim'—with, as Scruton says, a desire to 'find out' something about it (1979: 87). In psychoanalytic terms, 'ordinary' or, as I shall refer to it, literal perception[22] is the approach taken by ego-consciousness in its desire to appropriate the building to its own ends. To perceive the building imaginatively, by contrast, is to attend to it without an agenda, but nevertheless to discover something useful in it, by employing—as Scruton somewhat cryptically states—a 'different kind of understanding'. Our investigation will attempt to expose and clarify what this different kind of understanding actually entails.

Scruton goes on to assert that architecture can be perceived *only* imaginatively; it is never simply a 'mass of masonry'. He writes: 'It is not merely that architecture is the occasional object of imaginative experience (for what is not?), but rather that it is a proper object of that experience, and it cannot be understood except in imaginative terms' (1979: 87). For Scruton, buildings imaginatively order our experience, and in such a way that 'however much we divest our experience of interpretation, it retains the character of freedom which is one of the distinguishing marks of an imaginative act' (1979: 87). In other words, and in psychoanalytic terms, buildings encourage free unconscious expression, allowing our experience of the building to bypass the boundaries of rational understanding, subsequently directing our attention to possible meanings that are not available to our conscious mind through its literal perception of the building.

Scruton summarises his argument by alluding to the symbol as the defining character of architectural experience:

> [...] there are two ways in which experience and concept can combine: the way of literal perception, and the way of imagination. [...] [I]n the experience of architecture, it is the imagination that prevails. This means not

> merely that architectural experience is inherently interpreted, but that it can be modified through argument, remains free of literal-minded preconceptions, and acquires a status wholly unlike that of common perception, namely, the status of a symbol.
>
> (Scruton 1979: 260)

I suggest that the impressions we receive in our perception of architecture set in motion a flux of unconscious ideas, feelings, and experiences. In Chapter 5, I examine this sequence of events to explain why architecture in particular can be said to enlist our imaginative register of experience, and how we employ the surplus of meanings elicited by architecture to shape our sense of self. I shall there differentiate between the linear sequence of thoughts employed by ego-consciousness in its literal perception of architecture, and the wandering sequence of associated thoughts—often referred to as 'dream-thinking' or 'free-association'—that is encouraged by the unconscious in our imaginative perception of architecture. Scruton asserts that imaginative perception involves 'patterns of thought and attention' that are unavailable to literal perception. Psychoanalysis conceives unconscious activity in similar terms. Although chaotic and unpredictable, the unconscious is thought to configure its material in such a way that patterns of associated thoughts, feelings, and ideas can be loosely discerned. I shall argue that architecture captures our unconscious attention by compelling us to perceive its forms imaginatively, and in so doing it provides us with an invaluable opportunity to negotiate unconscious aspects of ourselves, including repressed conflicts, memory traces, and other fragments of experience.

Discovering ourselves through architecture

In this chapter we have begun to explore why buildings are regarded as dynamic events or dramas that invite us to participate in them. Our participation is encouraged when we perceive the building 'imaginatively'. Imaginative perception triggers impressions that cannot be discerned through our ordinary, literal perception of the building. This is because imaginative perception is guided by unconscious concerns that bypass our cognitive expectations, and lead us to experience the building in surprising ways. The impressions we acquire in the architectural event are muddled and loosely arranged as patterns or clusters of associated ideas. Later we see how this arrangement depends on the spatial techniques employed by the unconscious, which subsequently gathers together the impressions of the building with its own fragmented material and configures them into a narrative that is personally meaningful to us. The spatial techniques it employs are directed by our innate compulsion to merge with and detach ourselves from our environments.

In the architectural event the blueprints of psyche are put into practice. As we continue our investigation into the event, it will become increasingly clear that architecture isn't simply a metaphorical counterpart to the self, its abstract representative; architecture evokes the self, and invites us to re-evaluate who we take ourselves to be. Buildings embody and respond to both components of the divided self. They provide the ego, as the agent of consciousness, with an experience of abiding structure that it continually desires in order to ward off fundamental anxieties of self-doubt, instability, and annihilation. And they engage the unconscious through their elusive nature, described by many as a superabundance of meaning or undifferentiated forms—a nature that thwarts the cognitive ego in its attempts to understand it. Contrary to the lament of Roszak and other associated 'green thinkers', buildings are not edifices (of the ego) that express an ego-centric desire to have power over and to appropriate an uncertain terrain; they are symbols of the divided self or psyche as a whole. Buildings present creative opportunities for us. They are not inherently oppressive or defensive, but, on the contrary, veritable sites for the cultivation of personality, leading us, if we let them, towards a more objective attitude and perspective than ego-orientation can achieve acting alone.

In the chapters that follow I shall argue for buildings as occasions for the rediscovery of self, and opportunities for the negotiation of those aspects of our personality that are ordinarily hidden. I claim that the 'different kind of understanding', as Scruton puts it, that is activated in our perception of architecture is one rooted in an increased capacity for self-reflection and a greater appreciation of the built environments we find ourselves in. Architecture is a drama that resituates the perceiver within themselves and in relation to the buildings they use, enabling them to feel better oriented and contained.

I alluded to several theorists who define architecture as an event; and there are still others who support the idea that the event of architecture is specifically an existential event that reveals vital insights into the nature of our being.[23] Heidegger, for instance, famously concludes that we are ontologically connected to buildings; that they are places of dwelling that gather and disclose our being (1951). Hans-Georg Gadamer asserts that architecture exemplifies the symbolic nature of our being (1960: 119, 138–42). Architect Stanley Abercrombie maintains that 'man apprehends' architecture 'not as a remote object but as a close accomplice in his own reality' (1996: 168–9). Architect Bruno Zevi claims that architecture is 'the stage on which our lives unfold' (Zevi 1948: 32). As already quoted, architect Peter Buchanan asserts that 'one of the very most [*sic*] fundamental purposes of architecture, one underestimated by most architects, is as a means by which we create ourselves' (2012: 5). Designer Cecil Balmond defines buildings as personal 'journeys'; the 'structure' of the building, he says, 'reveals itself not as mute skeleton but as a series of provocations; sometimes explicit, at other times ambiguous' (Balmond and Smith 2002: 105–7). Psychoanalyst Stephen Sonnenberg, in response to Balmond's definition, underscores the existential significance of architecture, asserting that for Balmond, buildings are

> opportunities to be in the world creatively, unshackled from old routine, and rigidified emotional, cognitive, and perceptual aspects of human existence. The building is to him [Balmond] a vehicle opening up his mind to new, expansive ways of being, thinking, feeling, and designing.
> (Sonneberg 2005: 47)

Such assertions led me to question why there should be an ontological link between architecture and the self. That is to say, what is it in the nature or character of buildings that grants them power to shape us? Why are buildings, rather than any other object, so adept at disclosing existential truths? How does the architectural event actually work and why does it occur? And what exactly are the existential 'home truths' that we discover in the process? The remaining chapters will go some way to providing answers to these questions. But we shall end this chapter with some clues that will help us along the way. These arise in the salient work of psychoanalyst Christopher Bollas. I shall draw on his ideas and develop others as our investigation unfolds.

Bollas's ideas about 'evocative objects' and 'transformative objects' are particularly useful for our investigation into the architectural event. According to Bollas, as we go through life we articulate our character or personality through our use of objects. Our choice of objects and the way we use them is determined by their structural form or appearance. Bollas describes how our selection of objects amounts to a *collision* between our 'human form' and the 'object's structure' that results in our 'transformation'. We are, he says, 'nourished by the encounter' and gain from it the 'inner contents' of the object (1992: 60). Arguably, we articulate ourselves through any and every given object, which suggests that there is a vast and extensive array of potential structures that can be integrated into ourselves. The answer to why we are compelled to select buildings as a favourite object for the elaboration of ourselves lies in their structural form.

Given that our experience of objects and things is coloured by our subjective assessment of them, it is often difficult to talk about their objective quality. Traditionally, psychoanalysis and its related school of thought known as 'object relations theory' have shown little interest in differentiating between objects according to the therapeutic efficacy of their material form. However, by turning to Bollas's work we can begin to appreciate how psychoanalytic theories can be utilised and developed in that direction. At the beginning of *Being a Character*, Bollas writes:

> I have found it rather surprising that in 'object relations theory' very little thought is given to the distinct structure of an object, which is usually seen as a container of the individual's projections. Certainly objects bear

> us. But ironically enough, it is precisely *because* they hold our projections that the structural feature of any one object becomes even more important, because we also put ourselves into a container that upon re-experiencing will process us according to its natural integrity.
>
> (Bollas 1992: 4)

Bollas maintains that the evocative potential of any given object is dependent on the object's structural integrity, which is determined by the object's material features. The structural integrity of an object is intrinsic to it and independent of any subjective quality we may subsequently project on to it. Bollas concludes that each object puts us, its user, through a specific inner experience that corresponds to the object's formal character. For instance, if 'I choose to listen to a record rather than read a book, I select a thing that will elicit inner experiencings specific to the selection of a musical object, whereas if I had selected a book I would have fancied a thing that would have sponsored another type of internal experience' (1992: 22). Bollas refers to the inner experience that arises from our 'collision' or interaction with the structural form of an object as the object's 'processional potential' (2009: 88). 'Each thing in the lexicon of objects', he maintains, 'has a potentially different evocative effect by virtue of its specific form[,] which partly structures the subject's inner experience' (1992: 22).

Given that Bollas has written an essay titled 'Architecture and the Unconscious' (2000), which is one of just four selected for his anthology *The Evocative Object World* (2009), one would assume that his intention is to emphasise architecture as an especially important evocative object with a particularly rich processional potential. But the essay makes no explicit argument or claim to this effect. It does, however, imply as much through various assertions that resonate with and lend support to ideas I have already discussed. Thus, for Bollas, buildings are important evocative objects by virtue of their solid and enduring structural form, which imparts to us, as their users, the means to negotiate feelings of death and human mortality and the fact that these buildings will likely outlast us as their inhabitants. This idea complements my assertion that we are compelled to identify with the abiding structure suggested by our buildings due to our innate desire for self-preservation; by identifying with them, we identify with the structure that we desire for ourselves. The structural form of a building is therefore particularly poignant for us because it furnishes us with sought-after experiences of *abiding containment*: which is to say, a sense of ourselves as fortified, integrated, and securely in place. It can even impart to us feelings of immortality.

Bollas's work helps us to make sense of the processional potential of buildings and the important experiences of containment they evoke, both generally and in relation to our earliest experiences of transformation. Thus, in addition to sheltering us from the anxieties of death and destruction, architecture relates us to our earliest experiences in infancy, at a time when our self-awareness gradually emerged, with the realisation that we are autonomous beings, distinct from objects and other people. In our interactions with architecture, we awaken an experience that Bollas deduces to be an 'existential memory' or imprint of the earliest transformational experiences we had in relation to our original object of containment—which, for Bollas, is the mother (or primary caregiver). We cannot cognitively recall the momentous occasion of our earliest transformation into a self-aware being with identity. But what does remain available to us, Bollas claims, is the desire to replicate or relive the transformative process that led to our transformation into a self. It is this desire that compels us throughout life to search for objects that will impart similar experiences of transformation (1987: 4, 13–29).

If, as Bollas claims, our earliest transformation was set in motion by our experiences of containment (in relation to the nurturing caregiver), it follows that objects that appear to us through their material features as containers are primed to trigger our existential memory of transformation, and as such are especially attractive to us. Of all nonhuman objects that present themselves as containers, the building is arguably most compelling, and the building we call home most of all. Home contains us. As architectural theorist Andrew Ballantyne notes, the building we call home 'has witnessed our indignities and embarrassments' and 'seen us at our worst', but despite this it 'still shelters us and protects us, so we feel secure there, and have surprisingly strong feelings for it, even though they go unnoticed most of the time' (2002: 17). Underpinning our intimate identifications with architecture is the unconscious expectation that it will put us through an enriching, transformative experience.

Later I explore what other psychoanalysts have said about the earliest experiences of containment and transformation in infancy, in order to ascertain their repercussions for our experiences of architecture in later life. I shall argue that buildings are not objects for adult use only, but play a vital role throughout our lives. I shall go as far as to suggest that the built environment is integral to the earliest experiences of transformation—a somewhat controversial claim that assigns to architecture the noble role of accomplice to the mother (or other human caregiver), helping her to establish and cultivate the infant's identity and original, dawning experience of self.

I draw this chapter to a close with a word of warning and an outline of the chapters ahead. Just as Freud warns us not to 'mistake the scaffolding for the building' in our treatment of spatial metaphors, so too must we be mindful, as we proceed in our investigation, of the dangers of rationalising the contents of the unconscious and interpreting the symbolic nature of architecture in literal terms.

Given, as we are claiming, that buildings are dynamic events that reveal and conceal a myriad of possible meanings and provoke an imaginative response, any insights they purportedly evoke in the subject cannot be fully comprehended or fully deciphered in literal terms. Psychoanalysis allows for the decoding of unconscious language only to a degree (as we find, for instance, in its method of dream-interpretation). But to presume that a building can be appropriated as a passive object and made to give up its secrets is to deny its essential, symbolic nature. As Scruton reminds us, architecture is 'not so much a thing with discoverable properties as a way of envisaging the properties of its object', and this approach has no 'desire to "find out", no special preoccupation with facts' (1979: 79, 87). Thus it is with a degree of precaution and speculation that I proceed in my investigation, trying to make sense of the architectural event, and evaluating architectural features and designs for their evocative potential. Indeed, as I shall go on to conclude, those architectural projects that seek to engineer evocative affects, and thereby force an unconscious response in those who come to use them, more often than not produce buildings that appear ridiculous and akin to a parody of insight rather than genuinely insightful. The reason for this is that they fall into the trap of seeking merely to *represent* unconscious dynamics through their stylized designs, rather than evoking it.

In the chapters that follow I examine the architectural event to make sense of the psychodynamic processes that underpin it. For the sake of clarity, I wish to examine the architectural event according to what I consider to be its three interrelated components or phases. In so doing, I shall be able to highlight and scrutinise more effectively the more salient behaviours, instincts, and feelings of the complex mix that underpins our relationships with architecture. The first phase or aspect is the subject's initial encounter with the building, whereupon their identification with its features is triggered; the second describes the subject's detachment from the building and their withdrawal into themselves; and the final phase or aspect is marked by a moment of personal insight and transformation, as the unconscious mind of the subject discloses its material and brings about a new sense of self. Evident within each phase is the subject's fluctuating desires to connect or merge with the building and to disconnect or separate itself from it. Also evident within each is the integral role played by the subject's body, the subject's memories, and their corresponding experiences of embodiment and integration.

Our bodies and memories provide us with invaluable experiences of continuity, without which we would have no cohesive identity to speak of. It is therefore unsurprising that they should play so important a role in the architectural event, as the principal means through which we participate in it and experience its impact. Indeed, as we shall see, our bodies and memories are intimately involved in our 'imaginative perception' of the world, and the 'imaginative ideas' that are said to constitute the very meaning of architecture.

Notes

1 When unconscious material is denied its expression, it leads to a conflict in the personality, which results in all sorts of disturbances, including psychosomatic symptoms. Psychoanalysts refer to this conflict as a 'neurosis'. In severe cases, a 'psychosis' can result, which at its most basic level is when the ego-personality is fragmented by the onslaught of unconscious material. In neuroses and psychoses, there is a failure in the relationship between the conscious and unconscious aspects of mind.

2 See Huskinson 2004: 11–19. Interestingly, when the Apollonian impulse is at total variance with the Dionysian and is operating singularly and in its purest form, we find it most clearly expressed, Nietzsche asserts, in architecture (and other plastic arts): for there—within buildings, for instance—we are presented immediately with an undeniable structure and form, which constitutes the Apollonian aesthetic, alongside clarity, distinction, particularity, illusion, beauty, individuality, contrast, and convention. In its purest aesthetic form, the Dionysian is expressed in fine music, with associations of uncertainty, chaos, frenzy, contradiction, limitlessness, fertility, and the collective. In relation to modes of self-consciousness, the Apollonian impulse corresponds to feeling oneself to be distinct from one's environment, while the Dionysian impulse corresponds to the mental state of feeling conjoined to the rest of reality. The combination of music and architecture reminds one of the famous remarks made both by Schelling and Goethe: that music is architecture in a fluid state and that architecture is frozen music.

3 The psychoanalyst Michael Balint (1959) proposed similar spatial anxieties with his concepts *ocnophil* and *philobat*. These are two contrasting approaches to objects and boundaries that are perceived in our ordinary, everyday environments. If we respond to our environment with an ocnophilic state of mind, it appears to be a frightening and dangerous world of open expanses and uncertain happenings, punctuated by comforting objects that are clung to for support. This is therefore akin to an agoraphobic response, such as that demonstrated by Freud's clinging to the arm of Reik as he attempted to cross the street (Reik 1948: 15–16). In a philobatic state of mind, by contrast, the objects themselves are experienced as dangerous, and the wide open spaces as comforting (akin to a claustrophobic response). There is often a mixture of the two attitudes at any one time, one repressing the other; or there is an anxious instability, where one is experienced to excess, with either an unhealthy need to possess the object or a tendency to become paranoid, ever watchful for objects appearing out of nowhere, ready to possess the self.

4 Hillman describes the claustrophobic nature of Jung's Bollingen building when he criticises it as a 'self-enclosed stone-walled personality' (1993: §6).

5 Plato cites Heraclitus as saying: 'Everything gives way and nothing stands fast' (Plato 1997: 402A).

6 The Eiffel Tower in the centre of Paris is a well-documented case in point, its designs drawing controversy and criticism from the public and significant figures in the arts. A petition known as *Les Artistes contre la Tour Eiffel* ('Artists against the Eiffel Tower') was sent to the Minister of Works and published in the daily newspaper *Le Temps* (14 February 1887) with the following declaration:

> We, writers, painters, sculptors, architects and passionate devotees of the hitherto untouched beauty of Paris, protest with all our strength, with all our indignation in the name of slighted French taste, against the erection [...] of

> this useless and monstrous Eiffel Tower [...] To bring our arguments home, imagine for a moment a giddy, ridiculous tower dominating Paris like a gigantic black smokestack, crushing under its barbaric bulk Notre Dame, the Tour Saint-Jacques, the Louvre, the Dome of les Invalides, the Arc de Triomphe[;] all of our humiliated monuments will disappear in this ghastly dream. And for twenty years [...] we shall see stretching like a blot of ink the hateful shadow of the hateful column of bolted sheet metal.

7 Rainer Maria Rilke describes the incorporation of the memory of a house eloquently:

> Afterwards I never again saw that remarkable house [...] it is no complete building: it is all broken up inside me; here a room, there a room, and here a piece of hallway that does not connect these two rooms but is preserved, as a fragment, by itself. In this way it is all dispersed within me – the rooms, the stairways that descended with such ceremonious deliberation, and other narrow, spiral stairs in the obscurity of which one moved as blood does in the veins [...] all that is still in me and will never cease to be in me. It is as though the picture of this house had fallen into me from an infinite height and had shattered against my very ground.
>
> (Rilke 1910: §6: 30–1)

8 Bachelard speaks of the family home as a 'nest' of 'nooks and corners', and within 'each one of its nooks and corners' is 'a resting-place for daydreaming' (1957: 15, 30).

9 See Ostrihanska and Wojcik (1993); Shapland and Hall (2007: 183, 186, 191). Data from the 1983 British Crime Survey suggest that a third of victims of burglary suffer depression, sleeplessness, or other health problems (Hough and Mayhew 1985).

10 See, for instance, Roszak (2002), who writes: 'But what if [madness] derives not from the distant ancestral past but from something more recent: the beginnings of civilized life, the social and economic transition that rooted our species out [*sic*] of its original environment and relocated it to the city?' (2002: 83).

11 Here Roszak employs Wilhelm Reich's (1933) term 'body armour', which is an unconscious muscular defence that is caused by the tensions of emotional trauma. Body armour has similarities with Esther Bick's (1968) notion of the 'second skin'. Other scholars who argue for the split between the natural world and the built environment, by idealising the former and denigrating the latter, include Clinebell (1996), who asserts 'the need of city-dwellers to find healing in wilderness', because '[e]ntering the wilderness and its microcosms—gardens and parks—gives us an opportunity to reconnect with that instinct and rests our fragile psyches from the exhaustion of trying to stay intact in the civilized world, which is so alien to many of us' (1996: 46). Likewise, architect Yi-Fu Tuan asserts that 'the virtues of the countryside require their anti-image, the city, for the sharpening of focus, and vice-versa', and refers to 'city corruption and rural virtue' (1974: 102, 108; cf. 103–9).

12 This echoes Jane Jacobs in her criticism of Le Corbusier's utopian plans for the city. Jacobs asserts:

> No matter how vulgarized or clumsy the design, how dreary and useless the open space, how dull the close-up view, an imitation of Le Corbusier shouts "Look what I made!" Like a great, visible ego it tells of someone's achievement. But as to how the city works, it tells, like the Garden City, nothing but lies.
>
> (Jacobs 1961: 32)

13 Hillman and Roszak are further aligned in Hillman's published support of Roszak's work, the former having written a foreword to Roszak's *Ecopsychology: Restoring the Earth/Healing the Mind* (Roszak et al. 2002)—a foreword that is perhaps better known as Hillman's short essay 'A Psyche the Size of the Earth' (published in 1995)—and an endorsement of Roszak's celebrated work *The Voice of the Earth: An Exploration of Ecopsychology* (2002). The endorsement which appears on the back of this book is as follows: 'Because it's thorough, because it's right, and because it speaks the ideals of a passionate heart, Roszak's book lays a groundwork for the theory and practice of psychotherapy for the coming century.'

14 The note appears in Box Number: Hillman 185A in the James Hillman Collection, Opus Archives, Santa Barbara (see Hillman 1993a). Interestingly, Hillman makes a similar remark in the context of ceilings:

> What statements are these ceilings making? What are they saying about our psychic interiors? If looking up is a gesture of aspiration and orientation toward the higher order of the cosmos, an imagination opening towards the stars, our ceilings reflect an utterly secular vision—short-sighted, utilitarian, unaesthetic. Our heads reach up and open into a meaningless and chaotic white space.
>
> (1997: 196; see also Hillman 1986)

15 He says, 'I think when you go past a street where the buildings have been burnt, or where the windows are boarded up [and] the windows are smashed, it's a terrible feeling, it's like you're looking at a face with the eyes out' (Kidel 1993: 3). In his preparatory notes for this episode, Hillman emphasises the problems of windows that don't open, and those that are double or triple glazed. These windows, he says, 'reinforce the isolation or loneliness of the person inside. They come out of a paranoid fantasy that anything can come in on me, invade me, and so they reinforce our social isolation. You're absolutely hermetically sealed.' Compare this with architect Pallasmaa's comments: 'the polarized and darkened windowpanes of contemporary houses [...] are eyes blinded by some horrible illness; these are malicious eyes that secretly control the inhabitants themselves' (2000: 8–9).

16 In a handwritten note, dated 1993, Hillman boldly states: 'huge investment in [the] Front Door [e.g.] Oak door. Carved Door. SIGNIFY REPRESSION' (capitals are in the original note. The note appears in Box Number: Hillman 185A in the James Hillman Collection, Opus Archives, Santa Barbara; see Hillman 1993b). The door becomes, in other words, the means by which the ego can barricade itself inside and defend itself from all that is outside.

17 Jones is especially insightful on this notion, and cites several supporting claims from architectural and philosophical theorists including Mark Wigley, who refers to 'the irreducible strangeness of architecture' (1993: 28), and Charles Moore, for whom, 'a building itself has the power, by having been built right or wrong or mute or noisy, to be what it wants to be, to say what it wants to say' (in Cook and Klotz 1973: 242).

18 In Chapter 7, I shall consider the problematic repercussions of the building's capacity to evoke infinite meanings for those architects who design in order to convey specific meanings.

19 See also Deamer (2004:126): 'Psychoanalysis' aesthetic engagement has tended to stay at the level of content and not on form, due to the fact that architecture is largely non-representational art'; and Wigley (1993:28) who alludes to: '[T]he

irreducible strangeness of architecture'; and architect Tschumi, who employs the metaphor of a masked figure that reveals another mask beneath in order to convey the elusive and unknowable character of architecture (cited in Jones 2000: 24).

20 Indeed, unites all depth psychologists, perhaps most explicitly by Jungian analytical psychologists and archetypal psychologists.

21 With the publication of Edmund Spenser's epic poem *The Faerie Queene* in 1590.

22 I shall adopt Scruton's use of the term 'imaginative perception' in my investigation, but in place of Scruton's term 'ordinary perception', I shall use the term 'literal perception'. This is because, as I shall argue, imaginative perception is no less ordinary than the mode of perception that Scruton discusses here in contrast to it. Indeed, we employ imaginative perception on a daily basis, and far more often than is generally realised.

23 Of the theorists previously mentioned, Roger Scruton, addressing the value of architecture, concludes that 'aesthetic experience is not only a peculiarity of rational beings, but also an essential part of their understanding, both of themselves and of the world which surrounds them' (Scruton 1979: 261). Lindsey Jones asserts that 'architecture typically participates in the character of a homecoming, or a reunion with oneself and one's past' (2000: 76).

Chapter 4

The body's role in the architectural event

Fortification and containment

At the end of the previous chapter I alluded to the body and the memory as two vital components of identity that facilitate a self-awareness that is coherent and personal. We consider each in turn within the next two chapters, starting in this chapter with the body in order to explain how our sense of self is constituted through experiences of embodiment that arise when our body comes into contact with other objects. I shall argue that our bodily encounters with the built environment lead to an enriched and fortified experience of ourselves as integrated and self-contained. In the previous chapter I also discussed the importance of Bollas's ideas of evocative and transformational objects. There I explained how identity is formed through a 'collision' between subject and object, a collision that is unconsciously anticipated by the subject as a desire to repeat their earliest experiences of transformation (the original 'collision', so to speak), which led them to the formation of their ego-identity and to self-awareness. This chapter elucidates the psychoanalytic theory that underpins this account, and applies it to our earliest experiences of architecture—the 'original architectural event'—and outlines its repercussions for our subsequent relationships with the built environment.

We shall see that prior to the development of a cognitive ego—and prior, therefore, to the capacity to rationalise experience—the infant makes sense of its world through its bodily interactions with the objects it encounters. The comprehension available to the infant is comparable to the imaginative register of experience that I am keen to associate with the architectural event. Both involve the kinds of collisions Bollas describes, involving the psychological merger of subject and object, and the consequent incorporation of the object's features into the subject. The event that leads the subject to perceive these features not as qualities of an object that is independent and external to him or her, but as part and parcel of themselves. We shall trace this process of identification within a variety of psychoanalytic accounts to see how their differently nuanced interpretations of this vital process shed light on our relationships with architecture. The architectural event in this chapter is understood as the occasion of the subject's identification with specific material features of the building, and the mode of *participation*, as we described it in the previous chapter, is understood in psychoanalytic terms as the *incorporation* of the architectural features into the subject.

Unstable bodies, unstable architecture

We begin our investigation into the relationship between bodily experience and architecture from the perspective of those who have some sort of impairment to their body, body-image, or memory, for it is arguably in such cases that the correlation between the structural features of architectural image and self-experience is most noticeable. One might well question the architectural forms that are incorporated into those with impaired body or mind. We might ask, what are they and what are their repercussions for the architectural event? Later we turn these questions on their head, to consider the issue from the perspective of those architectural designs that appear to question our preconceptions about what a human body—or building—ought to look like, and how it should function, focusing on designs (often labelled deconstructivist or postmodern) that reflect, in their distorted, gnarled, and exploding features, a body-template that is comparably twisted and warped, decapitated, and fragmented. But here I note some interesting examples and illustrations that can be found scattered throughout psychoanalytic literature of people who have been diagnosed with psychosomatic illnesses of varying severity, and who appear to identify themselves with architectural imagery that is in one way or another unusual and unconventional.[1] The imagery that is reported tends to be treated as a representation of the disturbed mind of the patient or person who either designed it or demonstrates an attachment to it. In so doing, these psychoanalytic accounts suggest an identification between the impaired subject and an impaired architectural structure; but, as the accolades and awards given to many deconstructivist designs remind us, such supposed 'impairments' provide opportunities for immense creativity and reward.

I have already discussed the link between distorted forms of architecture and unstable experiences of self as one commonly experienced on those occasions when a familiar building undergoes substantial changes to its structure—for instance, in cases of radical renovation, erosion, demolition, or replacement by another, unfamiliar building. In such cases, the building's capacity to act as an 'abiding container' for the self is put into question, with palpable repercussions for the perceiver. We have noted, too, Freud's penchant for diagnosing his patients' ailments according to the architectural structures that appear in their dreams as deformed or not quite as they should be. But it is in the writings of other psychoanalytic thinkers on reported cases of pathological experience that we find the most striking correlation between a distorted self and a distorted architectural structure. Eugene Mahon (2005), for instance, describes the case of Miranda, a young girl who had become deeply traumatized by her parents' separation, and subsequently became preoccupied with drawing 'strange houses', with equally 'strange doors' that looked like 'large tears' in the fabric of the building. According to Mahon, Miranda's traumatized self is expressed through traumatic architecture. 'Architecture to Miranda', he asserts, 'was a torn blueprint that could only produce a cracked model, a crooked house.' Miranda's capacity to conceive a cohesive structure was impaired; the buildings she subsequently constructs reveal 'her own affects turned against the self'. Mahon continues to note that the effects of her trauma 'were undermining the architectural security of her body-image and mind-image'. Only when Miranda was able to 'retrieve her own sense of agency' from out of her desperate situation could she be said, Mahon tell us, 'to build better houses, so to speak, out of more adaptive, resourceful, non-neurotic blueprints' (2005: 29–30).

Thirty years before Mahon's account, we find a comparable case recounted by Donald Meltzer, this time of an autistic boy whose incapacity for self-reflection and lack of 'inner space' was articulated in his drawings of two-dimensional houses. As with Miranda, this unnamed boy became preoccupied with his architectural drawings. His designs comprised 'doors and gates, usually with complex wrought-iron grills', and took the shape of 'Victorian gothic houses'. As Meltzer recounts:

> One day he painstakingly drew an ornate house seen from the front on one side of the page, a house in Northwood, while on the other side he drew a back view of a pub in Southend. Thus the child demonstrated his experience of a two-dimensional object; when you enter by the front door you simultaneously exit by the rear door of a different object. It is in effect an object without an inside.
>
> (Meltzer 1975: 18)

The two-dimensional construction of the building, Meltzer claims, denotes the boy's inability to experience a sense of self-containment in his identification with other objects. In other words, Meltzer's diagnosis of the boy's condition suggests that the boy is unable to acquire the experience of *abiding containment* that is normally achieved in our identifications with architecture—which is to say, the boy is unable to experience himself as fortified, integrated, and securely in place. The boy identifies with architecture and uses the image of a building to articulate the quality of his inner world, but both are, as Meltzer, says, '"paper-thin"', 'without a delineated inside'. As Meltzer suggests, there is for this boy 'a primal failure of the containing function of the external object, and thus of the formation of the concept of self as a container', and this 'deficiency of containment is related to internal spacelessness of the self' (1975: 19–20).

The correlation between the structural form of an architectural image and that of self-experience is traceable across a spectrum of architectural compositions and psychosomatic temperaments; but, arguably, it is most noticeable in cases of instability, when for instance, a person is anxious or ill, or the architectural image is disordered and derelict. It is a correlation that architects often try to take advantage of by seeking to evoke specific feelings in the subject, such as feelings of pleasure and intrigue, or even unease and discomfort, all to varying degrees of success. In Chapter 7, I evaluate the efficacy of such attempts, but in this chapter I consider the psychological significance of the semblance of the material features of the building and a person's experience of embodiment. I have argued that the building captures our unconscious attention through its promise of the abiding structure and enduring containment that we desire for ourselves. I wish now to explore the role of the body within this attraction, and the identifications between body and building that subsequently arise. I shall argue that the building is an especially evocative object for us, not simply because of the perceived correspondences between its structural form and our bodily composition, but in the *expectation* that something will be achieved or acquired through this correspondence; that is to say, there is an expectation that the building will transform or enrich us through our unconscious recognition of our affinity with it.

As I noted in Chapter 1, analogies between the human body and architecture have been observed for centuries. Vitruvius's ideas about bodily proportion in particular continue to influence the designs of many a building to this day. While the symbolic meaning of the resemblance of bodily form and architectural structure has been emphasised—many studies, for instance, seek to explain its significance in terms of a measurement of heavenly or cosmological order, and of beauty—the usefulness of this semblance for elucidating our relationships with architecture, and its psychological impact on the perceiver and user of buildings, is rarely considered. My argument will go some way towards bridging these gaps by exploring the psychological repercussions of the semblance on a person's state of mind and wellbeing. I argue that awareness, at some level, of the affinity between the subject's body and the built environment gives rise to competing desires to merge with the building and to separate from it. The shifting dynamic between the two types of engagement with the building encourages significant changes within the subject, leading them to feel more integrated and better contained themselves and in their relationship to the built environment. The significance of the correspondence between body and building extends far beyond a specific measurement, or the proportionality of form; it suggests a fundamental experience of self as a flexible, dynamic identity, one open to new possibilities of being and self-expression. If one were merely to focus on the measurements and principles that unite the two, one could easily overlook the vitality each imparts to the other, a vitality that leads the subject to a heighted experience and deeper appreciation not only of themselves but also of the building they perceive.

How exactly does the perceived semblance between body and building exert an influence on a person? I alluded in Chapter 3 to the unconscious act of 'projection' as an explanation favoured by psychoanalysts and architectural theorists alike. With reference to the latter, we mentioned Peter Buchanan's assertion that by 'projecting our psyches into space' we 'create ourselves' as subjects who 'feel at home' in the world. We can also cite Juhani Pallasmaa, an architect who regards projection as an instinctive response that occurs when we recognise unconsciously the semblance between our bodily form and the structure of a building. 'Understanding architectural scale', he writes, 'implies the unconscious measuring of the object or the building with one's body, and of projecting one's body scheme into the space in question.' Furthermore, when we project our embodied selves into the building we feel a heightened sense of containment or, as Pallasmaa puts it, 'We feel pleasure and protection when the body discovers its resonance in space' (1996: 67).

Pallasmaa and Buchanan are just two of several architectural theorists who posit projection as the means through which we identify with the built environment, and utilise our perception of it to enhance ourselves. Pallasmaa describes projection as a 'curious exchange' that takes place between human body and building; it is a 'bodily interaction', like a voice in 'unconscious' conversation with another. If we 'project our emotions and feelings' on to the building, he says, it 'lends us its authority and aura', and through this interaction 'we meet ourselves', but in an enhanced version. I think it is this curious exchange, or 'collision' of forms, as Bollas suggests, that Jung experienced as a child with the large stone in his garden (where, to recall, Jung's understanding of his identity shifted between himself and the stone, such that at any one time he took himself to be the boy sitting on the stone or the stone upon which he was sitting), and is active within each of us in our daily encounters with architecture.[2]

If the act of projection describes the lending of ourselves to the building in our desire to converse or merge with it, the corresponding psychoanalytic notions of 'introjection' or 'incorporation' describe the response we receive in return from the building.[3] When we put something of ourselves 'into' the building, it responds in kind by lending us its characteristics—its 'structural integrity', as Bollas refers to it, or 'aura' as Pallasmaa suggests—and these are subsequently incorporated into us in return. In support of this notion, Pallasmaa maintains that, when we experience a building, its 'movement, balance and scale' are 'felt unconsciously' throughout our bodies 'as tensions in the muscular system and in the positions of the skeleton and inner organs'. He continues:

> When experiencing a structure, we unconsciously mimic its configuration with our bones and muscles [...] [T]he structures of a building are unconsciously imitated and comprehended through the skeletal system. Unknowingly, we perform the task of the column or of the vault with our body.
>
> (Pallasmaa 1996: 67)

The curious exchange that occurs between a person and a building can be explained by the dynamics of projection and incorporation that underpin it. It is a creative and vital exchange that goes by the name of mimicry or mimesis.

Mimesis

The exchange that takes place between the subject's body and the building reveals an act of mimesis that is highly creative for the subject in the cultivation of self. Translated from ancient Greek as 'imitation', the origin of the term 'mimesis' is often attributed to Plato, who employed it—in c. 380 BC in *Republic* (2013)—in a derogatory manner to refer to art forms that seek merely to imitate reality. Plato regarded such art as a corrupting influence on society, for it distracts citizens from seeking higher truths and from engaging with reality itself. Since Plato, mimesis has come to denote a complex array of dynamic meanings including, as Matthew Potolsky suggests, 'emulation, mimicry, dissimulation, doubling, theatricality, realism, identification, correspondence, depiction, verisimilitude, resemblance' (2006: 1).

Although the term is rarely employed in mainstream psychoanalytic discourse, a theory of mimesis is undeniably at the heart of its understanding of human behaviour, and, in particular, the manner in which we construct identity and establish relationships. Ideas of mimetic identification have influenced a wide range of disparate disciplines including, of course, architectural theory, where it has been suggested as an explanation for our bodily connection to buildings.[4]

Let us now trace this important notion of mimesis as it appears within key psychoanalytic theories about the construction of human identity in order to shed light on the dynamic exchanges that occur between us and the buildings we encounter. Our findings will underscore the vital significance of the semblance between architectural features and bodily experience for the perceiver of the building, and will help us to appreciate that our evocative encounters with architecture have greater bearing on our personal identity than we might otherwise realise.

We shall examine the notion of mimesis within two contrasting and often conflicting psychoanalytic approaches. Despite their disagreements, they agree on the fundamental point I wish to emphasise here, which is that personal identity is a creative achievement that is continually and unconsciously sought in our bodily interactions with the objects of our environment. We consider first Jacques Lacan's understanding of identity as the consequence of the subject's recognition of the semblance between the experiences they ascribe to their bodies and the mirror-image of their bodily form reflected back to them. On such occasions the body is perceived, Lacan says, as a 'statue' or stone replica, which the subject seeks to animate by taking on its structured form.[5]

Following our discussion of the role of mimetic identification in Lacan's theory of identification, we turn to object relations theory and its central claim that self-awareness is constructed through its relationships with other objects or parts of objects. This theory is associated with a number of prominent thinkers in the psychoanalytic tradition, but the ideas most pertinent to our investigation are those of Donald Winnicott, Esther Bick, and Didier Anzieu.[6] While Lacan's infant relies for the most part on sight, object relations theory tends to emphasise touch as and when the infant's skin comes into contact with other objects. The earliest experiences of this tactile encounter (most often described as the mother's touch) is regarded as the occasion for the earliest experiences of self, for they provide the infant with the required experiences of containment and integration to stabilise the frenzied impulses that otherwise overwhelm it, granting it the capacity to gather itself together into a more coherent and self-reflective being. Importantly, these experiences continue throughout life. Indeed, the quality of the infant's containing experiences is thought to establish the template for all future object relations, and thereby determines both the manner and extent to which a person is able to relate to objects of their environment, and subsequently use them in the elaboration of themselves. Also at stake in the earliest object relationship is a person's capacity to anticipate their environments and to trust they will deliver the experience desired and expected of them.

Psychoanalytic thought puts 'people' centre-stage as the primary 'objects' of our relating. Our earliest relationships with our parents are thought to establish the template for our later relationships, both with ourselves and others. The mother (or principal caregiver) is commonly assumed to be the crucial resource for the regulation of the infant's emotional wellbeing—through her touch, her smell, the tone of her voice, and her facial expressions. Certainly, I do not wish to downplay the vital importance of people or 'human objects' for establishing one's sense of self and wellbeing. However, their significance should not detract from the important role played by nonhuman objects. In other words, as I shall argue, if we register unconsciously a vital semblance between ourselves and other humans, we probably also register the semblance between ourselves and nonhuman objects, and in so doing we find in these nonhuman objects an equally valid resource with which to construct or elaborate ourselves. The 'nurturing environment', according to psychoanalyst and object relations theorist Donald Winnicott, refers explicitly to the bond between mother and baby; however, I suggest that it can and indeed ought to be extended to include the nonhuman environment—and not simply as an implicit or background influence on the mother's state of mind as she tends to her baby, but as a direct and explicit influence on the baby itself in addition to its mother. Moreover, I contend that just as the earliest object relationship, with the mother, continues to shape a person throughout their life, so too do the earliest relationships with the nonhuman environment.

Following our analyses of the contrasting accounts of the construction and development of self in the theories of Lacan and representatives of the object relations theory, I shall therefore move to consider the potential role and significance of the nonhuman environment in their accounts, with especial consideration given to the built environment. To develop my argument I shall later draw upon important ideas from unconventional psychoanalytic works—notably those of Harold Searles and J.W.T. Redfearn, whose insights into the affective nature of the nonhuman environment have been for the most part overlooked or ignored, due perhaps to their divergence from the mainstream of psychoanalytic discourse. We shall refer also to relevant ideas from the philosophy of Maurice Merleau-Ponty and Theodore Adorno.

Before we turn to consider mimetic identification within Lacanian theory and object relations theory, I think it helpful to consider briefly Freud's contribution to a general theory of mimetic identification from which Lacan and theorists of object relations largely derive and develop their own ideas. Although Freud concedes that bodily sensations shape the ego-personality,[7] he doesn't have a general discussion about their relationship, choosing to attend instead to the mental plane of human experience and its intrapsychic activity as the decisive factor in the development of the self.[8] Given his chosen emphasis, Freud's ideas will be more useful to this investigation in the next chapter, where I examine how our perception of architecture triggers a stream of unconscious ideas, feelings, and memory-traces that have largely been inaccessible to us. Nevertheless, and despite Freud's relative silence on the importance of the body, a theory of mimetic identification through bodily experience can be found at the heart of Freudian psychoanalysis and of his basic understanding of self-development and human relations. To this we briefly turn before outlining how Lacan and object relations theorists sought to develop Freud's understanding in different ways, each of which sheds light on the manner of our identifications with architecture.

Freudian mimesis

According to Freud, our lives are governed by our imitation of the characteristics we desire in others, and our experiences in the present, including our most deliberate actions and consciously conceived thoughts, are imitations of past experiences that we have forgotten and repressed. The Freudian self is a conglomerate of past occasions where the subject has unconsciously imitated the behaviour of others. As scholar Matthew Potolsky describes it, 'Selfhood and identity are not given at birth, but comprise a mimetic amalgam of those who have influenced the ego, Freud's term for the sense of self', such that 'we are the people we have imitated' (2006: 119).

For Freud, identity is flexible and is constructed and reconstructed in the light of emotional ties to other people (Freud 1921: 107). We cannot choose who we imitate, or influence who we are at any given time. The most potent identifications we make are those formed in our earliest experiences, with our mother (or primary caregiver) in prime position to take on the first and most commanding of models for our imitation; it is she who continues to shape us irrespective of our best efforts to resist.

Importantly, imitation for Freud does not signify a conscious act of emulation or replication, but a moment of unconscious *assimilation*, through which the desired traits of the other are incorporated into the self (Freud 1921: 113; cf. 1900: 150; cf. Adorno 1970: 162, 169). Imitation of the other does not result in a like-for-like representation of the other, but in a creative reinterpretation of it. In this respect, imitation is an act of self-creation or self-construction. Given that the self is founded on the assimilation of other people's traits, self-awareness will inevitably involve an awareness of an 'otherness' that cannot be wholly appropriated or possessed by the subject and integrated into them as them. As Potolsky observes, 'Identification installs an uncanny trace of otherness at the heart of identity, so much so that we can be surprised by the direction, intensity or emotional character of our identifications' (2006: 122). Within Freud's theory of mimetic identification we can therefore trace the two contrasting concerns or impulses of the divided self that are key to the formation and development of a person's identity and sense of self. On the one hand, there is a compulsion to *merge* with objects in order to incorporate their characteristics that we desire for ourselves—traits that bolster our sense of containment and subsequently help to alleviate our anxieties about disintegration. On the other hand, this merger involves the incorporation of something essentially 'other', an inconceivable otherness—or, to draw on a term I employed in Chapter 3, an 'infinite surplus'—that gives rise to an experience of the not-me within me. This could be interpreted as lending us an increased capacity for unconscious awareness, enabling us to discern an existential distance between ourselves and the objects of our identification—a capacity that subsequently helps to alleviate our anxieties of being quashed or suffocated by the other.

Identification, Freud says, 'endeavours to mould a person's own ego after the fashion of the one that has been taken as a model' (1921: 106). That is to say, when the subject forms emotional ties with another person, the attractive characteristics of the person are internalised by the subject as pervasive ideals that colour the subject's subsequent behaviour and outlook. This 'moulding' by the other is tangibly felt in the subject as an 'enrichment' of their own sense of self (1921: 113). Freud, as we know, restricts his theory of mimetic identification to the assimilation of attractive traits we perceive in people; but I wish to extend his theory to suggest that a similar scenario occurs in our perception of architecture and its desirable features. That is to say, the 'architectural event', as I have called it, describes the occasion when characteristics of a building's material form are unconsciously sought by the subject to bolster and furnish their sense of self with their promise of abiding containment. I therefore wish to broaden and develop human-centric models of psychoanalysis to allow for the architectural object as a potentially enriching and transformative 'role model' for the subject. Such a proposition is not so far-fetched if we take into account Bollas's assertion that we elaborate ourselves through our choice of any given object that attracts us by its structural form, and if we consider it alongside my claim that the structural forms of architecture are particularly compelling in their promise to contain and nourish.

Freud's understanding of the mimetic procedure that underpins our identifications with and use of others has been criticised for its paradox in presupposing the existence of a self-contained ego-identity to enable the ego to come into being. That is to say, if, as Freud maintains, the ego is formed through the bonds it establishes with others, we may well ask what then is the state of the ego prior to its bond-forming activity? Put simply, what comes before the ego to enable it to come into being as ego? Jacques Lacan sought to resolve this conceptual problem. His solution was to propose that prior to having established an ego, the infant is a chaotic flux of impulses, for without an ego the infant lacks the cognitive resources to establish bonds with others. The helpless infant must make sense of the world in the only way it can; and it does so, Lacan contends, through its bodily experiences. In the work of Lacan we find a model of mimetic identification that regards the recognition of the semblance between one's bodily form and another object as the decisive factor in the development of identity. For only through its awareness of this semblance can the infant find the resources to overcome its chaotic and turbulent environment.

Lacan's statue

Lacan outlines the significance of the body for the creation of the ego in his celebrated essay 'The Mirror Stage as Formative of the Function of the *I* Function as Revealed in Psychoanalytic Experience' (1949). The aspect that interests us in Lacan's proposed 'mirror stage' is its 'structural value', as he refers to it, and how it sheds light on the relationships between the body and the ego, and between the experience of self-containment that it achieves and the chaotic reality it overcomes.[9] In Lacan's discussion of the mirror stage we find useful parallels with the architectural event, not least in the significance of a stone-like structure for imparting to the subject who perceives it a vital and creative illusion of stability and containment.

Lacan asserts that the original identification made by the infant prior to its capacity to identify with others is itself. This narcissistic identification occurs when the infant first recognises its bodily image reflected back to it—hence Lacan's name for this occasion as the 'mirror stage' of ego development.[10] The recognition of the semblance between the embodied self and its mirror-image is an identification of body and psyche in one; that is to say, it is a spatial recognition of one's self as an embodied self. While infants have a fragmentary and chaotic sense of self—for their lack of coordination and mastery over themselves make them dependent on others to negotiate their bodily functions and needs for them—the image of the body they encounter in the mirror-reflection of themselves is unified, coherent, fixed, and autonomous. Lacan describes the mirror image as a statue. According to Lacan, the infant initially finds this image of wholeness threatening, so that its initial response to the statue is one of aggressive tension. The infant is compelled to alleviate this tension, and manages to do so, Lacan says, by identifying with its mirror image and assimilating itself to its coherent, statuesque form. It is in the process of identifying with the statue that the ego is formed. Lacan tells us that the moment of identification is one of jubilation for the infant, as it achieves an imaginary sense of mastery and a new-found capacity to negotiate and contain the chaotic tensions it had experienced. Importantly, for Lacan, and for our investigation, the process of self-discovery is founded on an illusion of stability and certainty: a false—and essentially creative— recognition of oneself as bounded, embodied, and contained within space.

For Lacan, the object that facilitates the discovery of self is the self in stone. The mirror image is 'the statue onto which man projects himself'; the 'statue' that looks back at us (1949: 76). According to Lacan, the self is continually rediscovered throughout life in our interactions with various objects, including architectural imagery, which, as Lacan writes, appear often in dreams as 'fortified structures', a 'fortified camp' or 'stadium' that contains within it 'the proud, remote inner castle' (1949: 78). We identify with the stone-self because it is 'replete with the correspondences that unite' our experiences of ourselves with it (1949: 76). The stone-self is an idealised image for the infant, for it is a body that is self-contained and stands erect without the need for support from others. The statue 'symbolizes the *I*'s mental permanence'; thus when the infant comes to identify itself with it, its inner world is enriched and furnished with a fortifying illusion of stability: the construction of ego as a 'proud' 'inner castle'.

The statue is the cornerstone of ego-identity and, given that the cultivation of self is an ongoing process, mimetic identifications between self and statuesque forms continue throughout life, making the stone-self an ever present companion in the construction of reality. The statue is not, therefore, a singular *event* that comes to a close in the original construction of ego, and the mirror 'stage' is itself never surmounted. Long after the child has mastered its mirror image, Lacan tells us, it continues to stare. Thus, the identity we fashion for ourselves is populated, Lacan says, by many statue-like images or 'automates' that continue to stabilise the gaze of our egos. Identity is an ongoing achievement, and the ego will continue to mould itself in the image of other stabilizing containers that it perceives, and these extend beyond one's body to include, Lacan concedes, 'even things around' us (1949: 93).

In my discussion of Bollas I suggested that we could feasibly project aspects of ourselves onto any object and use it as a psychological container for ourselves. Lacan likewise suggests that a great range of objects have the statuesque properties required to facilitate the development of ego. As one commentator of Lacan asserts, '*everything*' in Lacan's world, 'becomes a "statue in which man projects himself" and produces himself in front of himself' (Borch-Jacobsen 1991: 60). However, as I shall continue to argue, the material forms of the built environment are particularly captivating in this regard, and compel us to use them more than other objects for our containing needs. Lacan appears to suggest as much in his acknowledgment of our continual 'quest for the proud, remote inner castle,' 'fortified camp', and 'stadium'. Indeed, the convention in architectural discourse of explaining the material features of a building in terms of the bodily sensations it imparts to the perceiver adds further support to the idea, by presenting buildings as evocative objects principally in their capacity to incite a bodily response. The words of architect Pallasmaa cited earlier, for instance, explain this in terms that could easily have been lifted from a commentary on the Lacanian infant staring at the statue of his mirror-reflection. To repeat, 'When experiencing a structure, we unconsciously mimic its configuration with our bones and muscles'; '[u]nknowingly, we perform the task of the column or of the vault with our body'; it 'strengthens' our 'experience of the vertical dimension of the world' (1996: 67).

If Lacan were to design a blueprint of psyche to accompany those surveyed in Chapter 2, it would probably consist of a prominent, solid, and upright structure, one that expresses through its 'standing posture' and imposing form a character of 'stability' and 'prestige' (Lacan 1953: 15). Arguably, these criteria apply to some degree to every building, but it is perhaps the column or pillar that is the most obvious architectural feature to resonate with Lacan's account. For centuries the column has been characterised as the human body in standing posture (see Rykwert 1996). This is most strikingly illustrated by caryatids: sculpted female figures that stand upright as columns with entablatures on their heads, such as we find in the porch of the Erechtheion at the Acropolis in Athens, and in the neo-classical Greek Revival design of St Pancras Church in Bloomsbury, London (Fig. 4.1). The column is a particularly apt metaphor for the Lacanian integrated-self by virtue, also, of its function, for columns were traditionally incorporated into designs to enable the edifice to remain standing, as its load-bearing structure could negotiate and stabilise the various pressures, forces, and stresses incurred from the weight and mass of the edifice, and from unpredictable external influences such as wind and storms.

The emphasis given to the vertical, standing posture of the human figure that informs not only Lacan's statue but also the majority of blueprints of psyche is not without its critics. Such criticism is most readily voiced in reaction to the architectural convention inherited from Vitruvius of constructing according to the form and proportions of the human body (most often male) standing upright. Scholars and architects have questioned the privileging of this bodily stance by suggesting alternatives, such as the body in a different posture, as crouched low or lying down. Santiago Calatrava's architectural

Figure 4.1 Caryatids, St Pancras Church, London (William and Henry William Inwood, 1819–1822)
These caryatids are modelled from plaster casts of those of the Erechtheion, at the Acropolis, Athens.

designs are a case in point, for many of his designs are informed by his sketches of human bodies in dynamic postures. See, for example, his sketch of human figures with their heads lowered and arms fully stretched out to the sides (Fig. 4.2) – figures that are subsequently integrated into his designs, such as *Gare do Oriente* [*The Oriente Station*], Lisbon (completed 1998; Fig. 4.3).

Oscar Niemeyer's projects are influenced by the 'free-flowing sensual curves', as he puts it, of 'the body of the beloved woman'; and, as his sketches depict, his model is usually naked and in reclining repose (see Niemeyer 2000: 62, 169, 170) (Fig. 4.4).

Others go so far as to question our fundamental preconceptions of bodily form, with designs informed by mutilated, decapitated, and exploded bodies. Examples are Santiago Calatrava's *Turning Torso* (built 2001–2005), a residential skyscraper in Malmö, Sweden, influenced by his sketches of a decapitated, armless male torso in a twisting posture (Figs 4.6, 4.7; see Calatrava 2002: 94–5) and Frank Gehry's architecture, which often resembles his frenzied sketches of human figures that appear to be exploding in a frenzied tangle with their built environments (Figs 4.8, 4.9; see Rappolt 2008). Designs such as these resonate with the cases I reported earlier of the autistic boy who

Figure 4.2 Human figures, sketch (Santiago Calatrava)
© Santiago Calatrava LLC

Figure 4.3 Gare do Oriente / Oriente Station, Lisbon (Santiago Calatrava, 1998)
© Joao Pimentel Ferreira. Wikimedia Commons, CC BY 3.0

Figure 4.4 Centro Cultural Internacional Oscar Niemeyer / Oscar Niemeyer's International Cultural Centre, Ría de Avilés, Asturias, Spain (Oscar Niemeyer, 2011)
Niemeyer's sketch of a reclining woman adorns the auditorium of his International Cultural Centre.

expressed his lack of inner world through his drawings of two-dimensional houses (Meltzer 1975), and the traumatized girl who expressed her experience of self through drawings of 'strange' and 'crooked' houses (Mahon 2005).

The integration of the mental plane and the physiological constitution of the self is achieved in the subject's encounters with architectural structures that present to them idealised visions of autonomy, mastery, and containment that they subsequently proceed to incorporate into themselves. But importantly for Lacan, the establishment of ego, as with Freud's interpretation of mimetic identification, incurs not simply new-found experiences of stability and fortification, but also experiences of an uncanny sense of otherness. Scholar Borch-Jacobsen, in his chapter 'The Statue Man' (1991), draws attention to this important sense of otherness in Lacan's mirror stage in terms of the striking mismatch, as he sees it, between the image of the statue—which appears lifeless, inanimate, and object-like—and the self that is achieved through identification with it:

> Thus is the world described by Lacan so strangely petrified and static, a sort of immense museum peopled with immobile 'statues', 'images' of

Figure 4.5 Teatro Popular / Popular Theatre, Niterói, Rio de Janeiro (Oscar Niemeyer, 2007)
Niemeyer's sketch of dancing women adorns his Popular Theatre of Niterói.

> stone, and hieratic 'forms'. The world Lacan describes as strictly 'human' is simultaneously the most inhuman of possible worlds, the most *unheimlich* [uncanny], in any case: it is the world of Freud's doubles, a shadowy world, where every image of the ego is already an 'uncanny harbinger' of its death.
>
> (Borch-Jacobsen 1991: 59)[11,12]

The Lacanian ego is founded on an illusory correspondence between self and mirror-image. Indeed, the statue to which the infant assimilates itself is an incomplete and inaccurate image of the infant; for the mirror reflects an inverted image, and also fails to depict the infant as it appears from behind. Arguably, it is this essential mismatch (mis-recognition or *méconnaissance*, as Lacan refers to it) between the statue and the infant that installs within the resulting ego-identity a vital sense of a lack or 'otherness', which—as we discussed in relation to Freud's notion of mimetic identification—could inform and help to facilitate our desire to detach ourselves from our environments. The Lacanian statue provides the capacity for our competing desires for detachment and merger. By identifying with the statue, the subject acquires its rigid and ossified form, which furnishes their inner world with

Figure 4.6 Turning Torso sketch (Santiago Calatrava)
© Santiago Calatrava LLC

Figure 4.7 Turning Torso building, Malmö, Sweden (Santiago Calatrava, 2005)
© Knuckles, Wikimedia Commons, CC Figs. BY 2.5

Figure 4.8 Human figure sketch, detail from 'Don Giovanni' at Walt Disney Concert Hall
(© Gehry Partners, LLP)

Figure 4.9 Walt Disney Concert Hall, Los Angeles, California (Frank Gehry, 2003)
© Jon Sullivan, Wikimedia Commons, PD

an experience of abiding containment, while the uncanny sense of otherness that is experienced in the mismatch between the two ensures that a vital existential distance can be maintained between the subject and the objects of their environment.

Let us now turn to the psychoanalytic approach of object relations, one that emphasises the importance of identifying with objects that are decidedly more fleshy and animate. In contrast to the rigidity of Lacan's statue in a world that is 'visual through and through' (Borch-Jacobsen 1991: 60), object relations theory focuses on the warm elasticity of skin in a world that is formed and shaped predominantly by touch.

Touching the skin-ego

In Chapter 1 we noted the historical importance given by architects to an aesthetics of the visible, with its aspirations for clarity and detachment. By contrast, the immediacy of touch is a relatively new consideration within architectural design, and the recognition of the importance of sounds, and even smells, more recent still. Because these latter senses are highly prized within object relations theory, the latter's theoretical dialogue with architectural discourse could shed further light on the importance of these senses and the role they play in developing and improving meaningful relationships with the built environment. In object relations theory the self-reflexive experience of touch is key to the construction of self and for creating emotional bonds with others. The skin in this scenario not only defines the material contours of a person's body, but also gives rise to his or her capacity to think and self-reflect, and to establish relationships.

Within object relations theory we discover a notion of mimetic identification comparable to one proposed by philosophers Theodor Adorno and Max Horkheimer. Adorno and Horkheimer describe mimesis as a means to an authentic and natural self-knowledge, in stark contrast to the reductive knowledge of abstract reasoning that propagates, they say, an unnatural distance between the self and its environment. Adorno and Horkheimer criticise modern culture for its alienating tendency to promote abstract thought at the expense of emotions and instincts, and for valorising the sense of sight as the principal means for establishing subjectivity and self-knowledge at the expense of the other senses.[13] Mimesis is their remedy for the problem. Mimesis is achieved, they say, through tactile gestures—through 'touch, soothing, snuggling up', and 'coaxing' (Adorno and Horkheimer 1946: 182).[14] Tactile gestures animate the skin and pave the way for a reciprocal relationship between self and object where, for instance, the sensation of an object touching the self is experienced at one and the same time as the self touching the object.

Although Freud laid the groundwork for a psychology of the body by declaring the ego to be 'first and foremost a bodily ego', a mental 'projection of the surface' of the body (1923), he left it to others to address the implications of this claim and to develop a more comprehensive theory around it. The surface of the body to which Freud alludes has been widely interpreted as the physical self-reflexive skin of the infant that registers its various interactions with those who actively engage with it. From its tactile experiences—and those described by Adorno and Horkheimer seem particularly relevant here—the infant comes to recognise its autonomy as a distinct being in relationship to another. If the mother (or primary caregiver) is sufficiently caring of her infant with her nurturing touch and soothing voice, she will provide the containing environment required by the infant for the cultivation of its ego.

Esther Bick, in her brief yet seminal paper 'The Experience of the Skin in Early Object Relations' (1968), was one of the first to discuss the crucial role of the skin for 'binding together' the infant's sensations and enabling it to overcome the 'catastrophic anxieties' that otherwise arise from its unintegrated state:

> [I]n its most primitive form the parts of the personality are felt to have no binding force amongst themselves and must therefore be held together in a way that is experienced by them passively, by the skin functioning as a boundary. But this internal function of containing the parts of the self is dependent initially on the introjection of an external object, experienced as capable of fulfilling this function. Later, identification with this function of the object supersedes the unintegrated state and gives rise to the fantasy of internal and external spaces.
>
> (Bick 1968: 484)

The infant in its unintegrated state desperately needs to be contained, and so undertakes a 'frantic search', as Bick puts it, for anything that can hold its attention, even if only for a fleeting moment. Such an experience will furnish the infant with the containment and integration it requires. Significant for our investigation is Bick's suggestion that any object, including nonhuman objects, can facilitate the infant's containment. Although the touch of the mother's skin (specifically, she notes, the mother's 'nipple' in the infant's mouth, together with her 'holding and talking and familiar smell') is, she asserts, 'the optimal object', any nonhuman object that is capable of holding the infant's attention will suffice. Bick subsequently alludes very briefly to the efficacy of lighting and to smells other than those of the mother. We can freely extend this to other nonhuman objects, including a gamut of experiences pertaining to the architectural features that are registered by the infant—and not simply their visual and tactile qualities, but also the sounds and smells they disclose. Jung concedes, in a letter to Freud, that 'the first mimetic attempts' of an infant include its 'staring at a shiny object' (Freud and Jung 1974: Letter 126J; 125–6) Contrasting shades, shapes, and textures within the infant's architectural environment are likely to attract its attention should they fall within its perceptual range. Such focal points could include a crack in the plaster, light framed by a window, the decorative coving or moulding that separates ceiling and wall, the hum of hot water in a pipe, the textured walls of its own crib, the sound of a door closing, and the rhythm of the draught underneath the door and of footsteps on a staircase. Whatever the material source of the infant's containing experience—human or nonhuman—it will profoundly affect the infant; it is, Bick asserts, 'experienced concretely as skin' (Bick 1968: 484). When the infant's attention is captured by something, it experiences itself as being 'held' by it, an experience that Bick equates with the sensations registered by skin. The gathering together of its sensations leads the infant to an awareness and recognition of its own enclosed inner space.[15]

The psychoanalyst Didier Anzieu develops similar ideas to Bick through such works as *The Skin Ego* (1974), *A Skin for Thought* (1986), and *Psychic Envelopes* (1990). According to Anzieu, before the development of the cognitive ego, or 'thinking ego', as he terms it, the infant depends on something called a 'skin ego', which performs through various primitive functions the tasks that will eventually be performed by the cognitive ego. These include the maintenance of the infant's sense of self through its 'containment' and 'inscription' (1974: 195–203). The skin ego is not available to the infant from birth, but is gradually achieved in response to stimuli impinging on the surface of its skin. These stimuli lead the infant to construct a mental image of itself as a container that is capable of holding its experiences together (Anzieu 1985: 61). In the absence of a cognitive ego, the image that the infant establishes of itself is not rationally deduced from its experiences, but is 'phantasized': which is to say, the infant employs a primitive, imaginative register of experience to construct itself. At this early stage in its development, the infant is unaware of itself as an individual being, separate from its environment, and instead establishes through the reflexive structure of its skin the illusion of itself as a 'shared skin' with its human caregiver, a 'phantasy of reciprocal inclusion' and 'reciprocal empathy' (Anzieu 1985: 62, 63).

Although the skin ego is a surrogate for the 'thinking ego', it is not terminated following the latter's development, but continues to function throughout a person's life. As scholar Marc Lafrance notes, 'the thinking ego is always already formed and informed by the skin ego; or, put differently, the skin ego is the permanent support and ever-present backdrop of the thinking ego' (2013: 30). The skin and the sensations it processes continue their vital role in shaping identity, such that we continue to relate to objects, things, and other people through our imaginative perception of them, experiencing ourselves as if merged with them, with 'shared skin'. Whilst Anzieu discusses this phantasised union of the self and other in the context of relationships between people,[16] we can also apply it to our relationships with nonhuman objects, and architecture in particular, for we discover at the heart of the architectural event a dynamic self-reflexive and self-constructive experience that is comparable in its activity and function to the skin ego. When we perceive a building imaginatively, we identify with its containing forms, and experience ourselves as if merged with it and inscribed by it, as if embodying a common skin of flesh and stone.

Anzieu explains that the imagined merger of self and other, although repeatedly experienced throughout life, is itself a temporary experience, for the exchanges that occur through the skin surface of the subject lead them to become aware of the spatial boundaries of their body in relation to the other, and come to recognise it as a container for their own psychic contents, separate from the other. This awareness entails, he says, the 'suppression' of the 'common skin and the recognition that each has his or her own skin'. In contradistinction to Lacan, who associates the realisation of autonomy with feelings of jubilation, Anzieu describes it as an occasion for 'resistance and pain' (1985: 63).

The ability to shed the shared skin signals the capacity to imagine oneself as physically and psychically bounded and self-contained: as having, Anzieu says, both an inside and outside (1985: 61, 64, 124). In this scenario, the sensations of the body and its skin are transposed to the mind, where they are configured psychically and registered as experiences that belong to the self. In this respect physical, material, and psychic space constitute one another. According to Anzieu, the nature of this configuration and the manner by which bodily sensations are transposed into psychic contents is determined by the various functions of the skin ego that provide the self with its structure.[17] Although Anzieu is keen to employ specific images to describe this structure and its functions—including a bag, a screen, a sieve, and, later, a mirror (1985: 98)—his account of the development of the self is suggestive of an architectural scaffolding or an edifice under construction. In terms reminiscent of Lacan's description of the statue, Anzieu refers to the skin ego as a 'touchstone' for all sensations and perceptions (1985: 61), one that gives 'solidity' to the self, and 'support' to it by 'propping' it up (1985: 64, 98; Lefrance 2013: 26).

In the accounts of Lacan and Anzieu we discover an ego that is built upwards as if to prepare for its residence within a body in standing posture. This structural arrangement informs the majority of blueprints of psyche that we surveyed in Chapter 2—but not all, as we found with Freud's depiction of two rooms placed side by side. Indeed, before we go on to consider the impact of our earliest object relations on our relationships with architecture in later life, I want briefly to mention another architectural image that has been suggested in the context of the skin's role in the development of ego. This image lends support to a vertical structure that is built 'upwards', but with emphasis on the foundations upon which the construction is built. Object relations theorist Thomas Ogden develops psychoanalyst James Grotstein's (1987) notion of the sensory 'floor' to emphasise that the self-containment provided by the skin is a crucial 'grounding' of self, for it is upon this floor, Ogden says, that the infant constructs its identity (1989: 70). We may infer from this that identity is built from the floor upwards; but Ogden's focus remains firmly at floor level, so that when he considers the developing nature of identity he does not point to renovations in the structure of the edifice, as one might expect, but to the manner in which we 'reconstitute' this 'floor of experience'. Interestingly, Ogden suggests that we can reconstitute our 'floor' throughout our lives by engaging in various 'containing activities', including, he says, those that involve us interacting with architecture. By way of example, he refers to activities similar in kind to those occasions of integration that I proposed for Bick's infant. Ogden suggests 'focusing on symmetrical geometric shapes on the ceiling or wall, or using a finger to trace shapes on the wall' (1989: 70).

Psychoanalytic resistance to the nonhuman environment and architectural object

Lacan, Anzieu, and others may allude to architectural imagery to convey their understandings of the construction and development of ego-identity, but they are committed to the human object or its image as the role model and object of our earliest and subsequent identifications. If, as I have claimed, identity is established through the interplay of desires to merge and to separate from our environment, Lacan and the object relations theorists I have described understand this environment as the human body. Thus, the infant constructs its sense of self through its imaginative *merger* with the body of the mother (or his mirror image). This marks the occasion of the infant's mimetic identification with the impressions of containment provided by the other body in relation to the sensuous experiences of its own. But the fantasised union must eventually come to an end, for the containment imparted to the infant furnishes it with the integration of its experiences and the capacity to self-reflect. In the act of self-reflection, the infant differentiates itself from the other. This marks the occasion of the *separation* of self from the environment, of self-containment and autonomy.

I wish to draw attention, however, to the integral role of the nonhuman environment within the construction and development of self, and the architectural object as the mimetic object and role model for our earliest and subsequent identifications. This is a controversial position to take and goes against the grain of conventional psychoanalytic discourse, where the nonhuman environment and its objects are deemed arbitrary or irrelevant, and the architectural object or built environment is barely mentioned at all.

Winnicott's celebrated concept of the 'holding environment' is intended to define the interdependent relationship between the subject and their environment, but it extends only so far as the interpersonal plane of social relations (1965: 182–3). Grotstein, with his concept of the 'background object', attempts to extend the terrain of the affective environment further to include nonhuman components, by highlighting, for instance, the importance of the 'home' and the 'neighborhood' for the development of self, with its provision of 'a sense of *being* and *safety*' and the 'guarantee' of 'continuity of space and containment' (1981: 185; emphasis in original). However, the usefulness of this idea for our investigation is somewhat curtailed when we discover that Grotstein interprets the nonhuman in terms of social, cultural, and religious traditions; he is not interested in the material characteristics of nonhuman objects. Thus, the affective environment that Grotstein has in mind is constituted not so much by the architectural fabric of the home, nor by the streets and urban layout of the neighbourhood, but by the social interactions that happen to have taken place there (1981: 369).

Why is the material fabric of our environments passed over in silence? Psychoanalyst Harold Searles, in his largely overlooked and now out-of-print work *The Nonhuman Environment in Normal Development and in Schizophrenia* (1960), suggests that psychoanalysts just haven't had the time to consider the importance of the nonhuman environment. Intrapersonal and interpersonal relations are 'so complex', he says, and of 'such pressing importance', that they have continued to preoccupy psychoanalysts instead (1960: 25). Nevertheless, as Searles points out, their failure to consider its impact as a decisive factor in their investigations into human behaviour leads them inevitably to absurd conclusions, and to postulate human life as 'lived out in a vacuum—as though the human race were alone in the universe, pursuing individual and collective destinies in a homogeneous matrix of nothingness, a background devoid of form, color, and substance' (1960: 3).

Jungian psychologist J.W.T. Redfearn, in his essay 'When Are Things Persons and Persons Things?' (1982), suggests the psychoanalytic disregard for nonhuman objects more likely betrays a deeper resistance at work:

> When some analysts talk about the child's first relationship being with parts of the mother, such as the breast, rather than the whole person of the mother, what bearing has this on the personalisation and 'whole person' versus 'part person' psychology? Are we not dealing with a period before there is a differentiation between 'persons' and 'things'? Or is this a cunning way of avoiding the question?
>
> (Redfearn 1982: 219)

Redfearn continues to suggest that psychoanalysts intentionally avoid the question. For to concede that nonhuman objects affect us in fundamental ways involves, he says, accepting 'primitive animism' as a viable position—a position that many find objectionable, he claims, due to a misunderstanding of what it actually involves. Redfearn points out that primitive animism is not, as the vast majority of psychoanalysts likely believe, 'the name of a peculiar religion that Stone Age people follow', but 'a basic truth about ourselves and the real world which we all need to re-learn' (1982: 215). He continues:

> There is no question that internal conflicts are 'worked through' just as much with [nonhuman] 'things' as with 'people', provided that the passions are involved. If it is said that it is regressive or animistic or irrational to treat things as persons, one can only reply that this is in fact how we operate, that we operate best in this way, and certainly we operate naturally in this way.
>
> (1982: 217)

We encounter resistances even in those discourses that explicitly advocate the nonhuman environment as the principal site and occasion for the development and enhancement of personality, in their creation of unnecessary obstacles that prevent the built environment and its architectural objects from featuring in their narratives. As we noted in Chapter 3, there are, for instance, various 'green' discourses that establish an incoherent and unhelpful split between an idealised natural world with its resplendent organic objects that guarantee health and healing, and a denigrated built environment that leads to sickness and psychological disintegration.[18]

The psychoanalytic concession: architecture as memorial to mother

It goes without saying that the architectural setting has an inevitable influence on the mother's mood and wellbeing, which in turn affects her capacity to contain and nurture her infant. Bick readily concedes as much in her observations of a mother and her baby: 'There followed a move to a new house in a still unfinished condition. This disturbed severely the mother's holding capacity and led her to a withdrawal from the baby' (1968: 485). But, as we noted, Bick goes further than this, suggesting that nonhuman objects—with their various 'lights' and 'smells'—can perform the mother's task, if only for a brief moment, by capturing the infant's attention and providing it with the vital experience of integration. We noted, too, Lacan's acknowledgement of the power of architectural imagery to sustain the gaze of the statue's mirror image. These concessions, although relevant to our investigation, are mere glimpses into the potential role of the built environment in the construction of the self.

Generally speaking, when psychoanalytic theories grant power to architecture, it is as an object relation in later, adult, life. In other words, the built environment and its architectural objects are invested with significance only insofar as they facilitate pre-established identifications with *human* objects. Thus, the mother, as the first and foremost human object of our identification, is often presented in psychoanalytic discourse as the means through which we later develop our aesthetic sensibilities and our appreciation of architecture or art more generally. Perhaps most influential in this regard is Winnicott's notion of the 'transitional object' or 'transitional space', which he postulates in order to explain how our earliest experiences of the mother inform our capacity to play imaginatively with our environments in later life. In its effort to adapt to its newly acquired autonomy and estranged environment, the infant seeks to fortify its self-containment by exercising its mastery over other objects. Winnicott describes how the infant learns to play imaginatively with these objects, and invests them with the containing qualities originally provided for by the soothing mother. The teddy bear, blanket, or other favoured object becomes a 'transitional object' for the infant, an object that presents it with the desired illusion that it is merged with that object. The transitional object is imbued with a symbolism for the infant of being part-him or her and part-other. One day, Winnicott says, the infant suddenly discards the teddy bear. This is no arbitrary act, but an achievement of great significance that marks the occasion of the infant's capacity to contain itself without prop and to master its environment with confidence. The creative play with our environments as transitional spaces in which to negotiate ourselves continues throughout life. Our appreciation of aesthetic objects such as architecture is regarded by Winnicott as an example of this play and a re-enactment of our original identification with the mother, as we seek to make sense of our separation from her (1967; cf. 1971).[19]

I claim that there is reason to suggest that the built environment has a decisive impact on us in our earliest identifications, as an accomplice to the mother (or primary caregiver), acting with her to create the holding environment within which the infant's identity is shaped and the template for their future relationships is established. This interpretation would lend greater emphasis to the variety of architectural forms, textures, sights, smells, and sounds that capture the attention of Bick's infant, and out of which it creates the skin that envelopes and orders it. Greater significance would likewise be given to the background against which the Lacanian statue emerges. This background would then no longer be irrelevant or an unaccountable void out of which the bodily figure magically appears. Instead it would be granted a more realistic role as an environment that interacts continually with the subject's perception of it, changing in texture and tone according to the infant's bodily movements and in response to his or her gradual realisation that it is distinct from the 'statue' in the foreground. Speaking of backgrounds more generally, aesthetician Gilbert J. Rose aptly notes that they are more appropriately conceived as 'a dynamic oscillation between figure and ground than a steady backdrop for the projection of mental images' (1980: 4). Philosopher Merleau-Ponty similarly asserts:

> As far as spatiality is concerned [...] one's own body is the third term, always tacitly understood, in the figure-background, and every figure

> stands out against the double-horizon of external and bodily space. One must therefore reject as an abstraction any analysis of bodily space which takes account only of figures and points, since these can neither be conceived nor be without horizons.
>
> (Merleau-Ponty 1945: 101)

The background against which Lacan's statue emerges is, I claim, an important constitution of the self that should not be ignored but often is, on account of our tendency to focus on the foreground.[20] The infant inevitably interacts with the background environment to determine which aspects or features of it can be detached from it to establish the foregrounded image of the statuesque body. The features that are not incorporated into the foreground image are nevertheless vital to its creation and maintenance.

Reinstating architecture as mother's accomplice

Although there is a tendency in psychoanalytic discourse to regard the mother as the principal object of our earliest identification, and to regard the built environment as irrelevant, it is not uncommon to find examples of metaphor and analogy that identify architecture with the nurturing body or body parts of the mother, including her breasts and womb.[21] In such cases, the building is presented as a substitute for the mother, and thereby as an object that can provide the containment and encourage the transformative power required by her infant. As art critic and psychoanalytic scholar Adrian Stokes puts it, 'a fine building' announces itself as 'an inexhaustible feeding mother' (1965: 19–20).[22] I wish, however, to turn the metaphor of building as mother on its head, so to speak, to suggest that we consider the manner in which the mother is like a building—as part of the architectural environment with which we construct or build ourselves. In this respect, the mother can be construed as an architectural feature of the first building that gives rise to the original architectural event. To that end, we can revise Winnicott's famous dictum, 'There is no such thing as an infant' (1960[23]), to proclaim instead, 'There is no such thing as a building'. While Winnicott intended his phrase to express the psychological fact that an infant cannot be described or understood without alluding also to its mother or primary caregiver, I wish to emphasise that we are also inextricably linked to buildings through our earliest and subsequent mimetic identifications with them, so that the incorporation of the architectural object into the self establishes the containing environment through which both building and self are realised.[24]

There is a fundamental link between the nurturing mother and evocative architecture, and a connection between the subject's responses to each. Thus, the imaginative perception of the building that we outlined in Chapter 3 and the infant's precognitive mimetic identification with its environment both involve an illusory merger with and separation from an object that gives rise to a reconstruction or reconfiguration of the self. It would be absurd to propose the built environment as a viable replacement for the mother in the nurturing of her infant, and I certainly do not wish to entertain such a proposition. I wish simply to suggest that we consider the creative potential of the built environment as it impacts upon the infant in conjunction with his mother's care. In other words, I propose that architecture acts as an *accomplice* to the mother on the occasion of the infant's original transformative event, and not, as conventional psychoanalytic and developmental theories dictate, a *derivative* of the mother or *memorial* to her nurturing qualities experienced in later life.

There are two relatively unknown psychoanalytic accounts that go some way to supporting my unconventional claim. These are found within works by psychoanalyst Harold Searles and Jungian psychologist J.W.T. Redfearn. I referred earlier to both thinkers' criticism of the psychoanalytic field for ignoring the nonhuman environment as an integral factor in the development of human identity and human behaviour generally. Far from being an arbitrary or passive backdrop against which identity and human relations are forged, the built environment and its architectural forms are considered by Searles and Redfearn as vital resources for establishing the infant's sense of self and the template for its future relationships. Importantly, neither thinker denies the importance of the mother (or other human caregiver) in their schemes; they simply reconsider her role in the light of the infant's relationship to the nonhuman environment, and propose that mother and building work together to establish the containment required by the infant. But exactly how they work together and at what stage in the infant's development the work of the architectural object becomes most significant is interpreted very differently by each thinker.

Both Searles and Redfearn describe the affective nature of the built environment and consider architecture an important constituent of the nonhuman object-world. For both thinkers, mother and building are indistinguishable in the occasion of the infant's identification and illusory merger with its environment; but it is in the corresponding period of separation from the environment, when the infant discovers itself as autonomous, integrated, and bounded, that the difference between the theories of Searles and Redfearn is notable. Thus, according to Searles, the infant discovers itself in relationship to the nonhuman environment prior to its discovery of itself in relationship to the mother and the human object-world. For Redfearn, by contrast, the infant's relationship to the nonhuman environment indicates its successful separation from the mother. Let us now outline the salient features of their accounts.

The affective built environment prior to mother

According to Searles, the nonhuman environment and its objects are just as important for the infant's development as the human object-world, because the infant is unable to discriminate between the two. If we are to accept the conventional idea that the infant's sense of self is constituted by its relationship to the mother's breast, so that it perceives her 'nipple' as 'the centre' of its 'own personality',[25] we must concede, Searles asserts, that the infant who is fed by a bottle will similarly perceive this 'inanimate object' as the centre of its personality. Searles concludes that this nonhuman object will have an 'important, if subtle influence upon the course of later personality development' (1960: 32). The nursing bottle is accompanied by a wealth of other nonhuman objects that interact with the infant to attract its attention through its self-reflexive bodily sensations, including those architectural objects we noted earlier as capturing the attention of Bick's infant. Searles argues that these nonhuman objects are not symbolic representations of human beings, such as the 'mother' or 'nipple'; they are '*real* objects: things of the nonhuman world that are invested with aliveness by the infant's propensity to animate them'. Furthermore, prior to the infant's awareness of human objects as distinctly 'human', there must be, Searles contends, a phase in which the infant experiences a 'deeply felt kinship' and 'oneness' with the nonhuman environment (1960: 9).

We find in Searles's account distinct phases of the infant's transformation into a self-aware, autonomous being. The first and original transformative event is the occasion of its separation from the nonhuman environment: an event that is marked by feelings of being 'alive' in contradistinction to those 'inanimate' nonhuman objects with which the infant was merged. Following this, the infant has the resources with which to distinguish itself from 'the animate sector of the nonhuman environment' and experience itself, as Searles says, as 'not only alive but *human*'. (We might place Lacan's mirror-stage at this point, when the infant recognises itself as an animated version of the inanimate statue.) Only after the infant has negotiated its relationship with the nonhuman environment can it become aware of itself in relationship to its mother, as a 'living human *individual*, distinct from other human beings' (1960: 43–4).

The failure to differentiate oneself from the nonhuman environment has grave repercussions for a person's capacity to relate to other people in later life. By way of example, Searles describes the case of an adult male patient of his who, up until the age of six, had developed strong attachments to the attic room of his house. In this instance, the built environment is the affective nonhuman environment that Searles argues for. This room provided Searles's patient with a sense of security and containment, so that whenever he was made to leave the room he felt extremely anxious. With regard to the quality of his relations with other people, it was evident to Searles that the 'man had never really, as yet, left the attic, in terms of his feeling-orientation towards other persons'. This manifested itself in the man's enjoyment in manipulating people if they were objects to use and appropriate as one might an inanimate object, and his frustration with others—as if, as Searles puts it, they were 'large mechanical obstacles in his path' (1960: 90). Searles suggests that the infant's relationship with the nonhuman environment may prove more critical than its relationship with its mother and have greater bearing on the quality of its personality and later relationships, since a failure to negotiate with the nonhuman environment and to distinguish oneself from it can lead to severely problematic interpersonal relations.

In addition to establishing the 'emotional security' and 'stability and continuity of experience' required to construct the infant's sense of self, the built environment, according to Searles, continues to provide a person throughout life with the resources with which to establish healthy relationships with other people. He notes, for instance, that the nonhuman environment presents itself to the young child as a useful 'practice-ground' for developing the skills and 'useful capacities' that they will rely on in their later relationships with people (1960: 78, 85). He continues to note that the nonhuman environment enables children to discover that they are 'in various ways powerful, but not omnipotent', and helps them to appreciate and accept the value of other people (1960: 88, 120). It provides a person at all times in their life with a stabilising influence, by providing, as Searles puts it, 'relief from the tensions, and satisfaction for the hungers which arise in life among other human beings', by offering 'peace, stability, and companionship at times when interpersonal relationships are filled with anxiety and loneliness' (1960: 87). The built environment provides us throughout life with a containing space in which to explore our feelings free from judgements and censorship.[26]

Buildings facilitate vital separation from mother

The nonhuman environment has an important role in Redfearn's account of the development of identity on the occasion of the infant's separation from its mother and the discovery that it is an autonomous individual. To appreciate his account we need to understand the notion of 'depersonalisation' that underpins it.

According to Redfearn, the infant establishes its separation from its mother or other human caregiver through its depersonalisation of her. This activity is, he says, a necessary counterpart to our tendency to personalise nonhuman things by projecting human traits into inanimate objects and bringing them to life (an activity that Redfearn describes as primitive animism). Depersonalisation by contrast involves the removal or withdrawal of human qualities from objects—irrespective of whether these objects are human or nonhuman—to allow them to be comprehended in more abstract and simplified terms (1982: 218). I earlier described an act of depersonalisation with the Winnicottian child, who no longer needed his teddy bear and so threw it away. The bear is no longer needed because it no longer contains within it the child's projections of the soothing mother; the object is thereby depersonalised or divested of these maternal qualities of feeling, and loses its appeal.

This act of depersonalisation turns what had been an illusory part-subject and part-object into a banal and arbitrary object of reality that can be appropriated and discarded at will—a mere 'thing' that is no longer expressive of the child's imaginative play. The object's depersonalisation represents an important achievement in the child's development. According to Redfearn, depersonalisation is a helpful and necessary process in the infant's adaptation to reality, as it facilitates the infant's withdrawal from the illusory merger with its mother and its adaptation to a reality that is distinct from her (1982: 218, 229).

Redfearn describes the oscillating desires to merge with and to separate from the objects of our environment as desires to unite and to alienate through occasions of personalisation and depersonalisation. Redfearn's ideas echo various claims I have made in this chapter regarding the development of identity and the important role played by the body in its identification with architectural features. Thus, in the light of our tendency towards the personalisation of objects, he contends that 'when our instincts for unification or union are in operation [...] objects are naturally treated as self-projections or representations of the self, and this self always seems to have a bodily configuration'. He notes, furthermore, that this bodily configuration is expressed most clearly by the 'design of houses and cities', for these are 'fashioned to imitate and express the self and particularly the bodily self' (1982: 220). But we find that architectural imagery plays a crucial role in the act of depersonalising the human object and in instigating the separation of the infant's body from its mother's.

If, as Redfearn maintains, the act of personalisation involves experiences of embodiment, depersonalisation by contrast reflects a desire towards the disembodiment of the self that has merged with the human object (the mother) (1982: 221).[27] Depersonalisation occurs, Redfearn claims, when there is an overriding anxiety that one is too closely merged with the object; it is a defence against 'caring too much or fear of being too involved' with it (1982: 233). In this respect it provides the means to alleviate claustrophobic anxieties that arise when we feel constricted by our environments, by instigating our separation from them and encouraging our desire for self-containment. Disembodiment therefore marks the achievement of separation from mother, 'at a level where the mother's body image and one's own body image are identified'. This separation is brought about by the infant who employs, in the words of Redfearn, progressive acts of 'abstraction, mechanisation', and 'geometrisation' that seek to disembody the mother, and gradually change her image into something 'less personal', less human, and more abstract (1982: 222, 223). Redfearn asserts that this activity furnishes the child with the kind of 'scientific attitude' that is expressed and utilised in 'architectural activity and imagery' (1982: 223). Indeed, this vital developmental phase of the self is nothing short of an architectural construction, or, as Redfearn puts it, 'the great engineering project' (1982: 227). The building is for Redfearn the most apposite emblem for the autonomous self. Buildings, especially those in a state of ruin, most commonly express, he says, the disembodied, depersonalised mother; they are a geometricised image of her maternal affect (1982: 225).[28]

Just as Searles regarded nonhuman environments as useful 'practice-grounds' for children to work through their conflicts, preparing them for healthier relationships with others, Redfearn's conception of the building as an abstract and disembodied image of the mother grants us 'sufficient space' to negotiate the feelings and affects that continue in our experiences of the real, personal mother, and of other people who subsequently feature in our lives (1982: 231). Redfearn explains that dolls' houses, as an architectural image of the disembodied mother, function in the same way. The dolls' house encourages children to enact in their play their feelings towards other people in their household (1982: 230). Whether it be actual buildings, imagined ones, or dolls' houses, architectural images provide us with an efficient containing resource that enables us to negotiate feelings and conflicts within a safe environment, one that protects us from experiences of 'too much pain and overstimulation' (1982: 235).

Mimetic identifications with human or nonhuman objects, whether the mother or the building or a combination of the two, are creative transformations of the self. The mergers and separations of the self vis-à-vis its objects are essential to the construction of personal identity. Redfearn's conceptions of personalisation and depersonalisation can be understood in the context of these shifting orientations between self and environment. They lead, he says, to a 'transformation' of self, with 'the structuring of the mind', and the development of 'the containing, framing, and limiting functions necessary for remembering [oneself] as well as for art, religion, thinking, and the building up of the mind' (1982: 236).

The accounts of Searles and Redfearn give greater scope for architecture as an original object of our identification than conventional psychoanalytic discourses. While mainstream psychoanalytic theory regards architecture as a later object relation, one derived from the earliest nurturing experiences of the mother, Searles and Redfearn suggest its much earlier and more fundamental involvement in the development of identity, one that contributes to the template for a person's future object relations. As an amalgam of 'inanimate' nonhuman objects, architecture constitutes in Searles's scheme the first object in relation to which the infant discovers that it is self-aware, or 'alive', as Searles puts it. In other words, architecture will have an impact on us on the occasion of our first and original experience of transformation. If architecture were perceived as an 'animate object' (due to the infant's personalisation of it), it would still precede the mother and other 'human objects' in Searles's understanding of the construction of identity. Architecture in Redfearn's model, by contrast, is assigned the important role of triggering separation from mother, and providing the conceptual resources with which to think oneself into being. Here, architecture furnishes the self with its cognitive ego.

Conclusion: the flesh of the building and the building of flesh

In this chapter we have begun to explore how identity is constructed through the subject's bodily interactions with the built environment and its architectural objects. These interactions are guided by the subject's innate drive both to merge with and to separate from its environment. I have named the construction of identity in response to the built environment the *architectural event*, and, for the sake of clarity, I have divided it into three overlapping components or phases. To recap, these comprise the subject's initial encounter with the building or architectural feature, their withdrawal or detachment from it, and the disclosure of a new sense of self. Central to our investigation is how each phase or aspect involves the subject's bodily experiences and their unconscious thoughts and memories, for these are regarded as fundamental components of human identity, without which there would be no cohesive self to experience. I claim that the architectural event enriches and enhances our experiences of embodiment and integrates our unconscious thoughts, our memories, and other forgotten ideas and feelings into cognitive awareness. This chapter has begun to explore the first of these, with the body's involvement in the three phases of the architectural event as it interacts with the architectural object through a process of mimetic identification. Our investigation has drawn upon several psychoanalytic models of psychological development, each of which places the body centre-stage as the instrument we use to negotiate ourselves in relation to our environments.

The architectural event is an event that unfolds unconsciously in the subject's interaction with the material forms of the building. We have interpreted this interaction as an imaginative perception. Imaginative perception is the infant's only means of relationship and interpretation prior to having established the capacity for rational comprehension. It is a mode of cognition that continues throughout life, working alongside our 'ordinary', more conscious, perception of things that leads to our literal, rationalised understanding of them. In Chapter 3 we explained how buildings invite our imaginative perception of them, compelling us to regard them not as literal objects with their own distinct boundaries, but as *events* that encourage us to participate in their structural features, as if they were extensions of us, or we of them. Our interaction with buildings in this way can be regarded as a continuation of the mimetic identifications of our earliest relating. It is a fundamental mode of relationship, more fundamental than our capacity to rationalise, that gives rise to a deeper awareness of ourselves.

In the next chapter I consider how the imaginative perception of the adult is furnished by experiences that aren't available to the infant with its fledgling ego. I consider the architectural event in the light of the second of our two components of human identity, memory. I shall explain how our imaginative perception of architecture in later life involves our unconscious thoughts, repressed experiences, and forgotten memories, and how these subsequently shape the architectural event and are disclosed by it. We shall see that, in addition to making a mimetic identification with architecture, we engage with the three phases or aspects of the architectural event through a process called the 'dream-work'. This is a creative activity that utilises our perceptions of architecture to rework and reconfigure our forgotten and repressed material into a more manageable and containing form, one that enables us to engage with this material cognitively and to experience it anew.

I end this chapter by considering what it is exactly that we incorporate into ourselves through our bodily identifications with the built environment. I concluded in Chapter 3 that it involved an experience of *abiding containment*, which we strive to achieve out of our innate drive for self-preservation, by staving off its corresponding anxieties of disintegration and annihilation—anxieties that pertain, perhaps, to our earliest experiences prior to the discovery of the containing object. I also concluded that the containment we seek must be flexible enough to allow us the freedom to develop and to evolve, and to defend ourselves against anxieties of suffocation and restraint—anxieties that encourage our earliest compulsion to separate and detach from the objects with which we have merged. In the course of this chapter, several forms and images have been suggested as characteristic of the object that sets in motion this vital experience of abiding containment. Thus, Lacan describes the object of abiding containment as a vertical scaffolding, a fortification, and as having an essential solidity; Anzieu also describes it as a supporting scaffolding and distinguishes between its interior and exterior space; Bick suggests that it is a dynamic surface of various distinctive sensuous textures; Ogden refers to it as the laying of a floor that can be refashioned to accommodate different structural designs; Winnicott describes it as a safe and flexible space; and Searles alludes to it as a space that is peaceful, stable, and intimate. Collectively, these characterisations lead us to postulate that an architectural design which evokes abiding containment is one that resembles a three-dimensional enclosure, perhaps taller than it is wide, with various surface textures and openings. That is to say, something akin to a box! Although such a design may seem rather banal, it is, psychologically speaking, particularly evocative—when, that is, these enclosures are arranged in a variety of juxtapositions, as we shall see later. Indeed, as Adrian Stokes notes, 'The plain geometry of building, the simple volumes and lines, the prime shapes, are potentially so charged with feeling' (1951b: 62). Architectural theorist Thomas Thiis-Evensen propounds a similar idea, focusing on a building's essential components of 'floor', 'wall', and 'roof'—which together comprise a box-like enclosure with a base, sides, and lid that resonates powerfully with our own bodily constitution as an 'inside in the midst of an outside' (1990: 8). Given this, we are compelled, he says, to discover these fundamental forms within our environments as 'architectural archetypes'.[29] Each of these architectural forms resonates with our own bodily experience, but in slightly different ways in accordance with their different spatial arrangements. Thus, the floor for Thiis-Evensen denotes a bodily experience of 'above and beneath'; the wall, of 'within and around'; and the roof, 'through, over and under' (Seamon 2000). Thiis-Evensen goes on to claim that these architectural forms and their spatial arrangements are supplemented by the building's 'existential expression', by which he means the impressions it gives of its—and by extension, our own—'motion, weight, and substance' (1990: 21). But how does this box-like architectural structure convey the flexibility and freedom we require to develop and grow? How can we identify in its design the features that will encourage our detachment from its structure? Are we simply to assume that the box-like structure should incorporate several openings, which ensure that it does not enclose us too tightly?

In Chapter 3 we explored the 'infinite' nature of architecture with its superabundance of meanings, and in this chapter I explained how the subject incorporates this feature as an elusive and uncanny sense of otherness alongside its fortifying, structural character in their identification with the architectural object. Given its elusive quality, the infinite character of architecture is not immediately apparent or discernible within the material features of its design, but is suggested in those features that seem misplaced, hidden, missing, or not quite as expected. They are intimated by those architectural features that are out of sight, behind closed doors and under floorboards; within its unrealised and unplanned renovations; where the misplaced façade meets the walls of the building; and, as depicted by the blueprints of psyche of Chapter 2, within its indistinct, shadowy recesses and dark and expansive spaces.

The elusive 'infinite' quality of architecture is also intimated in the rhythms, flux, and movements of its forms, of those features that capture the attention of the infant, but often go unnoticed by the adult. Dynamic composition is difficult to measure and to locate within the building itself, as it is more often perceived unconsciously, and is identifiable most noticeably through its associated effects. Rose suggests that the formal arrangement of architecture (and artworks generally) resonate with the arrangements of the subject's mind and with the various shifts and movements that occur within the psyche or personality.[30] Speaking of the visual power of an 'artistic' arrangement, Rose asserts that it 'externalizes the moment-by-moment mental activity of the mind in slow motion, magnified and abstracted'; and through its 'delineated rhythms' it presents to us an 'image' of our own 'inner process' and 'inner, unreconciled struggles'. Rose continues by noting that we are compelled to follow and engage with the visual features of its image in order to feel ourselves 'nourished and enlivened' (1980: 13). Adrian Stokes presents a similar account of the visual forms of architecture. As a 'possessor of many bodily references', architecture, he says, 'mirrors a dynamic or evolving process as well as the fact of construction' (1965: 21). While Stokes concedes, and in a similar manner to Rose, that the visual play of spatial forms has, as Rose puts it, a special 'power over us', Stokes suggests that few would probably grant such power to the apparently 'static, physical forms' of buildings (1965: 20).

Nevertheless, we quickly discover that Stokes is keen to count himself among the few. Speaking of architecture, he asserts:

> Such immobility, however, often involves a sense of dragging weight, of the curving or swelling of a contour with which we deeply concern ourselves, since we take enormous pleasure [...] in feeling our way, in crawling, as it were, over a represented volume articulated to this end. [...] [Architectural designs] may invite a very primitive, and even blind, [or unconscious we might say] form of exploration. In one of their aspects, too, relationships of colour and of texture elicit from us the same sense of process, of development, of a form growing from another or entering and folding up into it.
>
> (Stokes 1965: 20)

I cannot end this section without referring to the influential phenomenology of Merleau-Ponty, and his understanding of our bodily perception of the world as key to our subjective awareness. Merleau-Ponty is similar to Stokes and Rose insofar as his account of 'objects', including architecture, emphasises their fluidity and synchronisation with our subjectivity and bodily movements. For Merleau-Ponty 'things' are only ever 'accessible to inspection by the body' (1945: 320), so that the meanings we ascribe to them are determined by our bodily participation in the building's form. His name for this interflow of body and its environment is 'flesh'. Flesh encompasses 'my body' as 'the fabric into which all objects are woven' (1945: 235).[31] As is the case with the notions of 'skin' proposed by Bick and by Anzieu, 'flesh' here implies the physical skin of the subject, but is not synonymous with it. 'Flesh' is more akin to an elemental medium, such as air or carbon, in which the meanings of the self and the world are constituted as one (Merleau-Ponty 1964: 139–40).

Significantly, for Merleau-Ponty 'flesh' is not restricted to the infant; nor does the mother or any other human being hold exclusive rights to that which flesh extends. Rather, we merge with any and every object we perceive and at every moment. Just as Bollas describes the 'collision' of subject and object, Merleau-Ponty speaks of the structures of object and subject 'opening' up or 'upon' each other, as a conjoined network of meanings, enfolded within the same flesh (1945: 229). He is less an inhabitant of the building he lives in than it is an inhabitant of him; his house, he writes, is 'a familiar domain about me only as long as I still have "in my hands" or "in my legs" the main distances and directions involved, and as long as from my body intentional threads run out towards it' (1945: 130).[32] His body and his house are constituted by each other.

If Merleau-Ponty were to speak of the 'power' of architecture, it would be in the manner of its sensuous arrangements, which ebb and flow in relation to our bodily movements. No single sense organ is privileged in our perception of the building; all the bodily senses work together, with one subsumed in the other, to 'open' us to the forms we perceive. Thus, Merleau-Ponty asserts, we don't simply touch 'the hardness and brittleness of glass' with our skin, we feel it through our eyes; we likewise see, he says, 'the springiness of steel', and the heaviness in the 'weight of a block of cast iron' sinking into sand; and hear the 'hardness and unevenness of cobble' stones (1945: 229–30). The mere sight, sound, touch, or smell of a building opens us to a full bodily engagement with its features, and this synesthetic engagement penetrates deeper than the physical surface of our skin, to construct a unique and personal identity and sense of self. The material features of architecture are, as Merleau-Ponty claims of any object or 'thing', 'correlative to my body and, in more general terms, to my existence, of which my body is merely the stabilized structure' (1945: 320).

In the next chapter I consider the role of thinking and memory in the architectural event. This investigation will help to continue the fleshing-out of the material features of evocative architecture beyond its rather crude depiction as a perforated, multi-textured box-like structure. I shall explain how the elusive unconscious mind interacts with the world through a currency of 'infinite excess', and as a result, our experiences of the world can disorientate and confuse us. We shall discover that our unconscious minds can be evoked, and to some degree accessed, by architectural designs which incorporate elements that are paradoxical, ambiguous, and surprising—designs that hold in creative tension features that are at one and the same time conventional and distorted.

Notes

1 Though not so extreme that a person is unable, for instance, to relate to others, to symbolise, or to imagine.
2 Jung himself referred to the experience of conjoining subject and object, not as projection, but as *participation mystique*. This is an anthropological term that Jung borrowed from Lucien Lévy-Bruhl to refer to the primordial fusion or identification of subject and object. We discuss this in Chapter 5.
3 Freud often used the terms 'introjection' and 'incorporation' interchangeably. However, I shall favour the use of 'incorporation', as the notion of introjection doesn't involve bodily boundaries (see Freud 1915b). Incorporation is a phantasy of taking objects from 'outside' the body and placing them within it (see Freud 1914/2004).
4 See, for instance, Adorno and Horkheimer (1946); Benjamin (1978); Redfearn (1982); Kahn (1991); Graafland (1996); Pallasmaa (1996: 66–7); Sanders (1996); Leach (2005, 2005b: 16–31). Pallasmaa notes: '"The brick wants to become an arch", as Louis Kahn said, and this metamorphosis takes place through the mimetic capacity of the body' (Pallasmaa 1996: 67).
5 Again we are reminded of Jung's experience of himself as the stone upon which he sat. Such experiences as this may have influenced Jung in his detailed studies of alchemy and the idea of the 'stone-penetrating spirit' and 'inspired stone' (1936: par. 406). Jung writes at length on the relevance of alchemy to the development of personality. The alchemical stone has parallels with Lacan's statue; it is, Jung says,

'nothing other than the total man' (1952a: par. 471). See also, Jung (1934–1939: par. 406), where Jung discusses Nietzsche's allusion in *Thus Spake Zarathustra* to the soul sleeping in stone: 'a wonderful image is sleeping in stone'; 'within the stone there is something that is alive, but is dormant'.

6 Several other thinkers could have been selected to convey the essential points I wish to make—including, for instance, Wilfred Bion and his ideas of container/containment (1962), or Melanie Klein and her concept of projective identification (1946).

7 A point underscored by his maxim that the ego is 'first and foremost a body-ego' (Freud 1923), and illustrated clearly within Freud's earlier blueprints of psyche (see Chapter 2). When Freud briefly expounds on the meaning of 'body-ego' in a footnote to the English translation of his work (a footnote that was authored by Joan Rivière and added on Freud's authority), he makes clear that the significance of the body is in its mental representation: 'The ego is ultimately derived from bodily sensations, chiefly from those springing from the surface of the body. It may thus be regarded as a mental projection of the surface of the body' (Freud 1923: 26).

8 See Smith (1985: 4).

9 Lacan refers to the relationship between the imagined sense of containment and the reality of chaotic fragmentation as the relationship between the 'Imaginary' and the 'Real'. Lacan's work centred on a triad of ideas: the *Symbolic* is a set of differentiated signifiers, including language itself; the *Imaginary* serves as a mediator between internal and external worlds, and is oriented towards cohesion; the *Real* is that which is unsymbolized, always present, and outside language. For Lacan, all of these can be seen as spaces in which certain aspects of subjectivity operate.

10 Lacan considers that this occurs at the age of approximately six to eighteen months.

11 That Lacan's mirror makes the subject rigid is similar to Freud's account of the narcissistic gaze (the allurement of the sight of ourselves), which makes the subject 'stiff with terror, turns him into stone' (Freud 1940: 273).

12 Interestingly, Borch-Jacobsen interprets the static, lifeless, and 'inhuman' form of the stone statue as indicative of death, whilst several others—myself included—have endorsed a contrasting interpretation that regards these same characteristics of architecture as evoking the promise of abiding containment, which could be construed as the promise of immortality. I suggested in Chapter 3 that it is, rather, those buildings that surprise us with their lack of solidity and appear fragile or in a state of ruin or decay or demolishment that inspire feelings of 'death', instability, or loss of self. These buildings express well the uncanny sense of other, which, as I explain in Chapter 6, is an awareness of the unconscious at work. Nevertheless, the important point to take from Borch-Jacobsen's account here is that, in addition to the experiences of containment and integration, those of separation or displacement are assimilated into the subject in their identification with the statue.

13 It is important to note that their criticisms of sight do not apply to the use of sight in Lacan's model. For Adorno and Horkheimer, sight is a 'rational' activity that functions best at a distance from an object, whilst the sense of smell (and, I would add, touch) literally merges the self with the object. 'When we see', he says, 'we

remain what we are; but when we smell, we are taken over by otherness' (Adorno and Horkheimer 1946: 184). However, as we have seen, sight for Lacan fulfils a similar function. It does not establish a passive relationship or distance between subject and object, but instigates their merger. The statue actually forms the self it anticipates, through the gaze of the self upon it. 'The predominance of the visual functions', he notes, determines the 'mental progress' of the infant (cited in Borch-Jacobsen 1991: 49). For Lacan, the statue that confronts us in the mirror allows us to look not only at ourselves but through ourselves to the 'object that knows himself to be seen' (Lacan 1954: 215, cf. 78). For both Adorno/Horkheimer and Lacan, mimesis threatens the autonomy of the ego by establishing an inextricable link between self and other: but they emphasise different senses as the means through which this is achieved.

14 Freud himself suggests that a desire to look may be a substitute for the earlier, primary desire to touch (Freud 1905: 98; cf. Ulnik 2008: 23), and that subsequently the desire to look is both a 'visual libido' and 'tactile libido' present in everybody—which is to say that our instinctual energies are channelled through both eyes and skin in order to identify with their ideal object or role model for their own self-expression.

15 Earlier I hypothesised that the stronger the perceived threat of disintegration of self, the stronger the need to identify with a containing object to lessen the threat; and that a problematic perception of one's body or ego-self may lead one to identify with unstable objects. Bick contributes to this conceptual point by postulating the development of something called a 'second skin' in the problematic cases where the infant is unable to identify with a containing environment. The second skin is a poor substitute for the actual physical skin-experience (Bick 1968: 485) and develops out of the infant's own meagre resources, such as the sensation of tension in its muscles in response to its unintegrated experiences. Identification with this substitute skin can lead to a disorganised, fragile personality with a 'muscular shell' and 'corresponding verbal muscularity', as exemplified in several case studies described by Bick—including her analysis of a schizophrenic girl of three-and-half years, who at 4 months of age compulsively scratched her skin until it bled, and was physically 'hunched, still-jointed, grotesque like a "sack of potatoes"' (Bick 1968: 485).

16 By way of illustration of the phantasy of the shared skin, Anzieu describes the experience of two lovers who 'wrap themselves in their two imaginary maternal skins', experiencing themselves as 'a single psyche' and 'single body unique to the two of them, with a single skin' (1996: 246, 247; cf. 1985: 63).

17 There are nine functions with potential pathologies: holding, containing, protection against stimuli, individuation, consensuality, sexualisation, libidinal recharging, inscription, and toxicity.

18 See, for example, Evernden (1978); Fisher (2002: 3, 7, 123, 140); Roszak (2002: 294–6); Saari (2002: 7–8); Clayton and Opotow (2003: 6, 27, 92); Rust (2006).

19 See also Bollas, who maintains: 'The mother's idiom of care and the infant's experience of this handling is the first human aesthetic' (1978: 386); Rose: '[The] alternation of closeness and distance [of mother and infant] corresponds to the balanced interplay of tension and release which has traditionally described the aesthetic experience' (1980: 14). Adrian Stokes conceives aesthetic apprehension as one in which we are 'grasped' and experience ourselves as 'being joined' and 'enveloped

with an aesthetic object'. According to Stokes, these experiences express a kind of reunion with the mother—a reunion that he construes in Kleinian terms, as 'an identification with the good breast' (1965: 19). See also Jones (2000: 76) and Maclagan (2001: 37).

20 Indeed, as Anzieu notes in his discussion of the skin ego, 'every figure presupposes a background against which it appears as a figure: this elementary truth is easily forgotten, for our attention is normally attracted by the figure which emerges and not by the background from which it detaches itself' (1985: 38). One of the functions of Anzieu's skin ego is '*intersensoriality*', which he describes as the means by which the skin ego connects various sorts of sensations in order to '*make them stand out as figures against the original background*'. Connecting and arranging sensations in this way provides the infant with a coherent experience of its inner organisation and coordination (1985: 103; emphasis in original).

21 See, for example, Freud, who refers to a 'dwelling-house' as a 'substitute for the mother's womb, the first lodging' (1930: 87). See also Stokes, who describes 'the smooth body of the wall face' as 'the shining breast' of the mother, and the 'mouldings, the projections, the rustications, [and] the tiles' of the building as the mother's head, and her 'feeding nipple'. Here, the building, for Stokes, indicates 'the return of the mourned mother in all her calm and beauty and magnificence' (1951/1978: 137). We are reminded of Filarete's comparison of the architect to a mother, who carefully nurtures her child from the time of its conception to maturity (see Chapter 1).

22 See also Stokes's assertion: 'Like mothers of men, the buildings are good listeners' (Stokes 1972: 74).

23 Winnicott claims to have first made this comment in a discussion at a 'Scientific Meeting of the British Psycho-Analytical Society, circa 1940' (1960: 587, n. 4).

24 My discussion in the previous chapter about the building as unthinkable without and inseparable from the perceiver can be read in this light. For a brief allusion to the idea that 'There is no such thing as a building', see Rodman (2005: 59), where Rodman intriguingly mentions an, alas, untraceable article written, he says, by 'an Englishman', titled 'There is No Such Thing as a Building'. For Rodman, a building provides continual contact with our origins, and is a source of sustained nurturing and security. Anita Abramovitz endorses a similar proposition in her assertion that a 'building standing empty is not a whole building. It is only a beginning. We cannot understand it until we fill it with people, if only in our imaginations' (1979: 5).

25 Searles is here quoting the psychoanalyst August Stärcke (1921).

26 Somewhat cryptically, Searles suggests that we can enhance the containing function of our domestic buildings if we attend to the 'stability of [their] room arrangements'. This, he says, can have repercussions on the psychological stability of the child, and can 'give the child support in the struggle for individuation from the mother' (1960: 151–2). Presumably Searles is suggesting here that the distance/proximity of a child's room in relation to its mother's, or their relative size, is of significance.

27 Although often associated with disorders of personal identity, depersonalisation is not a pathological phenomenon per se. After all, 'individuation occurs', he claims, 'through succeeding cycles of disembodiments and *coniunctiones* [unions]' (1982: 226).

28 In presenting this image, Redfearn contributes the tradition I alluded to earlier of finding metaphorical parallels between the mother and the building, portraying the mother-as-building as an architectural ruin. His ideas offer an interesting critique on the value of architectural ruins, and why they are so evocative for us in later life. In other words, Redfearn suggests that images of 'ruined buildings' (and 'blighted landscapes') are aligned 'very close[ly] to depersonalisation', and thus also to our desire to separate and distinguish ourselves from our environments in order to find them less human and less personal. According to Redfearn, architectural ruins express at one and the same time the 'blighting of the word/mother/self image' (1982: 228–9). In this respect, for Redfearn, the ruined building symbolises an essential phase in a person's development, in which they are developing into a self-contained autonomous being, having recently distinguished and separated themselves from the environment that had up until that point become merged with the person. This transition is a vulnerable situation, as I noted in my discussion of architectural ruins and their propensity to evoke in adults deep-seated anxieties pertaining to the instability of the self and threats of possible dissolution. Redfearn's image of the ruined building certainly plays on these ideas, by conveying the loss or decay of the original container—the mother—and the exciting, yet daunting, prospect of finding new habitation with oneself, as if the self were undergoing architectural renovation, like a new building under construction. We find something akin to this transition, or the reconstruction of a ruined building to make one that is in pristine condition, played out in a personal anecdote of Freud's on the occasion of his visit to the ruined Acropolis. We will explore this in the next chapter as an illustration of the 'architectural event'.

29 Given its appeal to archetypal forms, we could read Thiis-Evensen's architectural account in Jungian terms.

30 Both Rose and Stokes describe the aesthetic experiences—of architecture and art—as an inner process that parallels the three phases or aspects I have assigned to the 'architectural event', suggesting an occasion of merger with the aesthetic object followed by a separation from it, and culminating in an enrichment of the perceiver's personality. Stokes contends that works of art have an initial 'power over us' that 'arises from the successful invitation to enjoy a relationship with delineated processes that enliven our own, to enjoy as a nourishment our own corresponding processes'. After responding to 'the first power' of art to invite us into a relationship, Stokes explains that the 'mother-like' artwork induces within us a kind of surrender, such that 'we find ourselves to some extent carried away', 'joined' with, and 'enveloped' by the aesthetic object. And our identification with it, he says, 'will have been essential to the subsequent contemplation of the work of art as an image not only of an independent and completed object but [also] of the ego's integration'. Through our integration with it, we will continue to find 'nourishment' (Stokes 1965: 19–20; see also Jones 2000: 76; Deamer 2004: 132).

31 Of his hand, for example, he notes: 'if I reach out my own hand to another object, I can experience a reversibility between touching and being touched' such that 'the world of each opens upon that of the other' (Merleau-Ponty 1964: 141); 'through the crisscrossing within it of the touching and the tangible, its own movements

incorporate themselves into the universe they interrogate, are recorded on the same map as it' (1964: 133).

32 The implications here of our embodied perception, of our body embedded within our built environments, and the mutual apprehension of building and self, are extensive for architectural design—not least that the merger between body and building provides the means to circumvent the conventional dualisms that establish an artificial conceptual distance between self and building, dualisms such as inner/outer, self/other, human/nonhuman, subject/object.

Chapter 5

Using architecture to think ourselves into being

Buildings as storehouses of unconscious thought

In the previous chapter we examined the architectural event in the light of the mimetic identifications that are forged in our perception of the semblance between our experiences of embodiment and the containing forms of architecture. This activity, we saw, is our earliest mode of relationship, and it continues to operate throughout our lives, informing our imaginative experience of things. Prior to the establishment of an ego with its capacity for abstract thought, the infant is compelled to negotiate the environment through its bodily response to the corporeal forms that interact with it. The cognitive capacity for self-reflection that gradually arises out of these bodily interactions grants a person greater resources for self-development and the construction of identity. In this chapter we consider the role of memory in the architectural event in order to explain how our interactions with architecture provide us with opportunities to renegotiate past experiences or impressions of ourselves that had been forgotten, made unconscious, or repressed. In so doing, we discover that architecture is an invaluable resource for the integration of self-experience and for shaping an identity that is coherent and abiding. I shall explain that in addition to our mimetic identifications with architecture through our bodily experiences, we participate in the architectural event through an imaginative register of experience that goes by the name of the 'dream-work' or 'dream-thinking' in psychoanalysis.

'Dream-thinking' is a method of identification that is available to the person with a mature and consolidated ego, one who has the capacity to think and to self-reflect. As we shall see, dream-thinking is a mode of unconscious 'thinking' that works alongside and often in conflict with our powers of reasoning, leading to surprising and unpredictable insights, and thwarting our expectations of ourselves and our environments.

In the previous chapter I discussed how buildings come to be experienced as if extensions of the subject's own body, with accompanying feelings of a more distinctive, fortified, and contained sense of self. In this chapter I describe how buildings enhance our capacity to self-reflect and to think more productively and creatively by granting us access to our mind at its unconscious level of functioning, with its repository of experiences that are otherwise inaccessible to cognitive thought, or to the conscious mind, with its more direct and literal way of thinking. I shall explain how we use buildings as incubatory containers for the transformation of our fragmentary unconscious thoughts into creative ideas, and, furthermore, how their architectural features compel us to use them in this way by providing us with sensorial 'cues' with which to interpret and translate their infinite surplus of meanings into useful, personal insights. In this scenario, the built environment grants us opportunities to discover ourselves anew by providing us with the means to engage with aspects of ourselves that are normally 'off limits', hidden, and kept out of sight.

For the most part we are not consciously aware of the architectural event as it unfolds. We are more likely to notice its effects, and be unaware of the built environment as their cause. This is because our participation in the event is unconscious, and is encouraged by processes—such as projection and incorporation—that cannot be consciously willed into action. The architectural event depends on the activation of an 'imaginative' register of experience, and this activity is itself dependent on the absence or suspension of our cognitive faculties of reasoning. While infants rely on an imaginative register of experience in the absence of critical powers of reasoning, the adult, who depends on such cognitive faculties for their orientation in the world, may experience the suspension of this faculty as somewhat disorientating and odd, causing them to feel 'out of sorts' with themselves or 'displaced' in their environment. The activation of our imagination indicates that our rational judgement, which accompanies our direct or focused attention to things, has been suspended so as to allow us to engage with ourselves and our environment in a less focused, more 'dream-like' manner. In this chapter I shall explain the activity and processes that underpin this mental 'gear change' and how it is activated in our interactions with architecture.

To help us in our investigation I shall turn to an intriguing and often overlooked anecdote reported by Freud on the occasion of his visit to the Acropolis in Athens in 1904. I shall use his account as a case study on 'dream-thinking' to illustrate how the unconscious mind of Freud utilises his perceptions of the Acropolis and its surrounding environment to access his unconscious thoughts and how he reconstructs his sense of self in the light of them. Freud's visit to the Acropolis gave rise to an uncanny experience that remained unexplained for him for several years, until he finally came to interpret it as a manifestation of forgotten memories and repressed feelings of guilt that he had been harbouring in relation to his father (Freud 1936: 247–8). Although Freud concedes that the building had set in motion a 'process of transformation' insofar as the process 'included myself, the Acropolis and my perceptions of it' (1936: 244), his explanation for the transformation focuses purely on the situation of his inner, emotional life; he does not entertain the possibility that the architectural environment contributed to its cause. The majority of scholars who have gone on to examine his account also ignore the affective power of the architectural scene, choosing, like Freud, to consider his mental activity as if it were totally removed and in isolation from the physical environment in which the event took place. In contrast, I suggest that the architectural environment did in fact have a role to play, and a significant one at that. I shall argue that it is through Freud's imaginative perception of the material features of the Acropolis that he discovers the means to access memories, ideas, and experiences that had been latent, forgotten, or repressed within him. Furthermore, these features include those that are physically present to Freud and those that are impressed upon him through their evocative absence—notably, in this case, the image of the building in its original, pristine condition as it appeared in Freud's imagination, as if superimposed on the ruined structure that was physically present. In other words, I maintain that the various material features of the built environment that Freud perceived encouraged him to access ideas that he couldn't have accessed through rational deliberation alone. His imaginative perception of the built environment provides him with the containing structure with which to configure or shape his unconscious material into an arrangement that can be disclosed to conscious awareness, and subsequently thought through and experienced as personally meaningful. Moreover, I suggest that Freud's experience is not unusual, and neither is the Acropolis in this regard. Rather, Freud's account serves to illustrate (albeit, perhaps, with an unusual degree of clarity) the way in which the unconscious mind uses the built environment to arrange and disclose its material.

We have already seen other accounts of the psychological impact of architecture that arrive at similar conclusions to mine in my interpretation of Freud's experience at the Acropolis. For instance, Searles refers to the freedom granted to us by the built environment for the expression of unresolved feelings and emotional struggles; Rose and Stokes both allude to architecture as evocative of our inner, unreconciled conflicts; and Jung speaks of the hidden and unconscious activity that occurs within the architectural fabric of cities, and causes 'unforeseen vistas' to open, 'unexpected things' to become conscious, and questions to be 'posed which were beyond [my] powers to handle' (Jung 1961b: 319). But, as we shall see, it is within the details of Freud's account that we find perhaps the clearest and most comprehensive description of the 'architectural event' within the psychoanalytic literature—one that allows us to trace its various phases or aspects as the event unfolds through Freud's imaginative perception of the building, from his initial identification with it through to the insights that are disclosed to him to help him to negotiate inner conflicts that were inaccessible to the cognitive resources of his conscious mind.

Before we turn to Freud's experiences, I must explain the essential differences between unconscious and conscious thought, and how the unconscious can be said to 'think' creatively and imaginatively. I do so by outlining the various roles that scholars have tended to ascribe to each type of thinking within the context of creative thinking and problem solving. Traditional models and techniques for problem solving involve a procedure or sequence of stages that are comparable to the three phases or aspects of the architectural event as I have described them. A closer look at their similarity will help us to clarify the kinds of thoughts the unconscious gives rise to, and their usefulness to us in the light of the limitations imposed by our rational judgements and our more consciously determined ideas.

'Thinking' unconsciously

In Chapter 3, I described how architecture defies rational definition by evoking a surplus of meanings, which subsequently 'open' the perceiver of the building to the expansive possibilities of their own nature. In this respect, buildings facilitate a different kind of thinking and understanding from that acquired through our literal perception of things and the rational comprehension it gives rise to. In contrast to prescriptive and presumptive reasoning, which directs us to the knowledge we seek, the type of thinking and understanding involved here is unpredictable. In comparison with the linear path of logic, it involves a tangled web of associative thoughts, feelings, and impressions that gravitate towards or converge around focal points of shared meaning, the content of which may seem bizarre and nonsensical from a rational perspective. When we approach things with a view to using them in a specific way, with expectations that they will fulfil a particular function or purpose, we tend to restrict our perception of their form and character, and notice them merely as objects for our immediate appropriation. We approach things unconsciously, by contrast, when we are not immediately preoccupied with them, and allow our minds to wander freely in relation to them, and thereby entertain sequences of thoughts that don't follow a prescribed agenda. By allowing our mind to wander in this way, unconstrained by our practical concerns and 'to do lists', we become more receptive to the surplus of meanings evoked by our built environments. The architectural event, we shall see, brings both types of thinking into creative dialogue.

Jung describes the difference between the two types of thinking in terms of their focus and direction. He says that we think and perceive things 'with directed attention' when our thoughts 'imitate the successiveness of objectively real things'. In such cases 'the images in our mind follow one another in the same strictly causal sequence as events taking place outside it' (1911–12: par. 11). In other words, directed thinking follows the logic of causal deduction, and fuels both our expectations and our presumptions about how things are and ought to be. It is a form of thinking that no architectural engineer can afford to be without; the buildings they design, however, elude rational conceptualisation, and impart instead a surplus of meanings that cannot be 'thought through' in logical fashion. Architectural designs lead us, in other words, to a different type of thinking, one that we described in Chapter 3 as imaginative and symbolic, and one Jung that refers to as 'non-directed'.

Non-directed thinking, Jung contends, is an 'automatic play of ideas' that 'leads away from reality into fantasies of the past or future' (1911–12: par. 18). We think without direction when we withdraw our focused attention from objects and 'no longer compel our thoughts along a definite track but let them float, sink or rise according to their specific gravity' (1911–12: par. 18). As I shall explain, whilst directed thinking draws upon logical correspondences between ideas and perceived reality, non-directed thinking perceives forms as a haphazard collage of unconscious associations, as 'images piled upon images' and 'feelings upon feelings' arranged 'not as they are in reality but as one would like them to be' (1911–12: par. 18). The unconscious thinks with non-direction by binding to a person's perception of things an array of images, feelings, memories, and sensations.

In Chapter 2, I distinguished between these types of thinking by contrasting the metaphorical building designed by Descartes, constructed according to precepts of certainty and reasoning that establish an edifice that is secure and abiding, with that of Freud, who creates his 'eternal' city-scape with 'phantasy' and 'imagination' to establish an architecture that is incoherent and incongruous. Freud employs the term 'free association' to describe this kind of thinking, and he likens its tenuous sequence of images to the 'changing views' one sees out of the window of a moving train (1913: 135). In the next chapter we shall see how our body in motion encourages this unconscious type of thinking, and how walking within built environments (especially when we wander without a prescribed route in mind) provides the unconscious with 'food for thought', providing it with a greater variety of evocative forms with which to configure and disclose its ideas.

When we are unrestrained by conscious directives, our mind wanders freely, moving from one idea to another in a seemingly arbitrary chain of associations, under the guidance or sway of our unconscious desires and inclinations. We often notice our engagement in this type of thinking just before we drift off to sleep, or when we catch ourselves day-dreaming; but psychologists assert that we are preoccupied in unconscious or non-directed thinking much more often than we probably realise: indeed, they claim that the unconscious affects us at every moment, influencing even our most carefully thought-out plans. By thinking in this manner we create trains of thought that branch out in different directions, each an expression of our unconscious interests at the time. If the conscious mind thinks causally in a logical sequence of ideas and concepts, the unconscious mind can be said to think imaginatively, drawing on a vast reservoir of impressions available to it. In this chapter I explain how unconscious thinking is an elaboration of a web of perceptions and experiences of actual objects in our 'external' environments that are mixed and juxtaposed with experiences and impressions housed within our 'inner' or intrapsychic world that we have acquired over our lifetime, some of which have been deeply repressed and otherwise forgotten, whilst others are more easily recalled as vivid memories.

Although unconscious thinking groups together materials that may seem unrelated, Freud and his followers were adamant that if one were to trace the various techniques employed by the unconscious as it gathers and collates its material, patterns could be detected that suggest a coherent and meaningful arrangement. Later I consider two of these techniques ('condensation' and 'displacement') in order to explain how they can be employed to deconstruct the 'architectural event' by isolating its various components (including the sensory impressions of the architectural design, memory traces of specific events, emotional feelings, and other remnants of experience and fragmented ideas) and discovering the common meanings that inform their arrangement.

By using Freud's proposed methods to attempt loosely to decipher unconscious activity, the material features of an architectural design and the subject's repressed personal experiences can, in theory at least, be disentangled to identify the meaningful associations that unite the two. For Freud, this underlying meaning points to an unresolved conflict in the person's life, one that has been made unconscious because it is too traumatic to contemplate and to have integrated into the conscious personality. The architectural event provides an occasion for this contemplation, with the containing forms of the building—experienced, as we saw, as a stabilising and fortifying extension of the self—affording a more comfortable and therapeutic environment in which to entertain difficult thoughts.

Creative potentials of unconscious thinking

Whether we think with or without direction, or perceive things consciously or unconsciously, depends on what we are doing at the time. When our concentration is disrupted and the corresponding linear paths of thought are interrupted, we can become more attuned to the unconscious associations we bring to bear on the objects of our experience. Although non-directed thinking cannot be consciously willed, it can be encouraged; and to discover exactly how, we can turn to well-established accounts of problem-solving techniques and methods employed to enhance creative and productive thinking.

Many empirical studies celebrate the efficacy of non-directed thinking for solving problems that cannot be resolved using logical strategies or rational deliberation. The cognitive psychologist Guy Claxton, for example, describes the 'hare brain' and 'tortoise mind' to argue that intelligence and the ability to solve problems increase when rational thought (the hare brain) is abandoned to allow the unconscious (the tortoise mind) to think for us. Claxton asserts that 'often our best, most ingenious ideas do not arrive as a result of faultless chains of reasoning. They 'occur to us', 'pop into our heads', and 'come out of the blue' (1998: 49). Often our best ideas occur to us at the unlikeliest times and in the unlikeliest of places: when we are in the shower, doing household chores, or going for a walk. In other words, they often occur on occasions when we are not *trying* to think and to force ideas into conscious awareness, but when we are attending to something else entirely.

I suggest that ingenious ideas and insightful thoughts do not appear out of nowhere, but are the product or consequence of a gradual process that employs both types of thinking, and utilises our imaginative perception of things to trigger and set in motion various unconscious thoughts, feelings, and ideas that have been latent within us. This process, we shall see, knits these various elements into a coherent narrative that is subsequently disclosed by the evocative objects within our environment. To clarify and explain this process, I shall first turn to the seminal account of creative thinking outlined by the mathematician, philosopher of science, and theoretical physicist Henri Poincaré (1854–1912). Poincaré's account is particularly useful for our investigation, for it differentiates between the roles of directed and non-directed thinking in the creation of insightful ideas; moreover, the phases he ascribes to the process of creative thinking correspond to those phases or aspects I have attributed to the architectural event. Thus, in Poincaré's account we find a useful framework for making sense of unconscious activity as it underpins the architectural event—from the gathering of its material to its dissemination as an evocative, insightful idea through the material features of the building.[1]

Henri Poincaré's creative distractions

Poincaré's brief account appears in the chapter 'Mathematical Creation' in his study *The Foundations of Science* (1908). There he explains the circumstances that led him to the discovery of several mathematical formulae, and thence to deduce from his experiences a generic method for problem solving and productive thinking. Thus, he tells us how he spent fifteen fruitless days trying to prove a theorem. 'Every day', he says, 'I seated myself at my work table, stayed an hour or two, tried a great number of combinations and reached no results' (1908: 387). But matters changed when one evening 'contrary to my custom, I drank black coffee and could not sleep'. At this point, 'ideas rose in crowds; I felt them collide until pairs interlocked, so to speak, making a stable combination. By the next morning I had established the existence of Fuchsian functions'. He thereby solved the mathematical problem he had not been able to do through his concerted rational efforts, and 'had only to write out the results, which took but a few hours' (1908: 387).

Poincaré supports this account with other similar instances when the mathematical ideas he sought suddenly made themselves known to him on occasions when he was not preoccupied with them. For instance, a change in routine with a trip to Coutances, in Normandy, enabled him, he says, to 'forget my mathematical work'; but as soon as he stepped on a bus to continue his journey, he recalls how an idea he had been searching for came to him, with a feeling of perfect certainty. Upon his return home, he tested and verified the idea that had appeared to him as if out of the blue (1908: 387–8). On another occasion, when 'disgusted' with his failure to establish valid results through considerable effort, Poincaré decided to take leave of his studies and spend a few restful days at the seaside. 'One morning, walking on the bluff', he writes, 'the idea came to me, with just the same characteristics of brevity, suddenness and immediate certainty' (1908: 388). On still another occasion Poincaré describes how he sought to explain through rational deduction a number of mathematic functions that had continued to puzzle him. He began, he says, by making a 'systematic attack upon them and carried all the outworks one after another'. All of this work, he says, 'was perfectly conscious'; but 'my efforts only served [...] to show me the difficulty' of the problem. Poincaré recalls at this time how he had to give up his study in order to undertake military service—a change that left him 'differently occupied'. Soon after, he recounts how, when walking along a street, 'the solution to the difficulty which had stopped me suddenly appeared to me'. He now had before his mind's eye 'all the elements and had only to arrange them and put them together' (1908: 388).

Poincaré deduces from these experiences that rational deliberation alone is often unproductive, and only when one disengages from this type of thinking can a decisive idea or sought-after solution to a problem 'all of a sudden' reveal itself. Importantly, Poincaré concludes that the solution hasn't arisen simply because his break has allowed his reasoned thoughts and directed efforts the chance to rest and recuperate, but, rather, 'it is more probable that this rest has been filled out with unconscious work and that the result of this work has afterward revealed itself' (1908: 389). In other words, by preoccupying himself with a different activity, Poincaré was able to direct his rational thoughts elsewhere, and allow his unconscious the opportunity to get to work on the problem instead. The inspired thoughts that appear to come out of nowhere are regarded by Poincaré as the product of his unconscious mind revising and reconfiguring the work that had been started by his directed efforts. Unconscious work, Poincaré asserts, is fruitful only 'if it is on the one hand preceded and on the other hand followed by a period of conscious work'. Sudden inspirations can happen only after an occasion of conscious deliberation has failed to achieve its desired results; but such efforts, he maintains, 'have not been as sterile as one thinks; they have set going the unconscious machine' (1908: 389). Likewise, directed thinking is required after unconscious thought has disclosed its insights in order to verify them, and perhaps also, he says, to 'shape' or rearrange them a little so as to define them more distinctly.

How does the unconscious think and arrive at its inspired thoughts? Poincaré does not provide a definitive answer. He says that the unconscious is 'capable of discernment' and deduces its own 'combinations' of ideas from those arrived at through our initial rational deliberations. Furthermore, he says that the unconscious establishes a 'great number' of combinations of ideas, the majority of which are irrelevant to the problem at hand. Only those combinations that are 'harmonious and, consequently, at once useful and beautiful' will, he says, 'affect most profoundly our emotional sensibility' and thereby 'break into the domain of consciousness' to capture our attention. The remainder are left dormant, or, as Freud would contend, repressed. Our mind is therefore like a 'sieve', Poincaré says, which employs a special aesthetic sensibility to facilitate and determine which of the unconscious combinations are useful or 'harmonious' to our needs, and can therefore be granted conscious expression. Poincaré's understanding here is similar to Freud's figure of the 'watchman', whom we encountered in Chapter 2, standing at the threshold between the rooms of consciousness and the unconscious, and deciding which of a variety of mental impulses are allowed to pass into consciousness on the basis of whether they please or displease him.[2] Using Poincaré's account, we can begin to speculate on the methods we employ to engage with the surplus of meanings evoked by architecture and out of which meaningful insights are composed and disclosed. Through an unconscious, imaginative register of experience the perceiver of the building is able somehow to 'sieve' through this surplus of meaning to establish combinations of ideas that are relevant to their unconscious needs or concerns, and are subsequently revealed to the subject at the culmination of the architectural event.

In order to make use of Poincaré's model of creative thinking for our investigation into unconscious activity—specifically, the manner in which it uses impressions and images of the built environment to configure and disclose its inspiring thoughts—we need to clarify its various stages and relate these to the phases of the architectural event. To help us, I shall call upon the assistance of the social psychologist and economist Graham Wallas, who sought to establish a four-stage model of creative thinking on the back of Poincaré's account:[3] and also Freud, with his method of the 'dream-work'; and, once more, Bollas and his important idea of the transformative object.[4]

Stages of creative thinking

In his influential work *The Art of Thought* (1926) Wallas delineates four clear stages or sequences in Poincaré's account of creative thinking. The first, 'preparation', is a period of directed thinking that indicates our preoccupation with activities that require our rational judgement and deliberation. Such focused thinking cannot be sustained indefinitely and invariably comes to an end, especially when we are confronted with a problem we cannot resolve. At this point, the second stage, 'incubation', comes into play. Here our mind 'switches gear' and disengages from the strategies of directed thinking that have proven insufficient to our needs. The period of incubation marks a change in our mode of thinking. Here the conscious mind becomes distracted by other activities that encourage it to dispense with its fixation on the former task. Poincaré describes various activities, including a bus journey, a walk on a beach, and having a cup of coffee. These activities may seem trivial and wholly unrelated to the tasks that preoccupy our conscious minds, and even detrimental to our conscious needs. However, as Poincaré, Wallas, and Claxton maintain, these activities are vital for creative thinking and problem solving, for they provide cognitive nourishment, or 'food for thought', by bringing to bear on the task or problem at hand a different perspective from that afforded by our more measured approach through logic and reasoning. When occupied in distracting activities, we are less influenced by the rational judgements of ego-consciousness and more receptive to the creative and imaginative play of the unconscious.

The period of incubation can be traced within the architectural event as the occasion when the building is perceived imaginatively, and the subject experiences themselves as somehow merged with it. At this time, the person's rational faculties are temporarily suspended, thereby allowing them to disband with their literal perception of the building and engage with its more elusive features, which are otherwise unnoticed. Buildings, I have argued, are especially evocative for us, and in the context of our current discussion we can explain this quality in terms of a building's capacity to distract us and compel us to entertain ideas that we haven't been able to figure out through concerted effort.

The stage of incubation comes to an end with the sudden disclosure of an inspired idea.[5] Its presence is usually accompanied by feelings of surprise, as the proverbial 'bolt from the blue'. Its felt presence marks the third stage of Wallas's creative process, 'illumination'. The fourth and final stage, 'verification,' employs directed thinking once again in order to evaluate the surprising idea, to corroborate its validity, and possibly to reshape it a little to emphasise and clarify its meaning. In psychoanalytic terms, the third and fourth stages are difficult to distinguish. In Freudian terms, the stage of illumination signifies the return of a repressed thought and thus the disclosure of an important experience that had until then been forgotten. In Jungian terms, by contrast, the illumination is a revelation of an archetypal truth that up until that point in time was largely unknown and unfamiliar to the recipient. Following the illumination and disclosure of this hitherto concealed and unconscious material, the subject must either accept the thoughts 'given' to it or reject them.[6] The subject's ego must decide what to do, and their response is equivalent to the verification stage. If the ego decides to reject these thoughts, it will seek to keep itself cut off from them by repressing them or dissociating itself from them, thereby setting them up to return at a later stage. If accepted, the material is integrated into the conscious personality, whereupon the personality is enriched, with a more rounded and more objective attitude.

In this chapter we are concerned principally with the transition between stages two and three—where the period of incubation, in which one thinks without direction, leads to the illumination or revelation of insight or inspired idea—in order to shed light on the architectural event as it unfolds from the occasion of our imaginative perception of architecture through to the disclosure of its insights. Poincaré isn't very helpful when it comes to explaining the incubation stage and what exactly happens during this period of unconscious activity for it then to trigger the illumination. Neither is Wallas. Indeed, studies within cognitive psychology generally aren't. Of all the stages in the creative thinking process, the period of incubation attracts the most attention and criticism on the basis that it is arguably its most essential part, but the least understood.

The most popular hypothesis seems to be one that postulates the insightful idea as a *combination* of elements or ideas that are suddenly made known to us; but many are bewildered as to how these combinations occur, several believing them to be the product of random, chance events.[7] If we turn to psychoanalytic theories, however, we can construct from their ideas a coherent explanation for these combinations, one that assigns purpose to the incubatory period as a hub of organised activity, motivated by unconscious impulses that seek conscious expression. In this interpretation, the incubatory period is a particularly active time for the unconscious as it revises and reconfigures the thoughts and ideas that were arrived at earlier through efforts of rational deliberation. Poincaré's account was arguably the first to claim that unconscious activity does not randomly generate combinations of ideas, but establishes those that are of especial use or interest to the subject. In the next section I develop this important idea, by drawing on Freud's theories of unconscious thinking—specifically his concepts of free association and the dream-work—and Bollas's theory of transformative objects. By implementing Freud's ideas we can articulate the methods of the unconscious as it *gathers* and *orders* its material into meaningful combinations; and with Bollas's theory we can elaborate a coherent explanation of the methods of the unconscious as it *disseminates* its gathered material in such a way that it captures the conscious attention of the subject and induces (within him or her) feelings of enlightenment.

After this discussion of the ideas of Freud and Bollas I shall be in a better position to formulate a hypothesis about the psychological efficacy of the built environment in ordering our thoughts and reconciling us with ideas, feelings, and experiences that have been lying dormant and unconscious within us. I suggest that the period of incubation is an occasion of heightened unconscious activity, a time of distraction during which the unconscious *gathers* the various images and impressions we have acquired of our environment (such as the scenery that flickers past the window of Freud's moving train), and *selects* and *directs* us *to* those objects or things in that environment that resonate most strongly with the material it seeks to convey. In this process, objects in our environments capture our attention with their unconscious promise of releasing insights about us. By virtue of its abiding form and its surplus of meaning, the built environment is particularly resourceful and attractive to the unconscious, enabling it to go about its work efficiently.

To illustrate this hypothesis I shall return to the Acropolis and to Freud's insightful moment as he surveys the architectural scene before him. I shall deconstruct the architectural event in light of his account of his experience in order to illustrate how Freud's perception of the architectural features of the built environment encourages his mind to 'shift gear' and employ an imaginative register of experience, which sets in motion the unconscious construction and dissemination of Freud's personal insight. I shall conclude that the material forms of the built environment encouraged Freud to engage with forgotten or repressed experiences that had been too difficult to negotiate and think through in a directed, conscious manner.

The 'dream-work': building blocks of unconscious insight and evocative architectural design

I have described unconscious thinking as a gathering together of impressions we receive from our environments with those that populate our inner worlds, such as latent memory traces, disowned desires, and disallowed impulses. I have also described the gathering as a grouping together of various fragments of experience into clusters or combinations of associated meanings. But by what method does the unconscious do this? Jung gave us a clue earlier by suggesting that the unconscious 'shuffle[s] things about and arrange[s] them not as they are in reality but as we would like them to be' (1911–12: par. 19). We noted, too, Poincaré's allusion to a special aesthetic sensibility that sifts through the ideas made available to the unconscious mind to determine which 'fit' together. But it is to Freud that we turn for a more comprehensive account of the methods employed by the unconscious as it groups the mass of thoughts and impressions accumulated by a person into the meaningful experience that is disclosed within the architectural event.

Freud famously said that the interpretation of dreams is 'the royal road to a knowledge of the unconscious activities of the mind' (1900: 608). Furthermore, he maintained that if we trace the methods employed by the unconscious in the design and construction of dreams—the method of 'dream-work', as Freud referred to it—we can begin to interpret the underlying meanings of our dream-like experiences, including those non-directed streams of thoughts that occur when we perceive objects imaginatively. The dialectic between conscious and unconscious thinking and between literal and imaginative perception is therefore comparable to the contrast between waking and dreaming.

Dreams, like buildings, are symbolic in nature, and therefore their meaning cannot be conveyed directly in literal terms. Thus, their manifest appearance doesn't signify their definitive meaning, but conveys or evokes a multitude or superabundance of possible meanings. Furthermore, dreams, like buildings, are designed and constructed out of a variety of materials and according to methods and techniques that are not immediately evident. The building blocks of dreams are those materials (thoughts, perceptions, memories, desires) that

Figure 5.1 Santuario di Santa Maria dei Miracoli / Sanctuary of St Mary of Miracles, Saronno, Italy (c. 1498): façade (1596–1613)

This building illustrates Freud's analogy well, with its contradiction in style and scale between its façade and the rest of the building.

©Klausbergheimer

the unconscious busily gathers from our waking experiences into the various meaningful clusters from which it constructs our dream-narratives.[8]

Ever keen to elaborate ideas with architectural metaphors, Freud envisions the relationship between the dream as it presents itself to us upon waking, and its hidden, unconscious meaning, as an Italian church with a 'façade' that barely resembles and has 'no organic relation with' the structure lying behind it (1900: 211). Freud refers here to the Italian tradition of adding façades of a later architectural style to older buildings in order to make the analogous point that dreams as they present themselves—their façades—conceal meanings that cannot be immediately discerned in their presentation.[9]

Freud is, however, eager to draw attention to an important distinction between the construction of buildings and dreams. In a parallel with his distinction between the methods and approaches taken by the architect and those of the psychoanalyst (where the architect, you may recall, is thought to follow prescribed blueprints in his construction work, while the psychoanalyst builds more haphazardly, composing the plan as and when he builds), Freud suggests that the façade of a dream is unlike that of a building, because the dream's façade is 'disordered and full of gaps', and so much so that in many places 'portions of the interior construction' will have 'forced their way

Figure 5.2, 5.3 Numbers 23 and 24, Leinster Gardens, Paddington, London: façade (c. 1860)
These façades give Freud's analogy a modern twist. Although they appear to be two Victorian town houses in a terrace of five similar five-storey houses white stucco façades, complete with balconies, columns, railings and other architectural ornamentation, the astute observer will notice that their eighteen windows are blacked-out, and neither has a letterbox. A walk around the back of the building immediately reveals the façade to be just that—a prop placed in front of an empty space where the rest of the houses used to be. If you were to peer into the void, you would see the underground railway line, and possibly a train travelling between Paddington and Bayswater. Numbers 23 and 24 Leinster Gardens are not townhouses but the frontage to an air vent for the discharge of smoke and steam from the London underground train network. © Alex George

through' to appear within it (1900: 211). This difference is sufficient, Freud thinks, to revise his metaphorical description to one that reflects the nature of dreams more accurately.[10] Interestingly, he decides not to dispense with architectural imagery altogether, but chooses simply to modify the specific design features of his architectural metaphor to allow for the incoherent arrangements of a dream's construction. He subsequently refers to dreams as if they were buildings that have been constructed from bits and pieces extracted from the ruins of earlier buildings. By way of illustration, he alludes to the ruins of ancient Rome—Freud's eternal, unconscious city—'whose pavements and columns have provided the material for the more recent structures' of the city, including its 'Baroque palaces' (1900: 492).

Dreams often appear nonsensical and absurd upon waking because they are composed of parts that have been selected by the unconscious from a vast repository of seemingly disparate materials across different periods—including the recent and the distant and forgotten past—and subsequently arranged according to their unconscious associations. Dreams, like the Baroque palaces of Rome, plunder the spoils of earlier periods for their own composition. As Ken Frieden observes, 'In the construction of dreams[,] as of some buildings', there is 'a temporal gap between work on the foundation plans and the façade'. Thus, by 'alluding to the temporal gap between stages of an architectural construction, Freud reinforces his conception of dreams as combinations of childhood materials [memories] and recent events' (Frieden 1990: 35). What concerns us, however, is what the analogy tells us about our unconscious identifications with architecture, and which architectural features or designs are likely to capture our unconscious attention most readily.

I have already begun to describe various architectural features that stir and evoke our unconscious response, including those of great expanse, dark spaces, and those features suggested by their marked absence. In Freud's discussion of the composition of dreams and dream-like imagery, we learn about the spatial arrangements that underpin these features and the array of materials that go into their construction. We shall discover that the unconscious is disclosed through a bricolage of materials that are juxtaposed in confusing and irregular designs. It is the distorted and perplexing features of architecture that most readily captivate our unconscious minds and set in motion the creative thought processes that underpin the architectural event. Ambiguous and surprising architectural features provoke us into disengaging from our 'ordinary' or literal perception of buildings, causing us to hesitate and to engage with them imaginatively, in a non-directed manner.

For centuries architects have sought to incorporate complex and confusing features in their designs in order to undermine the expectations of those who interact with them, and instil within them feelings of tension and unease. Such attempts are often seen as a counteraction to architectural conventions that seek, in stark contrast, to design according to utilitarian principles, conveyed by simple, functional, uniform designs. As we have seen, the effects of the unconscious are most viscerally felt when the expectations of ego-consciousness, with its penchant for certainty and orderliness, are thwarted. An architectural design that captivates our unconscious attention and sets in motion our imaginative perception is likely, at first, to appear to follow conventional orders of design, but upon closer inspection departs from them, through their incorporation of curious spatial alignments that surprise and confound the onlooker. As I later argue, these distortions must be subtle and ambiguous, and not so obvious that they draw immediate attention to themselves as the building's central feature, for this will likely result in a parody of the unconscious and its effects, by merely representing the unconscious rather than evoking it. Such designs mock our sensibilities rather than calling them into question, and often appear more ridiculous or naff than evocative. I shall now elaborate on what I mean by these subtle distortions by outlining how other architects and theorists have conceived them and sought to employ them within architectural designs.

Architecture that distracts, perplexes, and surprises

Fred Botting refers to Gothic revival architecture as a reaction against neo-classical architecture; it is, he says, the 'shadow' that 'haunts' and runs 'counter to the ideas of symmetrical form, simplicity, knowledge and propriety' (2013: 30). While neo-classical architecture seeks to delight and entertain the conscious mind with the precision of its calculated proportions, the Gothic confounds it with intricate and complex ornamentation, 'uncanny shadows' and 'boundlessness' (2013: 2). But it is perhaps the mannerist style that illustrates most clearly an intention to subvert the architectural conventions of its time by maintaining elements of conformity but rearranging them into an uncanny composition that is at once familiar and unfamiliar, curious and ambiguous. The mannerist style originated in Italy as a reaction against the uniformity and equilibrium of form and proportions propagated in the Renaissance, and came to the fore more recently in the 1960s and 1970s as a challenge to the bland, utilitarian designs of International Modernism.

The principal difference between mannerist architecture and all other architecture, as art historian Arnold Hauser asserts, is that mannerist architecture

> creates a conception of space irreconcilable with empirical spatial conceptions and involves a confusing antagonism of the criteria of reality. All architecture that is not purely utilitarian to an extent raises the beholder out of everyday life, but that of mannerism isolates him from his environment, not only in the sense that it takes him to a higher plane, places him in an unusual, ceremonial, harmonious framework, but also in that it emphasises his alienation from it.
>
> (Hauser 1965: 280)

Figure 5.4 Vestibule, Laurentian Library, Florence (Michelangelo, 1524)

This vestibule demonstrates mannerist elements clearly. According to Hauser (1965: 281), it renounces the uniformity, balance, and harmonious rhythms of classical architecture, and also its tectonic logic. The dimensions of its features are out of sync with their functional attributes. Thus, the stairs are massive in relation to the limited space available for them, the heavy frames of the shallow windows are exaggerated yet reveal no view; the heavy consoles seem all the huger due to their lack of purpose. Other, less striking factors contribute just as much to the discomfort of the total effect, such as the columns in the niches that have no function, the consoles that seem to lean backwards rather than forwards as we would normally expect, and corners that appear to come towards the observer rather than recede. The articulation of the walls creates the impression of a *palazzo* façade, but here the street façade is forced into an interior, the bounds of which it threatens to burst.[11]

Mannerist architecture, Hauser asserts, finds its 'purest and most striking expression in paradox' by accentuating 'tensions between stylistic elements' (1965: 12). Its arrangements are similar in kind to the dream-like compositions of the unconscious. Thus, the tensions and paradoxical nature of mannerist architecture depend, Hauser maintains, on its 'defiance' of the

> naively natural and rational, and the emphasis laid on the obscure, the problematical, and the ambiguous, the incomplete nature of the manifest which points to its opposite, the latent, the missing link in the chain [...] The conflict expresses the conflict of life itself and the ambivalence of all human attitudes.
>
> (1965: 13)

Through its visual playfulness mannerist architecture challenges our feelings of control and self-containment, inducing discomfort through uncertainty, leading one to feel, as Hauser puts it, 'bewildered, uprooted, insecure, removed to an artificial spatial structure that seems abstract in relation to ordinary experience' (1965: 280). By way of response to this anxious state of affairs, the subject is compelled to renegotiate the architectural spectacle by employing a more introspective approach, one that brings into focus their intimate involvement with the building and secure grounding both within it and within themselves. This is achieved by disengaging from an 'ordinary', literal perception, which attempts unsuccessfully to rationalise the spectacle from a distance, and exercising instead an imaginative perception of its features.

In similar terms to Hauser, architect Robert Venturi in *Complexity and Contradiction in Architecture* (1966) argues for an architecture that circumvents the orderliness of the rational mindset—one that incites, he says, 'a feeling for paradox' that 'allows seemingly dissimilar things to exist side by side', and through 'their very incongruity' arrive at a 'different kind of truth' (1966: 16). This 'different kind of truth' is achieved through a register of experience that allows paradox and distortion. Venturi's allusion to a 'different kind of truth' that arises in our response to complex and incongruous architecture is comparable to Scruton's 'different kind of understanding' that is evoked by architecture more generally (see Chapter 3). Both, I claim, arise out of unconscious thought processes that can be accessed only when our directed efforts of consciousness, with their desire to ascertain certain knowledge, are relaxed or, better still, suspended. Venturi suggests that a temporary suspension can be achieved through the 'simultaneous perception of a multiplicity of layers' and other complex architectural features on the grounds that this 'involves struggles and hesitations for the observer' (1966: 25). Venturi elaborates on these complex architectural features; they incorporate, he says,

> elements which are hybrid rather than 'pure', compromising rather than 'clean', distorted rather than 'straightforward', ambiguous rather than 'articulated', perverse as well as impersonal, boring as well as 'interesting' [...] redundant rather than simple [...] inconsistent and equivocal rather than direct and clear [...] messy vitality over obvious unity.
>
> (Venturi 1966: 16)

Venturi later extended his list of elements and described them as features that comprise a 'mannerist architecture of today'. The following elements, when incorporated into the fabric of architectural design, increase the likelihood of hesitation and struggle in the perceiver:

> Accommodation, Ambiguity, Boredom, Both-and, Breaks, Chaos, Complexity, Contradiction, Contrast, Convention broken, Deviations, Difficult whole, Discontinuity, Disorder, Dissonance, Diversity, Dualities, Dumbness, Eclectic, Everyday, Exceptions, Generic broken, Imbalance,

Inconsistency, Incorrect, Inflection, Irony, Jumps in scale, Juxtapositions, Layering, Meaning, Monotony, Naïveté, Obscurity, Ordinary, Paradox, Pluralism, Pop, Pragmatism, Reality, Scales (plural), Sophistication, Syncopation, Tension, Terribilità, Vernacular, Wit, Wrestling.

(Venturi 2004: 76–7)[12]

Architectural theorist Kevin Lynch, in his celebrated work *Image of the City* (1960), suggests that the element of surprise can be incorporated into the design of any given building so long as it includes 'small regions' of visible 'confusion' within the 'overall-framework' of the building (1960: 5–6). Lynch attributes the power of the built environment to its 'legibility', and characterises this as a relationship of contrasts, with a capacity on the one hand to 'offer security'—or ego-containment, as I have explained—and on the other to 'heighten the potential depth and intensity of human experience' (1960: 5). For Lynch, the most evocative environments are those that are both vivid and surprising: in other words, those that appeal to the sensibilities of both ego-consciousness, with its desire for distinction and convention, and the unconscious, with its tendency to counter the expectations of ego-consciousness. The small regions of confusion embedded within a design will incite surprise, he maintains, so long as they don't compromise the overall distinctive structure of the building. Although Lynch doesn't explicitly say so himself, we can assume from his argument that too great a region of confusion within a design would result in a disruptive and illegible environment.

Lynch's description of surprising architectural design is suggestive of the stages of creative thinking. Thus a building, he maintains, will elicit 'new sensuous impacts' on a person only if it confuses or bewilders. These subtle confusions will contribute to the 'distinct' and 'vivid' image of the building and will allow 'meaning to develop without our direct guidance' (1960: 8). The surprising building is one that is 'open-ended, adaptable to change' and encourages 'the individual to continue to investigate and organise reality' through their subjective expression (1960: 9).

Jane Jacobs, in her influential investigation into American cities, speaks of the need for 'visual interruptions' within the built environment. Like Venturi and Lynch, Jacobs asserts that such visual breaks or distortions in the continuity of architectural form gives rise to a heightened awareness of the evocative character of the building or street and our participation in it (1961: 459). Interruptions, or 'eye-catchers', as Jacobs also calls them, are, she maintains, a 'seductive attribute' to architectural design (1961: 499)—they distract us and thwart our expectations of the built environment. Visual interruptions can be employed in any built environment, including, Jacobs maintains, the construction of a group of buildings so that their façades are 'set forward from the normal building line to make a jog, with the sidewalk cut underneath' (1961: 498).[13]

Non-directed thoughts or unconscious thinking can be elicited through features that confound our ego-sensibilities with their expectations for orderliness and consistency. Such thoughts are evoked by architectural designs that are in themselves, and in the context of their environments, curious, ambiguous, confusing, distorted, paradoxical, and irregular. In the examples noted above, we find design elements of this nature that are endowed with a power to provoke a heightened perception of the building or a more vivid awareness of its character, and this is exemplified in the subject's response, as a hesitation or bewilderment followed by surprise or curiosity. In other words, these features can be said to incite the distractions required to set in motion an imaginative perception of architecture, in which our unconscious mind gets to work to gather, construct, and disseminate its material. Let us now turn to Freud's proposed methods of the dream-work in order to ascertain how exactly such confusing arrangements lead to evocative insights.

The distracting spatial procedures of the dream-work

In Freud's account the unconscious employs four methods or procedures to construct its dream-like thoughts: condensation, displacement, representation, and secondary revision. Collectively these methods of the dream-work constitute the manner in which the unconscious 'thinks', and thus the means by which it both *selects* from the many meanings and experiences that are evoked in our imaginary perception of architecture, and *gathers* them into the meaningful insights that are disclosed in the architectural event. These methods are *spatial* operations that determine the arrangement of unconscious materials in the composition of dreams and evocative architectural designs. As Steve Pile asserts, they are '*spatial* operations, about convergence and divergence' (2005: 81), and they inform such arrangements and relations as 'setting, sequencing, juxtaposition, reversal, convergence, distribution, procession, movement, motion, proximity and distance, absence and presence, direction, architecture, comportment, combination, and composition' (2005: 47).

The two principal spatial operations of the dream-work that instruct and shape non-directed thinking or dream-thinking are *condensation* and *displacement* (the other two, 'representability' and 'secondary revision', take on supporting roles by furnishing the composition of dream-thoughts with the façade of its manifest narrative). Condensation gathers material together (ideas, thoughts, feelings, impressions, and so on) by merging it into one condensed idea or image. Poincaré's allusion to ideas having 'collided until pairs interlocked' to make 'a stable combination' suggests the activity of condensation. The idea or image established by condensation is a composite of several ideas and images that have no immediately obvious relationship to each other but, upon closer inspection, may suggest, Freud says, one or more of a variety of relationships through, for instance, their proximity, congruence, combination, composition, substitution, surrogating, or even their logical contradiction. Already we can begin to see how a dream-like image established by means of condensation, and with its confusing spatial relations, is comparable to the 'complexities and contradictions' of architecture that Venturi advocates, to the 'visual disruptions' proposed by Jacobs, and to Lynch's suggested regions of confusion.

Condensation reveals one image or idea as a point of convergence for several related chains of thought, each of which may suggest a different manner of relationship (Freud 1900: 279–304). We see such spatial operations at play in those architectural features that fulfil more than one function, for instance in a supporting structure that also encloses and directs space, or in a wall that is also a tower. They are also at play with renovated buildings that, in their changed use and expression, convey vestiges of past meanings at one and the same time as their current meaning—such as we find, Venturi asserts, with palazzi that become museums or embassies, and the pathways that surround medieval fortifications in European cities that become boulevards in the nineteenth century (1966: 38). To these we may add the many Victorian psychiatric asylums, hospitals, and prisons that have been turned into luxury apartments. According to Freud, 'the path of associations leads from one element of the dream to several dream-thoughts; and from one dream-thought to several elements' (1900: 284).

Condensation is the spatial operation that is responsible for the fact that dreams, as well as evocative architecture that invites our imaginative perception and dream-like thinking, seem from the perspective of reason (or literal perception) to appear, as Freud says, somewhat 'brief, meagre, and laconic in comparison with the range and wealth' of meanings it can evoke (1900: 279). Only when our reasoning is suspended can a rich array of meanings be entertained.

Displacement, the other spatial relation of the dream-work, gathers and arranges its material by replacing one element with another so that our rational interpretation of the dream upon waking has a different focal point from the unconscious meaning that it disguises (1900: 305–9). Displacement is responsible for distorting dream imagery, making it appear ambiguous, deceptive, and confusing. It imbues an image or idea with symbolic signification, extending its meaning beyond its literal appearance or function. We find this spatial operation at work in mannerist architecture, as Hauser explicitly asserts: 'the impression it creates is that the order of things that applies elsewhere has been displaced by another, fictitious order' (1965: 280).[14] More often than not, displacement employs relations of opposition and contraction to shift our attention away from those elements in the dream-image or dream-like thought that signify its actual meaning, and attract it to others that are less obvious, seemingly arbitrary, or unexpected. In an attempt to misdirect us, displacement often alters the emotional affects that we would normally attribute to specific images and ideas, by increasing or reducing their affects to an intensity they wouldn't ordinarily arouse, or by transferring the intensity of one experience to another, or by trading images that are known to have similar effects on us.

Read in the light of the Freudian dream-work, the incubatory period of the creative thinking process is a hub of unconscious activity, akin perhaps to an architect's sketch pad, where spatial operations of condensation and displacement are employed to reconfigure or 'redraft' units of experience into an evocative edifice that cannot be fully comprehended by the conscious mind. The unconscious draws upon a reservoir of experiences available to it in its designs and construction work. This reservoir extends far beyond the emotional encounters and meaningful relationships we have with people to include also the myriad forms and sensuous textures that we experience in relation to the nonhuman environment and that continually impress themselves upon us. Indeed, as Eugene Mahon aptly notes, 'If dreams can choose any item out of the flux and flotsam of day residue to build the manifest façade that cloaks the latent dream thoughts, it should come as no surprise that architecture might be a common structure pressed into usage by the dream-work' (2005: 32). In this respect, the unconscious doesn't discriminate between material objects in our external environment and the phantom presences of our inner worlds. Experiences of both are meshed together to establish the clusters of condensed and displaced material that captivates us and take us by surprise.

The unconscious, in Freud's account, is not simply a storehouse or repository for our past experiences; it is more akin, as Bollas suggests, to a 'dynamic factory of thought that knits together "infinite" lines of thought that combine and grow' (2007: 17).[15] If the construction work of the unconscious is allowed to continue—and its creations allowed to 'incubate'—without premature intervention from the conscious mind with its compulsion to scrutinise and to 'find out', then its work may generate sufficient intensity or density to break into conscious awareness in the form of a dream or other dream-like experience.[16] When this happens, the dream-experience imparts to the subject the feeling of an instruction or command, and instigates a shift in their conscious attitude that may go undetected; or, if it is particularly intense or dense, it can be experienced as a profound thought or insight. In either case, the shift in attitude can override previously held ideas and convictions—as we find in cases of problem solving where the sudden unconscious insight into the task at hand overrides the rational strategies initially deployed. The conscious breakthrough, as we noted, marks the stage of illumination, and encourages the ego to try to accept the fruits of unconscious thinking, and subsequently integrate them into the conscious attitude of the personality.

Kevin Lynch, albeit it unintentionally, illustrates the dream-work in operation in his explanation of the identifications people make with their cities. Lynch, like many others, as we have seen, interprets the built environment as evoking 'infinite' lines of thought, which we have interpreted as the non-linear streams or webs of associated meanings that impart dream-like experiences.[17] In Lynch's account we can trace a clear description of the architectural event, together with the dream-like perception that the cityscape elicits. He introduces his account as follows:

> At every instant, there is more than the eye can see, more than the ear can hear, a setting or a view waiting to be explored. Nothing is experienced by itself, but always in relation to its surroundings, the sequences of events

> leading up to it, the memory of past experiences [...] Every citizen has had long associations with some part of his city, and his image is soaked in memories and meanings [...] Most often our perception of the city is not sustained, but rather partial, fragmentary, mixed with other concerns. Nearly every sense is in operation, and the image is a composite of them all.
>
> (Lynch 1960: 1–2)

Clearly, for Lynch, we perceive the built environment—in this case, the city—imaginatively, as a dream-like encounter. Although he doesn't concern himself with psychoanalytic theory to elaborate his claims, his approach complements it. For instance, Lynch investigates what he describes as the "mental image" and the '"legibility" of the cityscape' (1960: 2), and thereby seeks to expose—in terms we would associate with the Freudian dream-work—the manner in which the fragmentary impressions of the city are mixed up with the perceiver's own 'parts' and are subsequently arranged, as Lynch puts it, into 'coherent patterns'. Lynch's account goes on to assign to the features of the 'external environment' what he describes as its 'definite sensory cues', which a person 'picks out' in order that they may somehow use them to 'organise' their sense of self and to 'differentiate [their] worlds' (1960: 3, 7).[18]

Lynch describes the city as a legible environment; and a method one can use to read or decipher its message is, I suggest, the unconscious techniques of the dream-work. By identifying how these techniques are involved in a dream-like narrative, Freud maintained that the underlying meaning of the narrative could be exposed. This involves untangling the components of the subject's emotional world from other impressions that are merged, condensed, and displaced within the overall evocative narrative—whether a narrative of a dream or day-dream, or the legible cues of the built environment.

Disclosing unconscious insights through evocative architecture

To develop the present account and help us to make sense of the unconscious as it discloses its material through our perception of architecture and its evocative cues, we return to the ideas of Christopher Bollas, and to his discussion of evocative and transformative objects. While Freud's methods of dream-work help us to envisage how the unconscious gathers and arranges its material during the period of incubation, Bollas's ideas help us in considering the methods employed by the unconscious to disseminate its work, and both why and how it uses architectural features to do so. We therefore find in Bollas's ideas a framework in which to conceptualise the unconscious activity involved in creative thinking and in the architectural event more generally, in its development from the stages of 'incubation', where it gathers and arranges its material, through to 'illumination', where it seeks to disclose its narrative as a meaningful insight.

Freud's account suggests that, by using its spatial operations of condensation and displacement, the unconscious distorts the impressions ordinarily acquired through our literal perception of things. It does so, first, by selecting from this variety of impressions those that resonate with its own concerns—which is to say, according to its instinctual drives, which are given their energy, shape, and direction by whatever experiences or desires the person has sought to repress—for these, Freud maintains, seek every opportunity to discharge themselves in the act of becoming conscious. Once selected, these impressions are integrated into the ever expanding cluster of unconscious fragments of experience, which also resonate with the underlying instinctive concerns of the unconscious. Out of this collection, the unconscious will construct its distorted narrative or 'dream-work'. As this collection expands, it draws upon instinctual libidinal energies from the subject's overall psyche, establishing a charge that, when strong enough, will compel the dream-work narrative to break through into conscious awareness, whereupon it is experienced as a dream or dream-like inspired idea or insight.

In Bollas's account, by contrast, the unconscious seems somewhat more cunning in its attempts to disseminate its material and bring it to conscious expression. According to Freud and Bollas, the unconscious works best when left to its own devices without interference from the scrutiny and directed attentions of the ego. However, in Bollas's account, the unconscious is arguably more efficient and resourceful, especially in the way it uses material objects to disclose its work. The unconscious for Bollas doesn't simply *gather* and *incorporate* the impressions we perceive in our environments into the narrative that, in Freud's account, eventually and somewhat arbitrarily becomes disclosed to the conscious mind whenever it has generated sufficient energy to do so. Bollas's unconscious actively *uses* the objects of our environment to convey its message. Similarly to Lynch, who maintains that we use sensory cues from the environment to deepen our awareness of ourselves (1960: 3), Bollas suggests that the unconscious impels us to 'seek out and find specific things' in the world that embody or represent its own interests (2009: 83). According to Bollas, the unconscious helps us to discover these things by 'intensifying' their evocative power so that they are more likely to capture our attention—thereby setting them up to be, in Lynch's terms, the 'definite sensory cues' that draw us to them. It is as if the unconscious leads us to the relevant location, through which it can more readily disclose or release its stream of thoughts. According to Lynch, the legible city provides myriad sensuous cues to trigger and set in motion creative experiences of ourselves, and to facilitate individual growth and emotional security (1960: 4). I claim that the built environments of cityscapes are evocative and transformative because they grasp our attention at a level deeper than is registered by our literal perception; and once we are engaged with them in this way, the creative processes of the architectural event are set in motion.

Bollas's account of the unconscious as it selects and uses objects in the subject's environment is significant for our investigation because we can trace within it the three phases of the architectural event and the three stages of the creative thinking process proposed by Poincaré and others who followed him. Let us now consider Bollas's account within the context of the creative occasion of the architectural event.

The construction and development of identity, I have argued, must negotiate both aspects of the divided self; they cannot come about by conscious willing alone, but involve also the imaginative activity of the unconscious. The unconscious seeks a constructive dialogue with ego-consciousness, calling upon it to integrate those aspects of the self that it has disowned and repressed. Without this dialogue, the person experiences life as sterile, flat, and wholly uninspiring—leading them, as Freud and others would have us believe, to develop all sorts of pathologies and neuroses. The unconscious communicates with the ego through imaginative registers of experience, through mimetic identifications and 'dream-thinking', which intensifies the objects we ordinarily perceive into evocative objects of transformation that, as Bollas says, 'give lived expression to one's true self' (1989: 110). Identity and the creative transformations that underpin it cannot be brought into existence by directed thinking alone. Bollas says that we may attempt to find evocative objects in this way, but more often than not we fail to do so. Instead, we tend to encounter them imaginatively, spurred on by our instinctual needs and unconscious concerns. The building, by virtue of its containing form and its elusive quality is, I have argued, an evocative object *par excellence*, a favoured nonhuman object for unconscious use, through which the unconscious readily expresses its material and captures our attention.

Echoing Poincaré and Wallas before him, Bollas asserts that, although inspired thoughts may appear to constitute an 'immediate knowing', such appearances are deceptive and 'should not obscure the fact that these thoughts are the outcome of sustained concentration of many types of unconscious and conscious thinking' (1992: 90–1, 76–7). The use of actual, external objects is a type of unconscious thinking that Bollas is keen to emphasise as a means of encouraging inspired thoughts. He argues that

> our encounter [with], [our] engagement with, and sometimes our employment of, actual things is a *way* of thinking [...] we select objects because we are unconsciously grazing: finding food for thought that only retrospectively could be seen to have a logic [...] whether we are pushed to thought by objects arriving or we seek objects to use them as forms of thinking, it is clear to us all that such existential engagements are a very different form of thinking from that of cognitive thought.
>
> (Bollas 2009: 92–3)

The type of thinking Bollas has in mind here is the creative play of the unconscious that underlies our imaginative perception of objects. In the previous chapter I described how this use of objects involves the incorporation of their structural form into an embodied experience of ourselves. I described how this identification is dependent on the *projection* of unconscious aspects of the self into the object (which will involve the person's instinctive desire for containment, as well as repressed material they seek to disown) and the *incorporation* of characteristics of the object into the self that resonate with the aspects that have been projected into it (that is to say, the return of repressed experiences in a more contained and manageable form). The oscillation between projection and incorporation underpins the kind of thinking that Bollas ascribes to the unconscious. It is a kind of thinking that involves the merger of subject and building so as to allow a person to use the built environment to think themselves into being. In other words, it is through the act of projection that we enter the period of incubation, and suspend our literal perception of things and our directed thoughts and deliberations about what those things literally mean. Bollas expresses the situation as follows:

> [A] person projects a part of himself into the object, thus psychically signifying it. This gives the object meaning, converting it into a tool for possible thought: the thinking that is special to the dream state. To do this, however, the subject must 'lose himself' in moments of experience when he projects meaning into objects [... this is an] action that must be unconscious and one in which the person is not being, as it were, thoughtful. Indeed, he must be a rather simplified consciousness, even out of touch with himself for a moment, in order to invest the object world with psychic potential. Viewed this way, this type of projective identification is ultimately self-enhancing, transforming material things into psychic objects, and thus furnishing an unconscious matrix for dreams, fantasies, and deeper reflective knowings.
>
> (Bollas 1992: 22–3)

Unconscious thinking begins, he says, with a moment of hesitation. This moment marks the occasion when a person disengages from a literal perception of the building to perceive it imaginatively, thereby allowing their mind to wander. This marks, we noted, the period of incubation in the creative thinking process. It is here that the evocative object announces its presence and the architectural object captures our attention. On such occasions we relinquish our capacity for 'being thoughtful', as Bollas puts it, and we subsequently behave much as the infant does in relation to its environment prior to the establishment of its cognitive ego. We are no longer preoccupied with deliberate, explicit thoughts, but become infant-like or, as Bollas puts it, a 'simple self' who is more prone to relating to the environment through acts of projection. In this state we allow our unconscious mind to think for us, and it does so, Bollas maintains, by selecting objects in the environment that signify by various complex associations its own unconscious concerns.

When we project aspects of ourselves into the architectural object, we receive in return those characteristics of the object's structural form or function that resonate with our unconscious needs at the time. This is the 'collision' Bollas speaks of, which I discussed earlier. It is an exchange that is experienced, Bollas says, as an 'uncanny fusion', an 'intimate rendezvous', and a 'deep subjective rapport' (1987: 31, 16). It is a curious relationship in which a person feels at once a loss of self, from having projected aspects of themselves onto the object, and the acquisition of a new sense of self, from characteristics they have acquired from the object. The object evokes in the subject, Bollas says, a 'sense of being reminded of something never quite cognitively apprehended but existentially known' (1987: 16). In other words, as I explained in Chapter 4, the psychological merger with the object provides a person with a 'symbolic re-enactment' of their original encounter with themselves and their earliest experiences of transformation from a nurturing environment (1987: 28). Thus, it is within the period of incubation, where the subject temporarily withdraws from their familiar sense of self to become infant-like and to establish by means of projection an affinity with the object, that the subject is led 'suddenly', as Bollas says, to discover themselves anew with the acquisition of new structural contents. This sudden discovery marks the 'illumination' stage of the creative thinking process, and marks the culmination of the architectural event with the disclosure of a shift in personality often accompanied by a meaningful insight into this shift. These insights are akin to a 'fundamentally new perspective' and 'new psychic structure' for the self (1992: 88). The reconfiguration of the subject is an illuminating experience, and has, Bollas says, the feeling of an epiphany; it '*feels* revelatory' (1992: 88).

Revisiting Freud at the Acropolis: Freud's memory building

Let us now return to Freud as he gazes in his dream-like state at the Acropolis before him, for I am now in a position to apply my hypothesis about imaginative perception and creative thinking to the occasion as he reports it, with a view to making sense of his relationship with the built environment. Freud's anecdotal account provides us with a useful case study for illustrating the principles of the architectural event, and specifically the manner in which the unconscious uses the architectural features of the built environment to awaken a new perspective within the personality and unlock aspects of one's identity and sense of self. We shall see that this new perspective involves for Freud the disclosure of thoughts, memories, and feelings that had until then been largely inaccessible to him.

I have mentioned that, although Freud readily concedes that his experience culminated in a 'process of transformation' that 'included myself, the

Acropolis and my perception of it' (1936: 244), neither Freud nor the majority of scholars who have examined his account consider the built environment or his perceptions of it as a contributory factor, preferring to attribute it completely to the emotional situation of his inner life.[19] The architectural scene of the Acropolis tends to be either ignored by scholars or mentioned only very briefly as a passive, arbitrary backdrop to the events that occurred there.

Just as Bollas is keen to emphasise the transformative object as a *re-enactment* of an earlier memory of transformation and not a *regressive* desire to return to a state of infantile dependence on the mother, I shall consider Freud's experience at the Acropolis as a re-enactment or event triggered by the architecture itself, the features of which Freud utilises as an evocative, transformative object to re-orientate himself and create himself anew. My interpretation seeks to explain how Freud's unconscious mind applies its methods of spatial re-alignment (condensation and displacement) to the architectural features of the Acropolis in order to juxtapose Freud's perceptions of them with other fragmentary ideas, feelings, and memory traces that had been latent within him. I shall outline, too, how his unconscious mind utilises the features of the architectural landscape to disseminate this network of associated meanings to Freud, whereupon he registers his surprise, and is granted insights into his personality (that he is able to validate only years later through his own diagnosis of the situation).

Our aims are similar to those of psychiatrist Stephen M. Sonnenberg, one of very few to consider the material characteristics of the Acropolis and their role in stimulating Freud's introspective self-analysis.[20] According to Sonnenberg, the fragmentary features of the Acropolis—notably, its structure eroded through time and the removal of some its parts (including the Elgin Marbles), and the efforts of restorers to retain others—trigger a comparable experience of fragmentation within the perceiver. He writes:

> The Acropolis, with its irregularities, its orderliness and its disorder, its missing frieze carvings and its remaining ones [...] promotes the same sort of experience in one who visits there. That visitor must negotiate a complex terrain with his or her eyes, legs, and mind. And at that point, if one is preoccupied with an aspect of one's own antique past, then those preoccupations may dominate that person's psyche.
>
> (Sonnenberg 2005: 51)

As Freud trod cautiously over broken pieces of stone and, with the help of his guidebook to the site, imaginatively reconstructed the building in his mind, restoring its image to its former pristine condition, he would most likely have experienced, as Sonnenberg puts it, 'a sense of the fluid interplay of inner psychological space and outer perceptual space' (2005: 46). Unfortunately, Sonnenberg doesn't suggest what this spatial interplay involves, beyond noting that it probably incurred for Freud an initial 'loss of temporal and spatial orientation, followed finally by the use of his imagination as he constructed a picture of what the Acropolis was once like' (2005: 46). Nevertheless, Sonnenberg's remarks coincide with my more comprehensive interpretation of Freud's account and with the various phases of the architectural event and processes of unconscious thinking that give rise to it.

Freud tells us that he didn't intend to travel to Athens but planned instead to take a trip with his brother to the island of Corfu by way of Trieste. The planning of his itinerary suggests the first stage of the creative thinking process (Wallas's stage of preparation). Here Freud and his brother attend to the task at hand with directed thinking until they conclude—with help from an acquaintance—that their plan is impractical, because it is too hot at that time of year to travel to Corfu. They decide they would more likely enjoy themselves if they went instead to Athens (Freud 1936: 240). The rational deliberations that were invested in their initial preparations prove fruitless, and consequently Freud and his brother disengage from this type of thinking, thereby causing their minds to 'switch gear', allowing a period of 'incubation' to settle in. This second stage is evident in Freud's account in two respects: first, in that both he and his brother engage in the seemingly trivial or *distracting* activity of 'wandering about town', as Freud puts it, for several hours; second, in their detached—or 'depressed' and 'irresolute'—frames of mind, which meant that they disengaged from each other and didn't even 'bother', Freud says, to converse with each other (1936: 240, 241). At this time, Freud and his brother are no longer interested in making further plans or composing new itineraries, as both seem incapable of focused and directed thinking; they are no longer—as Bollas would say—'being thoughtful', but are being 'simple-minded' and are 'out of touch' with themselves and each other. This is because they are immersed in preparations of another kind: unconscious preparations. They are getting ready, as Bollas would assert, 'to invest the object world with psychic potential' and to transform their environments into 'dynamic factories' for the creation of 'dreams, fantasies, and deeper reflective knowings'.

Freud doesn't comment on his brother's experiences from this point on, but he continues to give insight into the creative process that has been set in motion for himself. After alluding to his withdrawn mood, Freud's narrative moves quickly to describe the afternoon of his arrival at the Acropolis, whereupon he is greeted suddenly by a surprising thought. He writes that, as 'I stood on the Acropolis and cast my eyes around upon the landscape, a surprising thought suddenly entered my mind: "So all this really *does* exist, just as we learnt at school!"' (1936: 240–1). The sudden cognitive insight denotes the stage of illumination, where the unconscious reveals the product of its work to ego-consciousness. Given that the unconscious employs spatial procedures of distortion and association in its thinking, the thought it reveals to Freud's conscious mind is inevitably bizarre and, as Freud notes, 'incorrect and, indeed, impossible' (1936: 243). Freud exclaims: 'By the evidence of my senses I am now standing on the Acropolis, but I cannot believe it'

(1936: 243). The rest of Freud's account is his attempt to unravel the mystery that lies behind his perceived disbelief in the Acropolis.

Freud's explanation considers the role played by displacement and condensation in twisting his reasonable feeling of what he describes as 'joyful astonishment' at seeing the Acropolis into the bizarre doubting of its reality. From his inquiry into the associative links and spatial procedures employed by the unconscious to fabricate this distortion, Freud concludes that his visit to the Acropolis had occasioned feelings of guilt that he had been harbouring for some time towards his father. By contrast, in my reading of events, the Acropolis plays a more significant role in facilitating these feelings by lending their structural form to Freud's unconscious so as to enable it to convey the kinds of feelings that Freud surmises. When Freud's thwarted plans left him withdrawn and frustrated, his unconscious was free to work unimpeded for several hours, busily establishing associative links with previous, forgotten episodes in his life when he felt similarly frustrated and doubtful. This network of material may well have been developing for some time, gradually accumulating more images, memory traces, and experiences in Freud's life that resonated with his frustration—piling up image upon image and feelings upon feelings, as Jung would say. For, as Freud asserts, it is only when these clusters of experience generated sufficient intensity, energy or libidinal charge that they could break into conscious awareness. One might argue that the trip to the Acropolis happened to coincide with a time when a sufficient degree of intensity had been achieved. I suggest, however, that the ruinous architectural landscape of the Acropolis provided the crucial trigger for their release, one that allowed their dissemination within the security of its containing environment. Let us consider my claim more closely.

Freud concedes that his perception of the Acropolis inspired within him 'a sense of some feeling of the unbelievable and the unreal', and he is adamant that these feelings of doubt couldn't have been accounted for by the 'sensory impressions' of the Acropolis acquired through his literal perception of it, which, indeed, proved to him the reality of its presence (1936: 244). On that I agree; and although Freud does not express it in explicit terms, he leaves open the possibility that it is his *imaginative perception* of these sensory impressions that grants him his experience. In other words, that at this time he was not experiencing the architecture literally but imaginatively. For Freud concludes that the cause of his surprising experience is a displaced memory that was somehow associated with the object of his perception, the Acropolis, that had remained until that point in time repressed and cognitively unthinkable (1936: 244).

Freud goes on to analyse his fragmented memory of the occasion when as a schoolboy he first experienced feelings of doubt in relation to the Acropolis; and he identifies a number of experiences associated with this memory that help him gradually to expose the various elements that went into the unconscious construction of his bizarre epiphany upon seeing the Acropolis for the first time. He recounts how his doubt as a schoolboy was not about the existence of the Acropolis, but that he should ever get to see it at first hand. Starting with his memory, Freud allows his mind to wander (or 'freely associate' to use Freud's term) and thereby arrives at the following associated idea: that 'it seemed to me beyond the realms of possibility that I should travel so far—that I should "go such a long way"' (1936: 246). Freud proceeds to associate his schoolboy longing to travel 'so far' with his desire to 'escape' the pressures of his home life, by running away from home. From this thought, Freud imagines how the first sighting of new cities and lands, 'which for so long had been distant, unattainable things of desire', induce feelings of heroism, of having 'performed deeds of improbable greatness', and indeed, of having transgressed realms of possibility. Freud then considers again the occasion of his visit to the Acropolis, but this time in a heroic context, and imagines how

> I might that day on the Acropolis have said to my brother: 'Do you still remember how, when we were young, we used day after day to walk along the same streets on our way to school [...] And now, here we are in Athens, and standing on the Acropolis! We really *have* gone a long way!'
>
> (1936: 247)

For Freud it is a short move from this latest thought in a string of associated thoughts to arrive at the original meaning and motivation for the bizarre thought that was triggered by his perceptions of the Acropolis, but which, on Freud's admission, had already started to form, gestate, or incubate when he and his brother realised to their frustration that they could not go to Corfu. He writes:

> But here we come upon the solution [to] the little problem of why it was that already at Trieste we interfered with our enjoyment of the voyage to Athens. It must be that a sense of guilt was attached to the satisfaction in having gone such a long way [...] It was something to do with a child's criticism of his father [...] as though to excel one's father was still something forbidden.
>
> (1936: 247)

From this point in his account, Freud's detective work and analysis of events is restricted to the limitations Freud himself imposes on the nature of the unconscious and the repository of experiences from which it gathers and constructs its material in its dream-work—one that is limited to the subject's past emotional encounters (in contrast, for instance, to Jung's more expansive model of the unconscious that includes potential experiences that the subject has yet to encounter). Freud therefore understands the event at the Acropolis in terms of his past experiences of himself in relation to other people. When Freud and his commentators allude to the Acropolis in their considerations of the return of Freud's repressed memories and feelings, it is as a motif or 'theme', as Freud puts it, which suggests to Freud, through its cultural and historical connotations, the theme of 'the son's superiority' (1936: 247). The interpretation I wish to develop in the light of Bollas's ideas, however, suggests that Freud's evident emotional withdrawal and feeling out of sorts with himself in Trieste had left him 'simple-minded', impressionable, and susceptible to relating to his environment by means of projection, and subsequently prone to using—and being used by—the objects in his environment to express those unconscious concerns that were gathering momentum within him and couldn't be expressed or thought through in more logical or direct fashion. In other words, Freud was compelled by the architectural features of his environment to employ an imaginative register of experience in his perception of it.

Freud maintains that he identified with the theme of 'the son's superiority', and with his own feelings of guilt at having achieved something at the expense of surpassing his father. I suggest that the architectural forms of the Acropolis were unconsciously selected by Freud for their efficacy in attracting and drawing out his projections of his repressed memory and the difficult feelings associated with it. This projected material is subsequently embedded or inscribed in the architecture of the Acropolis in such a way that its forms are charged, 'psychically signified' or 'intensified' as Bollas puts it, providing Freud with cues with which to engage and interpret its inscription unconsciously. The architectural forms provide a nurturing, incubatory container for Freud's repressed material, one that discloses or reveals its material to Freud in a more manageable and transformed state, as an inspired thought.

In my reading of Freud's experience at the Acropolis, Freud identifies with its architectural features and incorporates aspects of their character into himself. In this 'architectural event', Freud inevitably experiences a loss of self or, as Sonnenberg suggests, a corresponding 'loss of temporal and spatial orientation'. The Acropolis as an evocative object provides Freud with an uncanny feeling of awe and disbelief, and a sense of having been reminded of something not yet cognitively known but, as Bollas states, 'existentially known' and recalled. By psychologically merging with the built environment, Freud incorporates within him the fragmented and disordered array of architectural textures that he perceives as he moves around the site. This would have included its complex terrain of recognisable shapes and missing features, its eroded and crumbling textures, and its quality of sound and smell, together with the image of the Acropolis in its pristine form and original condition as Freud had imagined it. I claim that it is through his mimetic identification with these fragmentary sensuous features of the built environment that Freud finds the resources to engage with his own unreconciled struggles and fragmented experiences that pertain to his own past.

Freud's imaginative perception of the Acropolis evokes within him clusters of associated fragments of ideas, memory traces, and unrealised feelings that had been gathering within him. Their complex arrangement and haphazard juxtapositions resonate with the fragments of marble and crumbling stone around him, some seemingly placed at random and others more purposively related and connected. As Freud mimetically identifies with those architectural forms that he perceives and incorporates into himself, their sensory impressions combine with other fragments in Freud's unconscious experience, where they are worked through and reconfigured according to the methods of the dream-work. The combination of the architectural features of Freud's environment and his past experiences of unconscious concern together establish through their interplay the uncanny experience brought to Freud's conscious attention. In this respect, the Acropolis was a veritable memory building, or group of memory buildings, for Freud—a mnemonic object that contained and preserved aspects of his self that he was not able to access or think through with concerted efforts of reasoning. The Acropolis was particularly evocative for Freud, and the memory it sought to convey through its fragmentary distortions equally so. Indeed, Ernest Jones, Freud's colleague and biographer, asserts that 'the amber-coloured columns of the Acropolis remained in his memory as the most beautiful sight of his life' (Jones 1955: 2, 24).

Conclusion: buildings are inscriptions of us

One of the concerns of this book has been to re-evaluate the significance of architectural blueprints of being and move beyond their conventional and somewhat limited interpretation as mere instructive aids for the recall and categorisation of abstract information, by considering them as symbolic narratives that point to a fundamental human need to identify with the architectural features of the built environment so as to acquire a more distinctive sense of self, one that is better contained and orientated in the world. I have sought to emphasise their existential significance and the existential repercussions of a perceived semblance between architectural image and human form. My investigation in this chapter has considered the legibility of the built environment and two different ways in which we can 'read' its architectural features to decipher or incorporate its message. One way is to read them in literal terms, by employing directed thinking and perceiving them at a distance as passive objects that may or may not be useful to our immediate conscious needs. Another is to read them imaginatively by implicating in our perception of them the non-directed thoughts of our unconscious personality that are driven by concerns that aren't immediately apparent or obvious to us. This imaginative approach deciphers architecture in symbolic terms, and therefore moves beyond the rationally construed like-for-like designations, postulated by the metaphorical blueprints of being to engage the subject's more elusive, unconscious interests. In my interpretation, architectural features are inscriptions of ourselves that, when read, furnish us with new perspectives and capacities to rethink and imagine ourselves anew. When I speak of architectural blueprints of being, I speak of the power of architectural forms to convey much more than metaphorical spectacle. It is a power to incite real psychological change.

In the previous chapter I explained how we come to identify with buildings as abiding containers for ourselves, which we subsequently use to stabilise and bolster our sense of self. In this chapter I have explained how we use buildings to rethink ourselves into being or to negotiate aspects of ourselves that we had forgotten or hadn't been given the opportunity to develop. The enrichment and development of self that we have explored in this chapter can be a destabilising experience for a person, as it involves a shift or rupture in the psychological containment they have sought and achieved through their bodily identifications with the built environment. As I have previously discussed, the architectural event discloses new aspects or attitudes of the personality that may replace or divert from those that were previously relied upon as familiar and habitual ways of relating to oneself and others. But the shifts and reconstructions of personality that occur in the architectural event do not threaten the ego-personality with anxious portents of its potential dissolution, because they take place in the safe containment of the architectural object, with which the subject has identified as if it is a psychological extension of the self. The shifts and resulting change in personality may be barely noticeable, but, if they are noticed, a person is inclined to experience them initially as an uncanny occurrence, and may feel bewildered, frustrated, and detached, withdrawing into themselves as the unconscious gets to work. Following this, a different kind of feeling comes to the fore, represented as a surprise, as the newly furnished self is realised. The moment of surprising insight in the culmination of the architectural event is akin to a wake-up call for the subject, bringing them to a more objective awareness of themselves, and a more attuned orientation within their environment.

The creative thinking of the unconscious and the insights it gives rise to are facilitated by an architecture that incites our curiosity and a desire to discover and explore its hidden features. This exploration may be attempted by our directed efforts and conscious attention, but the more powerful discoveries are those achieved through their imaginative exploration. This imaginative exploration is activated by the confusing and ambiguous features in architectural design that we spoke of, which cause us to hesitate, pause, and reflect, and it continues through an investigation of their hidden features, an exploration that involves us unconsciously reconstructing them according to our fantasies of what it is they conceal. They are the nooks and crannies clothed in shadow that invite us to expose their detail; the places that are no longer physically present but remain intact and preserved in memory; and other features that announce their presence through their absence, such as the room behind the closed door, and the planned extension that hasn't been built. The built environment allures us with its delineated rhythms that coincide with our own, and its promise to reveal and disclose to us the desires and secrets of our imagination that we unknowingly impart to its architecture.

In the next chapter I examine the stage of illumination within the architectural event, in order to establish what exactly is revealed in our interactions with architecture, and what kinds of ideas and feelings are evoked by the event as it unfolds. This will help us to conclude our investigation with a veritable framework for the design and construction of an evocative architecture that responds more effectively to our existential needs. By the same token, it will help us to understand why certain approaches to architectural design ought to be avoided due to their likely tendency to incite feelings of discord and alienation in those who use them.

Notes

1 I have suggested that the architectural event can be divided into three overlapping phases that are comparable to the stages often found in traditional problem-solving techniques and in creative thought processes. It should be noted that in reality the three phases of the architectural event can be difficult to distinguish. The same can be said of the various stages of creative thinking that are outlined by Poincaré and others. Indeed, there are many critics of stage theories; see, for example, Lowenfeld and Brittain (1987) and Sawyer et al. (2003: 22–9). See also Graham Wallas, who notes that, 'generally', stages of creative thought can be 'distinguished from each other', but 'in the daily stream of thought' they 'constantly overlap each other', so that 'the mind may be unconsciously incubating on one aspect of [a thought], while it is consciously employed in preparing for or verifying another aspect' (1926: 81–2).

2 Poincaré's 'sieve-like' mind anticipates Freud's idea of the censor, which selects which unconscious ideas can cross the boundary into conscious awareness. But, interestingly, Poincaré asserts that only some of us are receptive to the creativity of the unconscious, because only some of us will have 'aesthetic sensibility' (1908: 29).

3 Wallas's model was widely celebrated after its publication, many regarding it as pioneering, original, and innovative. Poincaré's formulation of it was by contrast largely forgotten (see Hakala, 2012). However, both Poincaré and Wallas attribute their description of the stages of creativity to the German physiologist Hermann von Helmholtz, who himself cites philosopher Alexander Bain as an influence (see Wallas 1926). Helmholtz noted: 'in all directions [...] happy ideas come unexpectedly without effort, like an inspiration. So far as I'm concerned, they have never come to me when my mind was fatigued, or when I was at my working table [...] They came particularly readily during the slow ascent of wooded hills on a sunny day' (cited in Wallas 1926: 37).

4 Interestingly, Bollas also cites Poincaré's ideas and acknowledges that his work is an influence on his own (1992: 76–7).

5 Empirical studies suggest this to be anywhere in the region of a few moments to several days and weeks: see for example, Ritter and Dijksterhuis (2014). Wallas notes that the time varies according to individual cases, and generally speaking varies greatly: 'Sometimes the successful train seems to consist of a single leap of association, or of successive leaps which are so rapid as to be almost instantaneous', but it must 'last for an appreciable time' for it to be 'sufficiently conscious for the thinker to be at least aware that something is happening to him' (1926: 47).

6 Material that originates in the unconscious can be experienced as overwhelming, and may be rejected on this basis. From a Freudian perspective, this material had been repressed for a reason. It may simply have been irrelevant to the needs of the ego-personality at the time, in which case its return during the architectural event may be easier to accept. But it may have been repressed due to its traumatic nature; in which case it may still be too difficult to reconcile with at a later stage.

7 See Campbell (1960: 390); Simonton (1988: 6–8); Sawyer et al. (2003: 24).

8 Freud argues that dreams invariably confuse us with their imaginative and often non-sensical narratives so as to hide the inner conflict they express. If they had presented these in a literal narrative, the person would wake out of concern. Their imaginative rendition ensures sleep.

9 According to Freud, the manifest content never bares the unconscious, but only a heavily censored copy of it. But other schools of psychoanalytic thought disagree with this view. Both Jung and object relations theorists lay claim to the view that the manifest content is an accurate picture of the unconscious self, even if what is portrayed is open to question. Jung rejects Freud's understanding of the dream and rejects his analogy: that is to say he rejects the dream as 'a mere façade, which conceals the actual meaning'. And he continues to denounce Freud's position, interestingly, by revising Freud's architectural analogy:

> For most houses, the so-called façade is [...] by no means a fraud or a deceptive distortion, but rather corresponds to the interior of the house [...] thus also is the manifest dream image the dream itself, and contains its complete sense [...] We are dealing with something like an incomprehensible text, which has absolutely no façade, but which simply cannot be read by us. Then we do not need to interpret behind it, but must rather learn to *read* it.
>
> (1954b: par. 319)

I shall explore the differences between these conceptions of Freud and Jung in the next chapter when I consider what we can know about the self that is evoked through the dream process.

10 We could argue against such a view by citing one of a vast number of possible examples of architectural designs that comprise a disordered array of various gaps and ruptures to the construction so as to confuse its interior and exterior. Indeed, the psychoanalyst Donald Meltzer, writing seventy-five years after Freud, refers to the ruins of Tintern Abbey in Monmouthshire, Wales, in this context, to illustrate the lack of distinction and boundary between the inner mind of a person and their material environment. Parveen Adams expounds on Meltzer's illustration: the lack of roof, he maintains, 'invites the sky in; through the damaged walls and glassless windows the landscape enters; the grass floor of the ruin belongs to the outside.

From without one can "see through" the building in the many places which would normally convince the eye of its solidity' (1996: 147). This description readily applies to many modern architectural designs, such as the iconic 'Glass House' of Philip Johnson (built in 1949) in New Canaan, Connecticut, whose glass-clad surfaces invite the surrounding landscape into the building as if to decorate its interior as its wallpaper. Coop Himmelblau's 'Open House', Malibu, California, is another case in point. Without a façade or predetermined divisions in the living area, this building, he says, evokes 'the feeling [that its] inside stretches the skin of [its] outside' (www.coop-himmelblau.at/architecture/projects/open-house; accessed 9/2016).

11 Examples of buildings that embody the complexities and contradictions Venturi seeks include those that call into question their shape and proportions. (Of Le Corbusier's Villa Savoye, Venturi asks, 'Is it a square plan or is it not?' and of Vanbrugh's fore-pavilions at Grimsthorpe, he asks, 'Are they near or far, big or small'?) Such buildings often have features that seem incorrect when viewed in isolation from the rest of the building. Venturi illustrates this issue with the example of Nicholas Hawksmoor's St George-in-the-East Church in London. This building has exaggerated keystones over the aisle windows, which when seen close up appear too big in relation to the opening they span, but when seen father back are, Venturi notes, 'expressively right in size and scale' (1966: 25).

12 Another means of achieving visual interruption that Jacobs describes is to have a diversity of buildings in both function and form, and older buildings remaining alongside the new (1961: 507). The juxtaposition of old and new buildings, Venturi notes, elicits a multiplicity of meanings (1966: 38); and, as we have seen, the rugged, crumbling surfaces of buildings ravaged by time elicit an uncanny response within us—conveying a threat to the containment we seek in them for ourselves—heightened, perhaps, when perceived alongside new buildings in pristine condition (as we find in Freud's account of his visit to the Acropolis).

13 Displacement is similar in function to the architectural device of inflection. Venturi writes: 'Inflection in architecture is the way in which the whole is implied by exploiting the nature of the individual parts, rather than their position or number. By inflecting toward something outside themselves, the parts contain their own linkage' (1966: 88).

14 Continuing the architectural analogy, Bollas notes: 'The course of associations sets up psychic patterns of interest, which, once established, constitute the architectural structure of the unconscious' (2009: 40). As he notes elsewhere:

> Some of the lines come together for a while and create nodal points, and because of their increased psychic weight may come into consciousness, but all along, of course, there are thousands and thousands of other lines of thought in this ramifying factor that continues separately.
>
> (Bollas 2007: 17)

15 The methods of displacement and condensation are often regarded as methods employed by the unconscious to distort the real meaning of its material, so that its activities can avoid detection by the ego and it can be allowed to continue its work. Thus Freud maintains that dreams are distorted to pass the censor of the ego, and allow the sleeper to continue dreaming. If the ego scrutinises the work of the unconscious prematurely, it may jeopardise the work of the unconscious. The

unconscious should be allowed freely to determine when it is ready to convey its material to ego-consciousness.

16 For an example of the dream-work within the practice of an architect, see Buchanan (2012). Buchanan briefly, and perhaps unwittingly, describes the creative, unconscious methods of the dream-work, notably the manner in which the unconscious gathers clusters of experience and uses material things—in this case, the building materials and design plans of architectural practice—to generate the momentum it requires to evoke and elaborate a heightened sense of self. Echoing the methods of condensation and displacement, Buchanan asserts that 'Architecture helps us to create ourselves, by compartmentalising experiences and setting these in calculated relationship to each other (so intensifying and adding meaning to them)' (2012: 12). Echoing the unconscious use of objects to express its latent meanings, Buchanan suggests that we have a 'compulsion to create buildings and cities of increasing complexity' and 'differentiation' in order to 'accommodate and communicate their contents' as well as 'explore and progressively elaborate' the complexity of ourselves. Finally, in parallel to the unconscious creative process, from incubation stage to illumination, he writes:

> We have progressively sliced up and compartmentalised (in distinct rooms, for instance) what would otherwise be the continuities of experience so that we can focus on and intensify each isolated experience [...] We also deploy those compartmentalised experiences in ordered relationships in space to further intensify and give additional meaning to these experiences [...] This compartmentalisation, differentiation and intensification are [*sic*] essential to how we have elaborated our many cultures – and equally to how we have created ourselves as complex acculturated persons. By separating out and dispersing our experiences spatially we also project and map our psyches in space so that we may then explore and progressively elaborate them. Thus one of the very most fundamental purposes of architecture, one underestimated by most architects, is as a means by which we create ourselves.
>
> (Buchanan 2012: 5)

17 Lynch here echoes remarks of architect Robert Venturi, who thirty years earlier asserted: 'A valid architecture evokes many levels of meanings and combinations of focus: its space and its elements become readable and workable in several ways at once' (1966: 16).

18 More often than not this anecdote is used to explore Freud's own unconscious wishes and desires, and also how these are evoked in his (transferential) relationship with Rolland (to whom he reported the case). See, for instance, Slochower (1970, 1971); Werman (1977); Masson and Masson (1978); Blum (1995); Bouchard (1995); Guillaumin (1995); Sugarman (1998).

19 Sonnenberg cites two others: Flannery (1980), who suggests that Freud unconsciously identified himself with the carved figures in the frieze on the Parthenon, which he would have seen, and also with those absent figures that had been removed and resituated in the British Museum; and Harrison (1966), who emphasised the fact that buildings and monuments elicit powerful reactions in their observers. To these we can add E.V. Walter (1988), who emphasised the sacred energies of the site, which 'moved' Freud 'in a way he did not understand, and that his mind had no scheme to grasp' (107).

20 Pallasmaa asserts:

> The gray stone staircase, detached from the walls of its cubic spatial container, awakens the image of a dark stream solemnly flowing down from the level of the library itself. One can almost hear the rippling of the solitary stream. This is a liquid stairway. The oddly placed consoles of the lower part of the walls and the columns, all but devoured by the walls, create an experience of the pressure of being underwater. The stream turns into an underwater stream. Michelangelo's stairhall speaks of another dimension of time; it speaks of the metaphysics of time.
>
> (2000: 14)

Chapter 6

The self that is disclosed through architecture

In the previous chapter I explained how the unconscious uses sensory impressions of architecture to gather its material and disseminate it as an evocative thought or creative insight. In this chapter I shall investigate the nature of this insight and what it can tell us about ourselves.

Crucial to the considerations in this chapter is the relationship between the aesthetic effects of architecture as we consciously experience them and the unconscious activity that underpins this experience. In Chapter 3, I explained how aesthetics and psychoanalysis, though different fields of study, are similarly concerned with the nature of symbolic experience and its surplus of meaning that eludes literal representation and comprehension, but nevertheless conveys through its psychosomatic effects important cultural and personal values. There I proceeded to examine how the sensuous impressions imparted to us by the built environment are subsequently incorporated within us through our unconscious identifications with them. Underpinning my argument is the inextricable link between aesthetic experience and unconscious affect. However, there continues to be, especially among Freudian scholars, a desire to maintain a conceptual distance between the two, by downplaying the value of aesthetic experience and the aesthetic object—and not simply 'artworks' or objects of 'beauty', but sensori-emotional objects more generally—as a means to achieving the depth of unconscious insight that I wish to ascribe to architecture. This position is symptomatic of the wider problem I alluded to in psychoanalytic studies: their tendency to undervalue the non-human environment in general. It is also perhaps an unfortunate repercussion of Freud's decision not to develop his ideas of the bodily ego into a more distinctive theory.[1] The downplaying of aesthetic experience is an approach that pertains to a limited and incomplete conception of the unconscious, as one exclusively concerned with the 'inner world' of repressed experience and intrapsychic relationships, and not, as I have proposed, one that also receives impressions from 'outside'. As Bollas likewise asserts, Freud's unconscious is in fact as much an organ of reception as it is of repression, and its aims are characteristically 'aesthetic' (1992). A more realistic account of the unconscious is one in which the unconscious responds to the sensory perceptions that impinge on us, and regards it as permeated by the aesthetic experiences we receive from the 'outside' as much as by our memories and other forgotten and repressed material. In this respect a person's inner and outer worlds are inextricably enmeshed.

Given that the disciplines of aesthetics and psychoanalysis are, as Maclagan puts it, embroiled in the same task of having 'to deal with' effects 'that are subliminal [...] and that are often almost beyond the reach of language' (2001: 40), any attempt to separate them will run into conceptual difficulties, and lead to conclusions that are complex and ambiguous. The difference between an aesthetic experience and an encounter with the unconscious is an unhelpful distinction for our investigation. Rather than examine them as different kinds of experience, it will be more profitable for our investigation to regard evocative experiences as a spectrum of unconscious affects and their accompanying feelings. These feelings will vary in kind and intensity according to the nature of the unconscious material that is disclosed in the experience, and the conscious disposition of the person who experiences it. Thus, when Jung asserts that the cities of London, Paris, Rome, and Pompeii 'can be enjoyed aesthetically', and that it is 'another matter entirely' when they affect you 'to the depths of your being' (1961b: 319), I suggest that he does not mean to insinuate that aesthetic experiences cannot also affect you profoundly, but rather that the particular feelings of 'enjoyment' probably indicate that the unconscious has not been stirred so deeply on that occasion. The same can be said of a similar comment made by geographer Yi-Fu Tuan, who in his consideration of the different affective ties one has with the built environment concludes that they 'differ greatly in intensity, subtlety, and mode expression', and include the 'fleeting' and often intense 'pleasures' of 'aesthetics', and, by contrast, the 'more permanent' and often indescribable existential feeling towards places in which we have personal investment, and which establish places as loci of 'memories' (1974: 93).

Rather than dismiss or downplay aesthetics or the 'aesthetic object' as an irrelevance in its capacity to affect us 'to the depths' of our being, I shall consider how the various effects and feelings that we experience in relation to architecture inform us about the extent of our unconscious involvement with its particular design features, and allow us also to speculate on which phase or aspect of the architectural event we are currently engaged with, and furthermore, on the nature of the insight that is evoked in the culmination of the event. In other words, I shall suggest that the aesthetic experience of a building and the sensations and feelings it evokes are largely dependent on whether the unconscious is in the process of utilising the subject's impressions of the building in order to gather material for its dream-work (and is thus occupied in the incubation of ideas) or is using them to disclose its work in the form of a creative thought (illumination). The feelings aroused by architecture can also indicate, I suggest, different levels of intensity of unconscious activity, depending on the nature of the material it seeks to disclose—whether it be a particularly poignant memory, for instance, or something comparatively trivial. Certainly, as we shall see, the sensations of 'enjoyment' and 'pleasure' alluded to by Jung and Tuan—sensations that are often associated with 'beautiful' and 'harmonious' architectural designs—would appear to arouse the unconscious less intensely and capture our unconscious imaginative attention less noticeably than feelings of discomfort and uncertainty aroused by the distorted, confusing, and even ugly features of other types of architecture.

What exactly it is that we notice in our imaginative perceptions of architecture and subsequently incorporate into our experience of ourselves will depend on the nature and dynamics of the unconscious mind that interacts with it. As I have established from the outset with the surveys of the metaphorical buildings of psyche in Chapter 2, psychoanalytic theories postulate different capacities and limitations of the unconscious mind, some postulating a greater repository of materials than others. Thus, rather than attempting to ascertain whether the symbolic experiences of psychoanalysis lead to 'deeper' or more permanent transformations than those conveyed by aesthetic affects, we will gain more by examining the essential differences between contrasting psychoanalytic theories on the nature of unconscious insight and its impact on us. This will help us to understand the kinds of things we can expect to discover about ourselves in the architectural event.

The models of Freud and Jung are two of the most prominent and influential in the psychoanalytic field, and their contrasting conceptions of the unconscious have important ramifications for our understanding of imaginative perception and the kinds of insights that can be disclosed by the architectural event. I shall examine some of the more salient differences as they pertain to the three phases of the architectural event, paying particular attention to the different sensations and feelings that are elicited in each case. I suggest that the key similarities and differences between an evocative experience of the Freudian unconscious and that of the Jungian unconscious can be illustrated by the overlaps and distinctions between the categories of experience traditionally known within philosophical discourses of aesthetics and religion as the uncanny, the sublime, and the numinous. The kinds of evocative experience recognised by Freud and Jung demonstrate striking parallels with these three categories; and, given that each of these three categories of experience has historical associations with architecture and the feelings and sensations architecture purportedly gives rise to, they provide a useful framework with which to examine the feelings and sensations of the architectural event as it unfolds and impacts upon a person's conscious awareness from both Freudian and Jungian perspectives.

Exposing the parallels between these categories of experience and the unconscious activity that underpins the architectural event will also help us to evaluate the extent to which those architectural designs that have traditionally been assigned the labels 'uncanny', 'sublime', or 'numinous' are worthy of their designation from a psychodynamic perspective, and whether these buildings can therefore be said to arouse the unconscious more powerfully or more likely to capture our unconscious attention than those designs that are deemed mundane by comparison. My discussion will go on to consider and reassess those banal and nondescript buildings that go unnoticed and thereby fail to captivate us, but contribute instead to an alienating, sterile, and anaesthetic environment.

By interpreting the psychodynamic models of Freud and Jung in terms traditionally employed in aesthetic discourse, and by the same token, giving these terms a psychodynamic grounding, it is hoped that our investigation will continue to go some way towards closing the alleged conceptual gap between psychoanalysis and aesthetic discourse.

Different models of the unconscious lead to different architectural insights

In Chapter 3, I mentioned that there is no definitive theory of symbolism to unite aesthetics and psychoanalysis or its related psychological theories. Jung openly criticised Freud's understanding of symbolism as limited and short-sighted; indeed, he didn't even think that Freud actually had a theory about symbols, but one about *signs*. According to Jung, Freud's 'symbol' fails to extend beyond the confines of the individual subject and the repository of their experiences, past and present. Symbolic experience in Freud's model is grounded within an unconscious environment that is regarded by Jung as severely limited. The Freudian unconscious is restricted to this personal repository of experiences (including, as I am keen to assert, the impressions a person receives from 'outside'), from out of which it gathers and constructs its evocative material. The insights that it proceeds to evoke therefore comprise material that the subject had experienced in one shape or another prior to its eviction from conscious awareness. According to Freud, then, it is the return of the repressed that surprises and transforms. Jung's criticism of the Freudian 'symbol' is demonstrated in his desire to redesign and extend the Freudian architectural blueprint of psyche. Freud's blueprint is for Jung an inadequate design with too few storeys, and too restricted a space within which to explore and discover the subject's potential. Jung's disagreement with the Freudian blueprint is also illustrated in the dream-image of the oppressive ghetto building with its low and narrow ceilings—an image that Jung dreamt while staying with Freud in Vienna, and that Jung himself associated with his dislike of Freud's approach to the psyche. In other words, from Jung's point of view, Freud's model of the unconscious heavily compromises the subject's creative potential, preventing the realisation of important psychological truths that pertain to the wider personality and identity of a person. If the Jungian subject were to explore Freud's house of psyche, they

would quickly find their movements restricted and frustrated, with no
granted to darkest depths of experience due to the lack of basement-
facilities and the absent cave of 'primitive man'. According to Jung, Fr
house is missing this all-important foundation-storey of the psyche—the collective unconscious—and the freedom granted by its more expansive space. 'How in hell can people live in such a place?', Jung exclaims in reference to his Freudian dream-ghetto (cited in Bennet 1985: 65). Without this crucial extension to the house of psyche, Freud's model prevents the more penetrating evocative experience and kind of insights that Jung claims as truly symbolic.

For Freud, then, a symbolic insight is an unmasking of a repressed conflict or wish, and the revelation of past experiences that hadn't been resolved or successfully worked through by ego-consciousness. This is illustrated in Freud's account of his experience at the Acropolis, where, as we interpreted it, the impressions of the built environment triggered within him the memory of a repressed conflict (the guilt he felt at having surpassed his father). His symbolic insight here comprised a personal memory intertwined with his perceptions of the architectural site, and the various personal associations that combined them together. The Freudian symbol is a symptom of a failure to negotiate a situation appropriately, and its felt effects point to there being an opportunity for the subject to renegotiate the unresolved experience and its underlying conflict. For Jung, on the other hand, the symbolic insight is progressive rather than regressive, and leads to an experience not simply of our *personal*, repressed past, but to human possibilities that are available to every one of us.

In Chapter 3, I explained how architecture is an *event of being* that encourages the perceiver of a building to participate in its material features, so as to impart to the perceiver a more vivid awareness and appreciation both of themselves and of the building with which they identify. I can now begin to explain what kind of information is disclosed in the event. Thus, if I were to perceive the built environment through a Freudian lens, the symbolic register of experience would lead me to discover a missing part of myself. For Freud the *event* in question is the awakening of a repressed memory; and if we are to speak of it as disclosing an existential truth, the Freudian building leads me to realise that I am more than I took myself to be, and enables me to recall who I was. From a Jungian perspective, by contrast, the architectural event awakens greater possibilities for me, and leads me to a more objective conception of myself than the totality of my past experiences. Perceived through a Jungian lens, the built environment is experienced imaginatively as the revelation of a priori 'archetypal' truths that resonate with each and every one of us. The existential truth that is disclosed by the Jungian building is also a realisation that I am more than I took myself to be, but on the basis that the building enables me to appreciate who I could become from the myriad of human possibilities available to me.

The respective models of Freud and Jung suggest that the unconscious can be oriented differently to establish different experiences of the self, and that it subsequently utilises the features of the built environment to construct and elaborate different aspects of a person's identity—emphasising their individual, unique, and personal history, or their wider, more objective and cultural human concerns. Let us now examine these differences as they play out in the phases of the architectural event, paying particular attention to the sensations and feelings they are likely to impress upon the conscious mind of the subject. We start with the incubatory phase of the architectural event, when the unconscious gathers its material and the subject experiences a corresponding disruption of their focused attention and concentration, with accompanying feelings of confusion that go by the name of the *uncanny*.

The uncanny: the unconscious as it gathers and unfolds its surprise

I have alluded to the uncanny several times already in the course of this investigation, principally in the context of the subject's illusory merger with the building and the feelings it gives rise to: that 'uncanny fusion', as Bollas describes it (1987: 40), and that 'most *unheimlich*', 'shadowy world' populated by 'weird doubles', according to Borch-Jacobsen (1991: 59). I suggest that an experience of the uncanny is an indication that the unconscious is busily attending to its creative work and preparing the way for its fuller disclosure into consciousness. The uncanny therefore denotes that we are distracted and preoccupied with unconscious concerns. In other words, uncanny feelings accompany the stage of incubation, when we sense the presence of something or anticipate that something is about to happen but we cannot cognitively comprehend what that something is.

Freud popularised the term 'uncanny' in his essay 'The Uncanny' [*Das Unheimliche*] (1919) by describing it as a feeling of something *strangely familiar*. The term *unheimlich* is often defined as 'unhomely', and is commonly associated with architecture that has an air of unreality about it, that makes us feel out of sorts or out of place—the haunted house often being highlighted as the most recognisable of uncanny themes.[2] In his analysis of the uncanny, Freud defines it as the 'unconcealed', 'unhidden', and 'un-secret', and he cites the words of philosopher Friedrich Wilhelm Shelling to describe it as an experience of that which '*ought to have remained...secret and hidden but has come to light*' (1919: 224; emphasis and ellipses are Freud's). The uncanny, Freud proceeds to explain, is a person's encounter with unconscious contents (various experiences, feelings, memories, desires, or ideas) that they had at one time managed to disown, but which have since reappeared, causing unexpected and often unpleasant surprise. The uncanny is, to cite a dictum of Freud's, the 'return of the repressed'.

The Freudian uncanny is a curious combination of double natures: of the familiar made strange accompanied by feelings of repulsion and attraction. It presents itself as an intriguing mystery with fragments of experience that had been forgotten but are now recalled to mind with little indication of what exactly they are memories of. They are experiences we thought we had discarded or outgrown, but which return to us as if new and original. The uncanny intrigues, but it also threatens to disrupt our habitual way of life by returning those aspects of ourselves that we sought to keep away. The return of the repressed thereby threatens to rupture and violate the ego's carefully maintained conscious identity, forcing it to confront its unwanted past, and to realise that it is no longer in control of itself or its environment—or, as Freud states elsewhere, no longer '*master in its own house*' (1917b: 143, emphasis in original). The uncanny return of the repressed can be likened to an intruder in the ego's home, or in more intense and potentially pathological cases, an intruder that threatens to evict the ego from its home, making it altogether homeless. In such cases, the non-rational unconscious mind takes control of the personality and eclipses the familiar ego-personality.

The uncanny can be frightening as it threatens to challenge our rational preconceptions and expectations, and rudely remind us that we are not in total control of our lives, and that life is not altogether as certain as we made ourselves believe. But the uncanny is potentially enriching, too, as those hidden, neglected, and repressed aspects of ourselves that it harbours can enlarge our attitudes and approach to life, and can even overcome unhelpful prejudices that we may otherwise embrace. In our everyday experiences, we inevitably prioritise all that is familiar, 'normal', comfortable, and stable, but an uncanny experience provides us with a wake-up call to other possibilities that are not immediately obvious to us; it enables us to traverse the boundaries of all that is conventional and all-too-familiar to arrive at perspectives that are otherwise hidden and unorthodox. In terms of the creative process, the uncanny marks the occasion when we switch gear from our 'ordinary' or literal perception of our environments, in order to suspend our focused attention and rational judgement and to enlist an imaginative perception—one that enables us to notice the ordinary and familiar in unordinary and unfamiliar ways. It is an orientation that encourages us to experience ourselves not as separate individuals going about our own business, but as participants within a unique and characterful environment.

Important to the present investigation is the notion of the 'double' that underpins the uncanny. As Freud maintains, uncanny feelings tend to accompany the fundamental experience of the 'doubling, dividing and interchanging of the self' (1919: 234). Uncanny feelings are therefore useful indicators of our unconscious identifications with architecture, and markers for the moments of our psychological merger with it. It denotes the incorporation of architectural features into ourselves, which establishes the building as our existential 'double'. In this respect, the architectural event is inevitably an uncanny experience, for it is a creative act of doubling, self-division, and interchanging of self. The architectural event elicits uncanny feelings as it disturbs the familiar sense of self, leading one to feel both present and absent, or 'de-realised' as Freud says of his experience at the Acropolis. But, as well as disturbing, the uncanny allures and compels us into a state of mind where our rational, thoughtful self is temporarily suspended, and our unconscious is allowed to use the material fabric of our environment to think for us. We are still present in the experience, but as 'simple beings', as Bollas notes. We thereby sense that interactions are taking place between us and our environment, or we may intuit that something is happening or about to happen, but we are not cognitively aware of what exactly. Psychoanalyst Adam Phillips aptly notes that the relationship between the uncanny and buildings is to do with containment, the 'house or mind' acting as a 'container' for 'disturbing, ghostly, hidden presences' (Phillips 2013).

Disclosing unconscious material: sublime and numinous surprises

If the uncanny describes the strangely familiar presence that is evoked during the period of incubation—when the unconscious begins its creative activity of gathering material into its network of associated ideas, and the agendas of the conscious mind are put on hold—I suggest that the notions of the sublime and the numinous can be employed to help us describe the experience of the architectural event at its culmination, when the unconscious disseminates and discloses its work to the conscious mind in the form of the creative idea or insight.

The sublime and the numinous have a long history of being confused with each other and used interchangeably to denote a profound and deeply evocative experience. The first documented use of the term 'numinous' in English was in 1647, when it was used to convey the power of divine presence. At this time 'sublime' was already in use as a term associated with spiritual and metaphysical qualities. However, in the following two centuries, the numinous and the sublime parted ways, the latter taking on secular connotations and being used predominantly in aesthetic and philosophical discourses to refer to awesome experiences; it was popularised by such figures as Edmund Burke (1757) and Immanuel Kant (1764, 1790). In 1917 the religious connotations of the numinous were emphasised by Rudolf Otto, who sought to redefine religion and set it apart from the prevailing Kantian perspective of the time, which had reduced religion to abstract ideals of reason and morality. The numinous, through Otto's popularisation of it, came to denote the terrifying yet fascinating non-rational experiences of God (and the 'daemonic') (1917).

Jung sought to couch his psychology within a framework of the numinous, and often alludes to Otto's religious understanding of the term in his own characterisation of the collective unconscious and its emotional, affective experience. The numinous, Jung says, is 'an experience of the subject independent of his will' that 'causes a peculiar alteration of consciousness' (1938: par. 6); it has a 'thrilling power' (1945: par. 393) and 'deeply stirring emotional effect' (1952b: par. 454); it is 'inexpressible, mysterious, terrifying' (1961b: 416); capable of 'transformations', 'conversions, illuminations, emotional shocks' and 'blows of fate' (1942: par. 274). Although Freud does not associate his notion of the unconscious with the sublime, the essential differences between Otto's notion of the numinous, with its religious connotations of infinite otherness and limitless expanse, and the Kantian sublime with its celebration of the cognitive powers of the human mind—can help us map out some of the salient differences between the kinds of insights that are disclosed in the architectural event when considered from contrasting Freudian and Jungian perspectives.

While both thinkers, I maintain, would concede that the architectural event is a distinctly uncanny occasion, Freud and Jung disagree on the nature of the unconscious insight that it discloses. This is because they understand the unconscious differently from each other, and consequently also have contrasting ideas about the dynamic relationship between the unconscious and the cognitive ego, and the nature of the symbolic experience that this interactivity gives rise to. For Freud and Jung, the symbolic experience can elicit similar feelings and emotions, but these arise in the ego's response to unconscious impulses that are differently oriented and motivated in either case.

An evocative experience from a Freudian perspective is intended to be surmounted and appropriated by the ego, and its material integrated into consciousness. The material disclosed in the architectural event is therefore knowable, was once known, and can to some extent be deciphered and translated back into cognitive terms, so long as there is a mediator that can provide appropriate translation and turn the incomprehensible, troublesome material into more manageable and containing terms. The therapist provides that role in conventional psychoanalytic settings; but, as I have argued, the built environment can also provide this service. Importantly, the translation, as I have stressed, cannot be a definitive or correct interpretation, but a representation that renders the unconscious material useful and personally meaningful. Once an appropriate interpretation has been made, the unconscious material is deemed in Freudian terms to have been successfully integrated into the cognitive ego, whereupon the experience loses its evocative effect.

Because the unconscious for Freud is bound to the subject's personal past, the insight that is achieved in the architectural event originates in the subject and is activated in their identification with the building and subsequent response to it. The insight is experienced when the subject is able to appropriate and overcome the incomprehensible and seemingly infinite object. Jung, by contrast, emphasises the ambiguous nature of the interaction between the subject and the evocative object, and suggests that the insights arise within their relationship, which is never fully overcome. The unconscious for Jung extends beyond the subject's personal past and is open to a collective realm of a priori impulses and archetypal patterns of experience. In this respect, the subject is more limited in their powers to appropriate and comprehend the insight, for the material of its composition has not been exposed to them prior to the architectural event. In this regard, it is 'new' and remains wholly other. Unconscious material for Jung is too expansive for the individual to reduce to personal terms, because the insight according to Jung does not originate in the subject's own powers to overcome the evocative object, but is gifted to them from the 'object' itself. Let us clarify these positions, by turning first to the notion of the sublime.

Sublime insights

This investigation will draw on the popular idea of the sublime drawn from the philosophy of Immanuel Kant (1790), whose ideas about perception and understanding were discussed earlier in relation to Scruton's explanation of imaginative perception. Kant describes the sublime as both a frustration and an elation that enlarges the mind. According to Kant, the sublime comprises two stages. The first is a distinctly negative experience—known as the 'negative sublime'—in which the subject encounters something astonishingly vast, difficult, or obscure. In response they feel powerless to make sense of it, since it appears to their imagination and perception as something that cannot be represented or fully comprehended. This feeling of powerlessness before something vastly greater than themselves can induce additional negative emotional responses—such as, Kant says, anxiety, terror, and pain (1790: §27).

In terms of the psychodynamic account of the architectural event that I am offering, the negative sublime describes the occasion when the cognitive ego is confronted with the enormity of the incomprehensible and unbounded architectural object, which cannot be comprehended by literal perception alone. In response to this frustrating powerlessness, the incubation period is triggered, wherein the mind switches gear so as to think differently and accommodate or contain the confusing spectacle. Here the directed, linear thinking of the conscious mind is suspended to allow the more creative, non-directed workings of the unconscious to take charge—in such a way as to be able to grasp and utilise the superabundance of meanings embodied by the architecture. Kant likewise asserts that, just as we are forced to acknowledge our limitations and our failure to gather the vast, difficult, or obscure experience into a coherent and unified conception, so we discover 'within us a power of resistance of quite another kind, which gives us courage to be able to measure ourselves against the seeming omnipotence' (1790: §28:5:261). It is on this occasion, when we discover our capacity to approach the situation through a different power, that the second stage of the sublime is triggered, the 'positive aspect', as Kant refers to it, when the mind releases its 'stronger outflow of vital powers' (1790: §23:245). At this point the mind is able to contain the frustration instigated by the perception of the vast object by formulating a conceivable idea of it—that is to say, a conception of 'totality or infinitude' (1790: §27:258).

The key point here is that, common to the movement of the Kantian sublime and to the psychodynamics that underpin the architectural event is the occasion when the subject experiences a shift in their cognitive perception (of the building) and moves from a position of powerlessness or bewilderment to one of enlightenment and vital insight. Kant describes this discovered capacity to engage and appropriate the experience of vastness as an overwhelming experience of elation, with a corresponding 'enlargement of mind' (1790: §26:255).

The sublime for Kant is a subjective category that is instigated by the mind of the subject. '"Sublimity"', Kant writes, 'does not reside in any of the things' we perceive—and not then within the material forms of our built environments—but 'only in our mind'. Everything that 'provokes this feeling in us' is 'improperly called sublime' (1790: §28:264). The sublime is, for Kant, the experience of the power of reason that overcomes and surpasses the human capacity of imagination or sensibility. When imagination is confronted with an object that is too vast in its magnitude or too dynamic for us to comprehend, the rational capacity of the mind is triggered, as if coming to the rescue, to contain and appropriate the nonsensical evocative object. We can understand this positive moment of the sublime in Freudian terms as the ego's capacity to appropriate and integrate the formerly unfathomable meaning of the evocative object into its own terms. Thus, the experience, daunting and *uncanny* at first as the subject encounters the incomprehensible object, turns to elation once they (or their ego-personality) are able to rationalise the experience and feel enriched by it. The sublime designates the triumph of ego as it overcomes the perceived threat of the return of the repressed, and marks the transformation of the unthinkable into thought. It therefore also marks the dissolution of the uncanny, for the hitherto hidden and 'unconcealed' work of the unconscious has been disclosed and integrated into the ego-personality as a creative idea or useful insight.

It is an error, Kant maintains, to regard a building, or any other object, as sublime (even though its initial evocative power may deceive us into perceiving it as such). But from a Freudian perspective, this error amounts to a very useful and creative illusion. To attribute qualities to the building that actually belong to the self is an act of projection that allows us temporarily to discard unwanted aspects of ourselves, putting them into some place other. As I explained, this activity psychologically 'intensifies' or 'animates' the building, charging it with an evocative power that compels the subject, making it appear both alluring and potentially threatening. But by externalising their unwanted characteristics within the contained space of the built environment, the subject creates the opportunity to engage them anew, and renegotiate their relationship with them. By using the built environment in this way, the subject is able to depersonalise—to cite Redfearn's use of the term—the contents of their troubling repressed material, and strip it of its more traumatic, emotional content. In exchange, the architectural object gives back the projected material in a transformed state, one that is more contained, manageable, and thinkable. The reception of this material and the subsequent withdrawal of the subject's projections into the building marks the occasion for the sublime experience. The sublime building read in this light is therefore the building that embodies the compelling illusions that we unconsciously impart to it, and is the building that we utilise as a therapeutic resource for negotiating personal conflict. In this respect, the Acropolis is a prime example for Freud personally of a sublime building or group of buildings.

Numinous insights

If the 'positive aspect' of the sublime marks the successful comprehension of unconscious material and its subsequent integration into the conscious mind, the numinous by contrast continues in the vein of the initial 'negative' stage of the sublime, insofar as it underscores the sheer magnitude and obscurity of the evocative object, rendering its superabundance of meaning absolute, thereby preserving the uncanny experience that accompanies it. Whilst the Kantian sublime marks the occasion when we recoil or withdraw back into ourselves in order to find within us the resources to comprehend the elusive object and subsequently rationalise and appropriate its meaning, the numinous sustains the moment of ego-powerlessness in the expansive, infinite experience, so that our perception of the evocative object continues to exceed our capacity to understand it. While the positive sublime emphasises the triumph of ego, the numinous underscores the limitations of ego and calls its powers of reason into question. I suggest that these different emphases exemplify the contrasting approaches of Freud and Jung to the unconscious and to the nature of symbolic insight.

Otto describes the powerlessness we experience before the numinous 'object' as 'creature consciousness' (1917: 8–11, 18–23), wherein, he explains, we find ourselves 'utterly cowed and cast down', rendering us mute and dumb (1917: 31); and also as 'awe' that overwhelms us (1917: 15–16). Otto compares the Kantian sublime with the numinous and asserts that both evoke feelings of elation and an 'impulse' of fascination that causes us to try to appropriate their perceived source (1917: 31). But the numinous 'object' cannot be comprehended fully and reduced to rational terms; strictly speaking, we cannot regard it even as an *object* with which we find ourselves in relationship, for to do so would be to presume that we know something about it and can therefore measure ourselves against it. The numinous presence continues to call the ego into question, never allowing it to rest.

In Freud's model, the building becomes evocative and uncanny as a result of the subject's having projected their unconscious material onto or into it; but in a Jungian scenario, when the collective unconscious is concerned, all is received; nothing is returned. In this respect, 'projection', as Jung puts it, 'hardly conveys the real meaning of this phenomenon. Projection is really an act that happens, and not a condition existing a priori, which is what we are really dealing with here' (1921: par. 495). Jung prefers the term *participation mystique*, which he takes from anthropologist Lucien Lévy-Bruhl, to convey the a priori merger and interaction between subject and object, wherein the object 'obtains a sort of magical—i.e. absolute—influence over the subject' (1921: par. 781). It has 'such a powerful effect that the subject is forced into introversion' (1921: 495). Otto asserts that we are nevertheless able to ground our experience of this Otherness in symbolic terms, by employing analogies that allow us to render its experience meaningful and purposeful. Symbolic experience here is not created or consciously fashioned in our own image (or from our past experiences), but is, Jung asserts, *discovered* outside us (1942: par. 400). As Jung asserts, 'I cannot "conquer'" a numinous experience, 'I can only open myself to it, let myself be overpowered by it, trusting in its meaning' (1959: 864). I must give myself up to it in 'will-less surrender' (1947: 383). For Jung, the evocative experience of the unconscious continues so long as we allow ourselves to remain open to its experience.

Within the context of the architectural event, the perceiver of a building that is deemed 'sublime' will report feelings and experiences similar to those of the perceiver of a 'numinous' building, but the nature of unconscious insight each achieves will be different. Both will experience the same kind of uncanny feelings upon their initial identification with the building. These feelings may go largely undetected, or, as Otto says of the uncanny, appear as if a 'mere fleeting shadow passing across his mood' (1917: 16). But these uncanny feelings denote for our two perceivers the conscious effects of two differently oriented unconscious minds at work, making preparations for the disclosure of different facets of the personality. On the one hand, the sublime building, in our Freudian reading of it, interacts with unconscious material of the subject's past. The meaning of this material can be appropriated and interpreted in the subject's own terms, and the feelings that accompany the encounter may be anxious and overwhelming at first, before turning to elation. The numinous building, on the other hand, interacts with unconscious material of an a priori nature, the meaning of which is gifted to the subject in terms that open them to a more objective perspective. The encounter, as Jung describes an experience of the collective unconscious, is 'often accompanied by peculiar symptoms', such as physical sensations of being too large for one's skin, or too small, of feeling that one is 'in a strange place' or 'a stranger' to oneself, as well as hypnagogic feelings of endless sinking or rising, confusion, disorientation, and dizziness (Jung 1928a: par. 250).

But what of actual architectural designs that purport to be uncanny, sublime, or numinous? What differences can we point to in their respective designs?

Uncanny, sublime, or numinous architecture? How to tell the difference

Given the phenomenological similarity between the uncanny, the sublime, and the numinous, it is difficult to pinpoint when architectural designs evoke one rather than another of these experiences. Their confusing overlap is demonstrated somewhat ironically in Otto's own attempts to explain the *sui generis* nature of the numinous in the context of Gothic architecture, which for him is the 'most numinous' of the arts (1917: 67). However, he also asserts that Gothic architecture owes its peculiar impressiveness to its 'sublimity' and sense of 'magic' (1917: 67). To compound the confusion, 'magic' for Otto is none other than the 'shudder of the uncanny' (1917: 117–19).[3]

Despite his conflation of these experiences, Otto suggests that we can distinguish between them simply by looking at an illustration provided by art historian Wilhelm Worringer—a contemporary of Otto's—in his book *Form Problems of the Gothic* (1911) (Fig. 6.1). The illustration in question is an image of the Gothic tower of the Minster at Ulm in Germany. Without

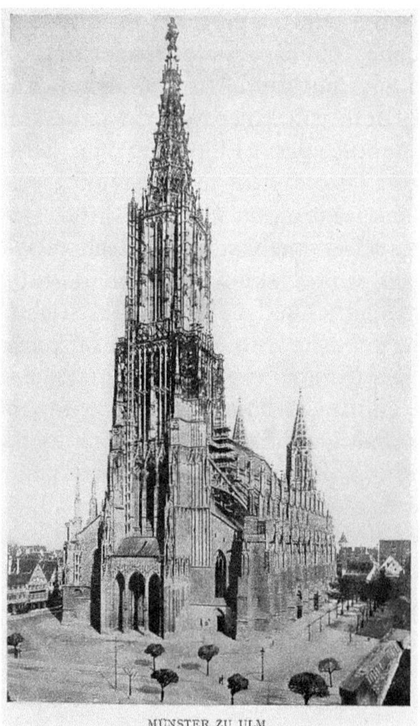

Figure 6.1 Ulm Minster, Germany (plate from Worringer's *Form Problems of the Gothic*, 1911) © Creative Commons

further explanation, Otto claims that it reveals a tower that is 'emphatically not' uncanny (or 'magical'), and 'more' than 'the effect of sublimity'; 'it is', he asserts distinctly, '*numinous*' (1917: 68; emphasis in original).

The lack of explanation and reliance on the visual impression of the cathedral tower (and on this particular image rather than any other) leaves us somewhat confused.

Although Freud and Jung conceive the unconscious differently, as having different orientations and concerns, our actual experience of the effects of the unconscious in either case is phenomenologically equivalent, with similar accompanying feelings. The evocative objects that are selected for use by the unconscious (to disclose its material) in either case are likewise difficult to distinguish between, with no discernible characteristics to separate evocative objects of a Jungian nature from those that are distinctly Freudian in kind. My psychodynamic interpretations of the uncanny, the numinous, and the sublime may put different emphases on the nature and dynamics of the unconscious, but none of their evocative experiences can be isolated from the others on the basis of the visual appearance of architecture considered abstractly and apart from a more substantial, embodied interaction with the building.

What, then, is it about an architectural design that makes it distinctly uncanny, numinous, or sublime? To be fair to Otto, we should not take him at his word and assume he intended that we need merely to *look* at the image of Ulm Minister provided by Worringer in order to discover how its Gothic design evokes the numinous as Otto intended. Rather, we need to visit the building and experience its full sensuous impact for ourselves. As Jung intimates, the difference in the quality of these feelings is a matter of 'trust'. The evocative nature of architecture, whether it be uncanny, sublime, or numinous, is established in the unconscious *exchange* between subject and building, and thus through the bodily interaction between the two. It requires the intimacy of a mimetic merger of forms, and not simply the abstract contemplation of its visual components.

Anaesthetic architecture: the problem of the 'American sublime', and the need for ugliness

The unconscious processes of identification that underpin the architectural event are intimately involved with the body and its full gamut of sensations. Any investigation that seeks to expose the 'uncanny', 'sublime', or 'numinous' characteristics of architecture through an investigation of its visual elements alone will arrive at unrealistic conclusions, and will adduce a skewed and limited array of architectural examples to illustrate their claims—with the numinous, for instance, assumed to reside only in buildings designed for religious purposes, such as cathedrals, mosques, and temples. Arguably, it is in part due to an emphasis on the visual image above other sensory considerations that scholars have tended to interpret the awe and power that underpin sublime and numinous experiences somewhat rigidly in terms of enormous size, lofty height, and extensive solidity and mass. Their intention is to convey the insignificance of our ordinary everyday experiences by presenting our bodily proportions as tiny and lost in the shadows of the overbearing object. By way of architectural examples, buildings that are characterised as sublime or numinous by virtue of their impressive geometric measurements and feats of engineering include the ancient pyramids of Giza and St Peter's basilica in Rome (cited by Kant), and various Gothic cathedrals with their lofty towers. Indeed, it is perhaps not incidental that Otto chose the tower of Ulm Minster to exemplify the numinous, given that this building, by virtue of its tower, is the tallest cathedral in the world.

There have been notable attempts to warn against such rigid architectural characterisations of profound evocative experience. Thus, Edmund Burke, in his influential treatise on the sublime, asserts that buildings made 'vast only by their dimensions are always the sign of a common and low imagination' (1757: 74); Ruskin likewise asserts that 'mere weight' is a 'clumsy way' of making an impression (1849: 82); and as we have noted, Freud and Breuer warn against the limitations of spatial imagery for conveying the affects and dynamics of the unconscious. However, it would seem that such warnings have gone unheeded, and are in large part counteracted by the architectural ideals that inform and shape the built environments we inhabit today. I argue that the conflation of evocative power and geometric vastness is emblematic of many of the problems we face today with architectural designs and urban planning. Part of the problem is that we have come to associate evocative architecture with those examples that are already in the public eye and are viewed as having something special about them, so that their popular reputation precedes our actual experience of them. Evocative architecture tends to be equated with buildings that enjoy iconic status, either through their historical associations, or, as is most often the case with modern architecture, thanks to the impressive feats of engineering and geometric measurement that made them possible—buildings that lay claim to being the tallest in the city, the most expensive, the grandest, the most intricate, and so on. By contrast, the majority of buildings that we encounter on a daily basis—those that line our streets and fill our neighbourhoods—have come to be regarded as ordinary, mundane, and altogether unremarkable.

Psychologist James Hillman laments our modern 'obsession for geometry' and our compulsion to build ever skyward. It is a problem rooted in our desire for what he calls the 'American sublime' (1995c: 168). Although he doesn't make the connection, we can understand this as a twisted and misappropriated version of the Kantian sublime, one rooted in a desire for an architecture of ever increasing geometric proportion and visual spectacle.

Hillman joins other scholars (such as Theodore Roszak) in declaring this desire a symptom of our modern, megalomaniac mindset. It is an architecture that is designed merely to satisfy the demands of ego-consciousness, and thereby involves the neglect or repression of our aesthetic sensibilities, which in turn inhibits the unconscious in its creative work. The result is an ego-centric architecture that appeals to the ego's values and ideals, but fails to capture our imagination. As Hillman asserts, it is an architecture designed according to naïve and superficial values, such as, 'the pretty, simple, pleasing, mindless', and 'easy' (1991: 172), the 'sweet' and 'sentimental' (1995b: 188), 'the practical, the moral, the new, and the quick' (Hillman and Ventura 1993: 129), the 'old-fashioned' (Hillman 1997: 195), and the functional, cost-effective, and efficient (Hillman 1997: 197).[4] Meeting the demands of the ego while inhibiting those of the unconscious leads not to the architectural event, but to the stultification of self or, as it is referred to in psychoanalysis, a 'false self' or 'ego inflation'.

The 'American sublime' tries to capture our attention with its impressive geometric feats, but its spectacle goes only as far as capturing the attention of ego-consciousness. The sublime building in this context may overwhelm us with its sheer monumentality but, as Hillman asserts, it will fail to surprise us. Hillman uses the example of the modern skyscraper to make the point. Skyscrapers may excite our ego-sensibilities through their magnificent heights and stature, but through their glass-clad surfaces they reflect to the perceiver exactly what they expect or want to see, without surprise. They have no secrets and disclose instead an 'empty vanity and superficiality' (1978: 21). In other words, their sheer vastness dissuades us from identifying mimetically with them, and from using their features for our own creative ends. If we were to identify with them, Hillman indicates that it would lead to a twisted and pathological bodily experience, for high-rise buildings with their 'glassy front' and 'hollow atrium interior sectioned by vertical shafts' are 'anorexic', 'skinny, tall, rigid, bareboned' and 'trimmed of fat' (1982: 104; cf. Hillman and Ventura 1993: 128).[5]

According to Hillman, architecture that is fashioned according to the ideals of the ego cannot command a healthy aesthetic response. Aesthetics involves an embodied response that often circumvents the desires of the ego. Hillman describes this in physiological terms as a 'gasp', 'startle', or 'shiver'; one that takes 'your breath away', makes 'your hair on your neck rise', gives you 'goosebumps, and brings tears to your eyes' (1995b: 188, 189, 190). If architects are to design buildings that engage us more effectively and productively, they need to ditch their ego-centric blueprints of ever impressive feats of geometry and engineering for those that impress upon us to ever greater 'depths' of being, as Hillman puts it. This is no easy task, given that our modern mindset, with its prioritisation of the visual sense and its heavy reliance on technology—as Hillman, and Jung before him, were at pains to point out—has been conditioned into repressing our aesthetic sensibilities. We tend, Hillman and Jung claim, to engage with the world from the perspective of ego-consciousness, through its measured responses, preferring that which is functional, efficient, economical, and systematised to experiences that are likely to disrupt such order. Experiences of chaos, disorder, and dysfunction are consequently resisted, denied, and repressed. A significant repercussion of this aesthetic numbing, Hillman argues, is that we are more likely to create and design objects that reflect the banal ideals that are valued. We come, therefore, to assume that the more economical or functional a thing is, the better its quality. Such repercussions have led to a profusion of neurotic and harmful architectural designs. Indeed, Hillman intimates that the majority of buildings that populate downtown areas of large cities are of this nature. They inevitably fail to incite visceral aesthetic responses in people, beyond a muted indifference.

The architect is charged, therefore, with the particularly difficult task of designing buildings that can stir us from our anaesthetic slumber and put us back in touch with our bodies, enabling us to reorient ourselves. In this respect, the architect's role is similar to that of a psychotherapist. Although Hillman, of all psychoanalytic theorists, is most accepting of aesthetics and appreciative of the importance of the aesthetic nature of our built environment for our psychological health and wellbeing, and goes so far to publish an anthology of essays called *City and Soul* (2006), his views on the matter are presented as a handful of comments, scattered through numerous books, essays, and unpublished notes, which we are forced to piece together in the absence of a sustained argument. He therefore doesn't go into detail about how the architect can go about this task; but he does leave us with one or two clues that can help us to establish some useful guidelines.

In Chapter 5, I explained that, if we are to stir the imagination, we need to distract our focused, conscious attention and put it on hold. This distraction causes us to disengage temporarily from our conscious register of experience, and engage instead with an imaginative register of experience that compels the unconscious to construct its creative patterns of thought. I noted suggestions made by Robert Venturi, Jane Jacobs, and Kevin Lynch about how we can incorporate distracting elements into architectural designs through methods analogous to the spatial distortions of Freud's 'dream-work', such as the inclusion of visual interruptions, regions of confusion, and complex and ambiguous features in otherwise conventional and familiar designs. The addition of these features distracts us and thwarts our expectations of the architectural object, causing us to hesitate and pause in response, and to approach them differently: that is, imaginatively. We noted, too, that Adrian Stokes and Gilbert Rose allude to the curving shapes of architecture and its rhythmic compositions as structural features that capture our unconscious attention by mimicking the movements of our unconscious processes. To these we can add Hillman's comments about the psychological value of ugliness and distortion, as I shall discuss in the next section. Together these perspectives provide us with a useful backdrop for considering the significance of distracting features for evocative architectural design.

Ugliness and distortion

When we find something disturbing, our unconscious is stirred. According to Hillman, this sets in motion our engagement with the unique features that characterise the disturbing thing (its 'soul', as he refers to it). For Hillman, ugliness, more than its aesthetic counterpart, beauty, incites a strong feeling-response within us.[6] A similar point was made centuries earlier by the practitioners of the art of memory, who regarded hideous imagery as the most evocative and memorable. According to Frances Yates, an ability to entertain the grotesque—a capacity that was often attributed to those with a 'tortured psychology' (Yates 1966: 112)—could increase one's chances of successfully recalling ideas to mind. Hillman alludes to the recognition of the ugly and twisted in similar terms, as a '*pathologized*' perception. This perception, he says, unsettles us, and dislodges the ego from its comforts, thwarting its expectations and forcing it to engage with unruly unconscious matters (1997: 203). Importantly, 'pathologizing' for Hillman is not an attempt to diagnose problematic illnesses according to established norms by means of rational deduction—which is how the term is commonly used. Rather, it describes the unconscious affects and creative impact that distorted and disturbing images have on the perceiver by drawing their attention to the particular characteristics of things. Thus, whereas an ugly building encourages us to notice its unique features, we fail to notice those of a conventional or banal building, because the latter appears to us just as we expect it to. In so doing, the ugly building bypasses our more measured responses to the environment and engages with us more deeply.

Hillman is by no means advocating the free rein of ugliness, or calling for architects to design hideous buildings! Indeed, buildings designed to emphasise ugliness (or indeed beauty) in concentrated form can lead to all sorts of problems, especially within a sterile and desensitised environment that is unprepared for its affects and doesn't know how to make good use of them. In alluding to an idea from the philosopher Plotinus, Hillman asserts that ugliness is unable to 'master the form it seeks to be', because it lacks composure and restraint (1997: 204). In other words, if ugliness is to be productive and transformative, it cannot be wholly repellent. Ugliness must usurp the ego's plans for an ordered, regulated environment; but if it is not kept in check, it will go too far and agitate the ego, causing a person to resist the ugly object, to turn away from it, and disengage with it. Ugliness becomes a problem when it is cut loose from the constraints otherwise imposed on it by the ego. In a brief unpublished note, Hillman identifies this problem as one that underpins urbanization: 'In urban sprawl, ugliness has the freedom to run riot within our desensitised streets' (cf. Hillman and Ventura 1993: 127).[7]

The 'beautiful' building is just as problematic, for sheer beauty can overwhelm us, provoking us into defensive strategies that attempt to control and restrain it. But when we exert too much control over beauty, Hillman says, it becomes segregated, and permitted 'to make its appearance only in certain scenes'. We are therefore hard-pressed to find beauty within our desensitised cities; it can be discovered only within such places as restaurants, art galleries, and museums, and within 'the privacy of homes', where it is 'closeted' off and kept out of sight (1995b: 187). Beauty rarely permeates into public, everyday scenes of 'normality', within the familiar 'streets and buildings of cities' (1995b: 187). Beauty 'hardly gets into downtown, to the lunch counter or cafeteria, the shopping mall and parking lots around them. Moreover, the retail strips, the industrial parks, commercial zones—forget it' (1995b: 187). Instead we find a built environment that is sterile and wholly uninspiring.

Our desensitised culture is unable to harness the creative opportunities of ugliness and beauty principally because we have a poor understanding of their psychological value and utility. Because beauty is conceived naïvely, Hillman says, 'it appears as merely naïve', and it 'can be tolerated only if complicated by [the] discord, shock, violence' of the ugly (1997: 195). This is an important point to bear in mind, for if we continue to design buildings according to naïve conceptions of aesthetic value and 'quality', we continue to perpetuate uninspiring and desensitised environments, which in turn continue to stultify our sense of self and general wellbeing. As Hillman suggests, this is a cycle we need to break, as we cannot continue to live this way. Something has got to give, and thankfully it invariably does—but in ways that are more often than not underappreciated and unrecognised for what they are. He writes:

> The soul that is uncared for—whether in personal or community life—turns into an angry child. It assaults the city which has depersonalized it with a depersonalized rage, a violence against the very object—storefronts, park monuments, public buildings—which stand for uniform soullessness.
>
> (Hillman 1978: 26)

These 'violent attacks' against the built environment are often cited as the central problem at hand, and not, as Hillman suggests, as attempts to overcome the more deep-seated problem, which goes unacknowledged. Such violence, he asserts, is an attempt, albeit an unconscious one, to restore aesthetic sensibility to a depersonalised environment—to its banal public buildings, uninspiring park monuments, and monotonous storefronts. Graffiti is an example of the kind of violence Hillman has in mind. Often deemed a social problem and an ugly nuisance, it is here reinterpreted by Hillman as an attempt to resolve our problematic architecture. 'Notice', he exclaims,

> what happens to our blank bank walls and office buildings, the merely functional fortresses [... with] their cost-effective, low maintenance, impersonal facelessness. They become refaced—though we say defaced—with graffiti, signatures, monograms, declarations of love, territorial markings, [and...] daring inventiveness.
>
> (Hillman 1997: 198–9)

The problem we need to concern ourselves with isn't ugly graffiti, but the sterile blank walls and buildings that call out for their 're-facement'. In this instance, the bank and office buildings cannot be tolerated without graffiti. Graffiti is a disturbance, but a creative one that seeks to restore an intimate participation in an otherwise alienating and expressionless wall. Here we find that graffiti is both a symptom of the repressed aesthetic sensibility brought about by the architectural design, and an attempt to heal it. Banal architecture is built according to rational precepts that seek to avoid shocks and surprise. But we require more than such designs allow if we are to identify with them—they engage only one half of our divided mind. Graffiti is an example of an attempt to establish a more comprehensive, and unconscious, identification with such buildings. It is a response that seeks to violate the building in order to loosen the constraints imposed on it through its orderly design, and thereby render it more evocative or, in Hillman's terms, 'soulful'.

Good architectural design, it would seem, from our reading of Hillman, requires both beauty and the shock of ugliness. Taken together, they express a notion of the 'sublime' as a beauty tinged with terror that evokes 'depths' of feeling (Hillman and Ventura 1993: 127). In contrast to Kant, whose sublime encounter with the disturbing object involves the subject recoiling back into themselves in order to summon the capacities to transform the disturbing experience into one of jubilation as the authority of the rational ego is affirmed and its powers fortified, Hillman suggests that the jubilation occurs in our celebration of the disturbing object, on the occasion we allow ourselves to be disturbed by it. In Hillman's sublime encounter, the powers of ego are suspended and bypassed to allow the 'deeper', unconscious aspects of personality to come into play. These aspects inform our creative relationship with the world—or, as Hillman puts it, with the 'soul of the world', in which we and 'all things' participate, including 'man made things of the street' (1982: 101).

I argue that we tend to become preoccupied with the superficial ideals of the 'American sublime', and we are often unable to appreciate a fuller, more embodied, and unconscious response to architecture. We therefore fail to notice the unique features of the otherwise ordinary and seemingly unremarkable built environments that we encounter on a daily basis, and reserve our attention for those few grand and iconic buildings that feature in tourist guide books.

It is my contention that all buildings have the potential to elicit the architectural event, but few are actually experienced as doing so. The problem is that the majority of buildings fail to stir our unconscious, and therefore fail to set in motion the processes that lead to the disclosure of sublime or numinous insight. In the concluding chapter I consider how we can address this problem by encouraging the architectural event and recognising its effects. A more evocative architecture is one that encourages intimacy and curiosity rather than distance and apathy, and celebrates the unique and personal character of a building and place. As Hillman puts it, we need 'a reduction in the scale of awe from a romantic and sublime immersion in vastness—the American way—to joy in pondering the particular' (1995c: 168).[8]

As the architectural 'blueprints of being' demonstrate, the architectural event involves both the subject and the building participating in each other, in an elaboration of both. If we are to understand how to encourage the event, we must consider how to do so from either side of the equation. So, in the final chapter, I shall, on the one hand, explain how we can enhance our capacity to *notice* our built environments, rather than simply *see* them, and in so doing become more susceptible to their evocative character, by recognising their unique and surprising features, even in those buildings we ordinarily perceive as lifeless and unremarkable; and, on the other hand, explore some principles that can enhance the designs and strategies of architects and town planners to help them to build more effectively for our existential needs.

Notes

1 The usefulness of Jung's ideas to theories of aesthetics is also overlooked, due in no small measure to the unfortunate but common tendency of some commentators to conflate Jungian psychology with that of Freud, without due recognition of their essential differences—particularly their contrasting conceptions of the nature and dynamics of the unconscious—a contrast which, as we shall see, has important implications for the nature of the insight that is evoked by the architectural event.

2 The most comprehensive study of various attempts to link the uncanny with architecture is Anthony Vidler's *The Architectural Uncanny* (1992), which explores, in particular, the numerous ways in which architecture and the built environment have become the favoured sites for the uncanny within literature and art since the end of the eighteenth century. He illustrates how the relationship between the uncanny and notions of architectural instability of 'house and home' is useful for reflecting more generally 'on the questions of social and individual estrangement, alienation, exile, and homelessness' (1992: ix). As I attempt to demonstrate in this chapter, so Vidler himself notes that it is through its links with architecture that the uncanny 'open[s] up problems of identity around the self, the other, the body and its absence: thence its force in interpreting the relations between the psyche and the dwelling, the body and the house, the individual and the metropolis' (1992: x).

3 Most cryptically, we find Otto on one occasion contradicting his earlier stance by stating that the relationship between the sublime and the numinous is actually much closer than a mere analogy of feeling: the sublime is rather an authentic conceptualisation of the numinous in its fully developed state (1917: 45–6, 63). Sadly, Otto does not elaborate on this curious comment beyond noting they are similar in 'structure' in that they both have in them 'something mysterious' and are both 'at once daunting, and yet again singularly attracting' (1917: 42). Yet they nevertheless will always remain, he says, absolutely different in kind (1917: 44, 24).

4 It is important to note that Hillman doesn't argue for this in a sustained or consistent manner; and his discussions of aesthetics and pathology are no less ambiguous and muddled than his remarks about the value of the built environment. However, the gist of this argument can be traced in his writings, and underpins much that he says.

5 As Robert Sardello notes, 'The eyes slide over them quickly, dazzled by their sparkle, but can find no detail, no interesting differences [...] These glass buildings are greasy to the eye, slick' (1986: 72).

6 Hillman's use of the term 'ugly' is also ambiguous. At times he refers to ugliness as a problem: for instance, when he asks: 'Why is the USA so ugly and what might be done about it?' (1995b: 189), and when he states that 'it becomes the citizen's duty [...,] above all, to work to protest actively against ugliness wherever it appears, or threatens to appear' (1995b: 193). Ugliness for Hillman is often a problem that is symptomatic of 'careless design' such as 'inane sounds, structures and spaces [...] direct glaring light [...] bad chairs [...] hum of machine noise, looking down at a worn, splotched floor cover, [being] among artificial plants [...] project housing' (1991: 176). At other times, he uses it more positively to refer to a sublime effect of the unconscious, or to feelings of distress, which are necessary reminders or wake-up calls to alert us to the kinds of problems we encountered above. In this second sense of the term, ugliness enables us to take leave of all that is ugly! Hillman writes:

> The cost of ugliness gains a further meaning. Ugliness costs us pain. We hate it, we are shocked, dismayed at so much ugliness everywhere. We find ourselves outraged, emotional life in disarray. But this pain to our senses may be the entrance fee, the cost required for attaching ourselves to the world, re-finding our love for its beauty. It costs ugliness to awaken our contemporary anesthetized consciousness.
>
> (1997: 203)

Although Hillman claims that the ugly stirs us more than the beautiful, elsewhere he takes a contrary position, noting that 'Nothing stirs the heart, quickens the soul more than a moment of beauty' (1995b: 188). Furthermore, there he equates ugliness with the very lack of having been stirred, with numbness: you must protest against ugliness; 'otherwise you remain "anesthetized"—without *aesthesis*, without the awakened aesthetic response—passive and compliant with whatever is going down' (1995b: 193).

7 The note appears in Box Number: Hillman 185A in the James Hillman Collection, Opus Archives, Santa Barbara (see Hillman 1993a).

8 However, this particular point does not sit well with a more positive comment he makes in the same essay regarding 'the experience of inspiration' that one may get 'from the towering structures of glass, steel, and aluminium' when 'walking down Fifth Avenue in New York' (1995c: 168)—a comment that clearly contrasts with his negative comments on towers that I cited earlier.

Chapter 7

Conclusion: architecture that captures the imagination

Designing and responding to evocative architecture

In this final chapter I shall examine characteristics of evocative architecture in order to explain how we can encourage the architectural event, and how buildings can be designed to maximise their evocative potential. Although we cannot consciously summon imaginative perception or force ourselves to think unconsciously, we can employ techniques and put ourselves in situations that make us more susceptible to this approach, and allow us to sustain it for longer periods of time. By the same token, although we cannot draw up plans for a definitive, one-size-fits-all evocative building that guarantees the architectural event for all who perceive it, we can deduce from the present investigation general principles for evocative architectural design and for encouraging our imaginative participation.

Making banal buildings evocative by enhancing our capacity to *notice* them

What is evocative for me may of course not be evocative for you. Likewise, the feelings induced by the architectural event on one occasion may be different on another. On some occasions the effects may be barely noticeable, and for some there may be no felt 'event' at all, as I have intimated—for instance, for those who have an impaired sense of self-containment, and those who, as Winnicott maintains, haven't had the opportunity to develop the aesthetic sensibilities required for the imaginative use of objects in later life due to a failure of nurturing containment in infancy. Others may demonstrate the opposite extreme, having developed a highly tuned aesthetic sensibility that induces them to project aspects of themselves, perhaps all too readily, into their environment—as we saw with Jung, who experienced himself to be the rock upon which he sat. A heightened aesthetic sensibility is as potentially destructive as it is creative, depending on whether it leads to a more integrated or disintegrated sense of self.[1] Then there are those who have a negative self-body-image, who may find the insights disclosed by the event distressing and unmanageable. And finally, affecting us all, are those inevitable occasions when the creative work of the unconscious is rejected, and potential insights remain undisclosed, unable to break through to conscious awareness.

Whilst Freud and theorists of object relations are keen to emphasise the infantile origins of evocative experience, other psychoanalytic theorists such as Jung and Hillman regard the pressures and influences of cultural expectations as key factors determining the extent to which we allow ourselves to be captivated unconsciously by an object. Whether we truly *notice* something and allow its evocative power influence over us is, they claim, largely dependent on whether there is a perceived immediate and measurable gain in doing so. In the previous chapter I mentioned that Jung and Hillman are just two of many scholars within a variety of disciplines who lament our technological age for having repressed our aesthetic sensibilities and our imaginative perception in favour of a more measured approach to life, one deemed more 'efficient' in its grounded values of logic, rationality, detachment, and abstraction. We have disengaged from imaginative thinking and have forgotten, they say, how to play creatively and allow our thoughts to wander, because such activity is deemed childish and irrelevant to the pressing demands and needs of adult life. The perceived problem with imaginative thinking is its inability to provide information and to provide it quickly. It doesn't get us from A to B in the most efficient way possible, but appears to dawdle aimlessly somewhere between the two. Furthermore, as we saw in relation to Hillman, the repression of our imaginative perception has led to the cultivation of a disenchanted environment—a repercussion that threatens the efficacy of the architectural event, since buildings have to work extra hard to capture our unconscious attention and activate the imagination that we have worked so hard to disarm.

If we are to consider how to encourage the architectural event, we need to find ways in which to subvert our habitual reliance on literal thinking and to distract ourselves into allowing ourselves the space and time for our unconscious musings to gather and to disseminate. We cannot summon the creative process into action, nor propel the unconscious in its search for viable architectural objects for its use.[2] What we can do, however, is employ distracting activities that can help in this regard, for these, as I explained, suspend our directed thinking and encourage our minds to wander freely and to graze on objects in the production of unconscious thought. However, the extent to which unconscious ideas are allowed to gestate without interference and interruption from our focused attentions is very much dependent on our ability to allow ourselves to remain in this dream-like state. Likewise, whether we allow these thoughts to continue once we become aware of their content, or prefer to reject them and cut them off, is largely dependent on whether we can allow ourselves to contemplate and to consider them appropriately. But in either case, the pressures of everyday life all too often get in the way. As Jung and Hillman maintain, the vast majority of us are too embroiled in our conscious agendas to allow their suspension even for a short while.[3] And when the unconscious does eventually find a way to break through, the bewildering and destabilizing experience it can induce may lead us to resist it by being even more rationally defensive.

Interestingly, Hillman adopts an approach that contrasts with our investigation, but appears to arrive at very similar conclusions. For Hillman, our aesthetic sensibilities are repressed to such an extent that our environments are largely anaesthetic and sterile. As a result, buildings are far less evocative for Hillman than they are in my account due to the way we tend to perceive them. For Hillman, buildings are simply passive objects that we almost invariably fail to notice, because we tend for the most part to perceive them literally, and appreciate them merely for their functional value and purpose. Part of the problem as he interprets it is that either buildings are designed solely with function in mind, which encourages us to perceive them in those terms, or they are built according to blueprints that we have come to expect, and consequently find unsurprising and uninspiring. Where Hillman and I firmly agree is on the value of interrupting our literal perception of buildings in order to begin to notice their unique characteristics and to allow ourselves the creative opportunities that arise when we participate more intimately in them.

Attending to the unexpected: noticing the unfamiliar within the most familiar of places

Without our literal perception of things we, of course, wouldn't be able to negotiate our environments effectively, and wouldn't get much done. But concentrating one's focus comes at a price, for it supresses the possibility for surprise and the desire for discovery. When we engage with our environments in this way, we are less likely to notice their unique features, and instead project onto them those aspects that we already expect to find in them. At its best, directed thinking trains us to scan the environment and attend to those features that respond to our immediate needs while ignoring those that don't. At its worst, it debilitates us, by supressing our aesthetic sensibilities and by limiting access to the environment's surprising features and its 'processional potential', as Bollas calls it. A consequence of this suppression is the tendency to perceive our environments as overfamiliar, tiresome, and uninspiring. As Alexandra Horowitz states in her popular book *On Looking*: 'by thinking about what you are looking for, your brain grows biased to see it: biologically, the neural processes are primed to spot objects that fit your expectation' (2013: 153). Over time we store mental representations or 'cognitive maps' of the places we have visited, and these become stored in our mind as templates or blueprints that regulate our expectations of new places that we come to encounter. Horowitz notes that

> whenever we arrive at a new scene we first compare what we see, hear, feel to various stored representations of previously constructed maps/places we've been in. if there's a match, we ignore what we see, unless something surprising, unusual, new, pops up, and we wander with confidence.
>
> (Horowitz 2013: 249)

When directed by our literal perception within our familiar environments, we are less likely to find it surprising because we are primed to notice features within it that we were expecting to find. To engage with them creatively, without directed attention, requires a different form of noticing, one that operates outside our preconceptions of what we have come to expect of our environments. It requires *notitia*.

Notitia is a Latin term, derived from *noscere* meaning 'to come to know', and it is employed by Hillman and his followers as an approach to the world from a perspective of not yet knowing, or presuming not to know, what is there. It is a useful approach for us to consider, as it is receptive to the possibility of surprise, and introduces the perceiver to a whole host of sensations and experiences made available to them in the places they visit, not simply those that are habitually expected or logically deduced. Hillman emphasises the importance of *notitia* as an attitude that calls our attention to the distinctive qualities and 'true form of things', granting perception of 'the particular shape of each event' (1982: 85, 115): which is to say, to the characteristics of our environments to which we are usually blinded by our preoccupation with their functional properties, and whether these properties can fulfil our immediate needs.

Notitia conveys an unconscious register of experience that allows us to perceive the unique characteristics of things, and this perception encourages us to establish an intimate rapport with these things. It is similar to Bollas's idea of the 'collision' between the subject and object, through which we come to experience the object's integrity, setting in motion the processional potential of that particular thing. By adopting an attitude of *notitia* we can give close attention to the tangible qualities and unique characteristics of our built environments, to their colours, textures, sounds, smells, even tastes, and become attuned to the dream-like associations that our buildings elicit.[4]

For Hillman, we *notice* an object, rather than simply *see* it (or touch, smell, or hear it), when we experience it and ourselves as participants within a wider event of being. In this respect, the object is not an object of literal perception in the subject's field of perception, but, rather, the very manner in which the subject perceives (Hillman 1982: 117). For Hillman, emotional qualities and aesthetic properties such as beauty and ugliness are within the world for us to notice. But such noticing is not a subjective response, or an occasion for us to project our personal tastes onto the world and shape it accordingly. Rather, Hillman says, the aesthetic quality is already in the world and is simply brought to light or 'intensified' in our engagement with the world. By 'noticing' or 'paying attention to the specifics of what is actually there', we enable it to 'become fully what it is' (Hillman and Ventura 1993: 52). By the same token, by noticing the distinctive characteristics of our environment, we become more aware of ourselves as participants in the event. As one commentator on Hillman puts it, by truly *noticing* something we are led into an aesthetic response that 'establishes an interior or imaginative reciprocity in which individuality unfolds as it is perceived' (Nicholsen 2002: 102).

According to Hillman, we are inspired when we perceive the uniqueness of things; and this experience is 'intensified' under specific conditions and in 'certain events', such as 'artworks'—but also, Hillman says, various 'man made things of the street', such as 'highways', when we are stuck in traffic, 'houses', 'malls and airports', 'open offices' (1982: 101, 1997: 196, 1982: 96). Thus, when a person walks along a street with an attitude of *notitia*, they become attuned to the unique characteristics of the urban scene around them. In so doing, they dissociate themselves from, or temporarily suspend, their normal perception of their environment, as if no longer aware of the functional properties and generic significance they had customarily assigned to its various buildings and other architectural features. Instead, the person notices the specific character of the built environment as if for the first time.

Popular commentator Alain de Botton, no doubt unintentionally, describes an experience of *notitia* in his account of a walk he took around Hammersmith in London:

> A row of shops which I had known as one large, undifferentiated reddish block acquired an architectural identity. There were Georgian pillars around one flower shop, and late Victorian Gothic-style gargoyles on top of the butcher's. A restaurant became filled with diners rather than shapes. [...] The neighbourhood did not just acquire people and defined buildings, it also began to collect ideas. I reflected on the new wealth that was spreading into the area.
>
> (de Botton 2002: 251–2)

Of course, *notitia* is not simply a matter of what one *sees*, or the disclosure of an object's unique character through sight alone; it involves our embodied participation in things that we perceive through the full array of senses. Moreover, as de Botton's comments show, it involves the train of associative thoughts that accompanies unconscious thinking. Thus, if it is a matter of *seeing*, it is about *seeing properly*: a point made by Hillman, who insists that it is 'critically important to see generously, or you will only get what you see' (1996: 259).

Notitia requires patience and time to allow the intimacy to develop between a person and their environment. To notice properly, we need to slow down. *Notitia* involves, Hillman says, 'attending to, tending, a certain care of, as well as waiting, pausing, listening. It takes a span of time and a tension of practice' to allow ourselves greater opportunities to notice the unique details of those buildings we have become accustomed to, and to become attuned to their more elusive and nuanced qualities of sounds and smell (1994: 56).

Notitia demands that we relinquish our sense of control and accept a degree of helplessness. As one commentator on Hillman notes, 'it requires the vulnerability of coming without a plan or of knowing that the plan we arrive at will soon dissolve as we find the ideas we have come with inadequate to the

Figure 7.1 'Look!' Detail of New York City street
© Lucy Huskinson

Figure 7.2 'Listen to this wall'. Haight Ashbury, San Francisco
'Listen to This Wall' is an initiative to bring a creative antidote to the ever increasing visual noise that crowds our urban landscape. Working with artists and designers to produce original works that offer new ways of seeing and being inspired in our city spaces (www.listentothiswall.com).
© Lucy Huskinson

Figure 7.3 'Daydream' from 'Daydreamer' graffiti under a bridge in Cambridge, UK
© Lucy Huskinson

situation we find ourselves in' (Watkins 2008: 419). It requires us to adopt a naïve attitude similar to a child's perspective on the world, one that has not yet been conditioned into expecting to experience specific things and seeing only what one expects.

As children develop into adults, their capacity to relate imaginatively to the world diminishes or becomes harder to access. Children tend to be surprised by things that adults have become indifferent to, as they haven't figured out what is 'meant' to be interesting and uninteresting. Reflecting on her young son's fascination with an otherwise nondescript walk around the streets of their neighbourhood, Horowitz remarks that for him 'the sidewalk and street are refreshed, each time we leave or arrive home. There is a constant rearrangement of things on the street and in the air that is seen only by those who do not know that gazing at the cars parked on the street is boring' (2013: 36). The 'boring' streets of the adult's perspective are for the child playgrounds for the imagination.

We often come close to a naïve and playful, childlike attitude when we find ourselves in unfamiliar urban environments, lost, or negotiating foreign cities. In the midst of people going about their day, seemingly in control, guided by their conscious agendas and directed thoughts, a lost person or tourist tends to notice what the locals dismiss as irrelevant. De Botton remarks that as tourists we irritate the locals by standing on 'traffic islands and in narrow streets' to admire what they take to be insignificant details. In doing so, we 'risk getting run over because we are intrigued by the roof of a government building or an inscription on a wall' (2002: 246).

The simple act of walking or moving about the built environment can encourage *notitia*, even within our local neighbourhoods and in the most familiar of places. In *On Looking*—the subtitle of which is *Eleven walks with expert eyes*—Horowitz describes an interesting experiment she undertook to re-aestheticize her overfamiliar neighbourhood in New York City, and thereby, she says, 'to knock' herself awake (2013: 3) from the slumber induced by a reliance on literal perception. Her experiment involved several walks along the same street near her home, each with a different walking companion. I have already alluded to her young son as one; the others are an urban sociologist, a sound designer, a geologist, a physiotherapist, a graphic designer, a blind man, and her dog. Each companion helped her to *notice* the fabric of her neighbourhood from a different perspective and, moreover, to encounter it anew, as if it were a place unfamiliar and strange. After being led around her street by the olfactory senses of her dog, she states, 'I was paying [...] little attention to most of what was exactly before us [...] what my dog shared with me was that my attention invited along attention's companion: inattention to everything else' (2013: 3).

Horowitz's ventures are by no means unusual; she follows in the footsteps of many who have undertaken similar experiments. Indeed, it is a common belief that wandering around built environments refreshes our mind by encouraging our imaginative perception of things, our susceptibility to surprise, and the creative flow of ideas, and in the next section I shall briefly consider some notable theorists who have developed ideas about it.

The significance of wandering for wondering

Buildings are most evocative when they engage us on the move. Our sedentary gaze will often perceive a building as a singular comprehensive image, but our bodily movement in relation to the building will encourage its forms to flex. The building is subsequently perceived as a dynamic stream of forms and textures that move in rhythm with our muscles. The dynamic effect of architecture is therefore enhanced by our bodily movements in relation to it. As Robert Venturi notes, 'This is especially true as the observer moves through or around a building, and by extension through a city: at one moment one meaning can be perceived as dominant; at another moment a different meaning seems paramount' (1966: 32).[5] I wish to suggest that by moving in and around architecture we increase the likelihood of creating pathways, rhythms, and connections not simply for our feet, but for the flow of thoughts and ideas that work in conjunction with our bodily movements in relation to the architecture we perceive.

Walking is regarded by many as a form of knowing; to walk about the built environment is, I suggest, a means to encourage self-knowledge.

Poincaré suggests that walking helped him to disengage from his focused rational deliberations and encouraged more creative, unconscious thoughts. Wallas, who sought to develop Poincaré's creative methods, likewise recommends walking as a means to encourage the creative thinking process (1926: 43–4). Walking encourages unconscious thinking in a number of ways. For instance, as we move around we inevitably encounter a greater variety of impressions for the unconscious to 'graze upon', a more varied menu of 'food for thought', allowing the unconscious to be more selective in its choice of object with which to elaborate and express its concerns. A walk around a building will increase the likelihood of encountering its unexpected features and triggering our surprise. The rhythm and motion of our stride establishes a dynamic flux of impressions of the environment that resonates with the 'free associations' of unconscious thought, a point illustrated by Freud's comparison of unconscious thought with the fluctuating images that pass by the window of a moving train. Walking also brings attention to our embodied sense of self, a self that is contained, integrated, and sustained by the movements of our muscles and the support of our skeleton; and instigates greater opportunities for perceived correspondences between our bodies and the built environment.

It should come as no surprise that mobility encourages our creative thinking; after all, the art of memory requires us not simply to imagine a building of many rooms, but to imagine ourselves *walking* around them, for it is our movement between rooms that enables us to string together the various associated ideas we have placed within each of them. Freud himself claims that his celebrated work *The Interpretation of Dreams* is itself structured according to pathways through changing landscapes that he imagines himself walking within. The argument of his book begins, he says, within a dark forest with several paths, one of which leads to a hidden gorge, then to a dark cavern, and finally to a mountain summit (Freud 1899: 365; cf. Frieden 1990: 10–11, 15–16).[6,7]

It is unsurprising, too, that a great many philosophers were known to be prolific walkers.[8] The 'Peripatetic' school of philosophers in ancient Greece (which originated with Aristotle) are reputed—as their name implies—to have practised their teaching whilst walking. Edmund Husserl proclaimed that in walking 'my organism constitutes itself' (1931: 248). Jean-Jacques Rousseau (known for, amongst other works, his *Reveries of a Solitary Walker*, 1782a) remarks in his *Confessions*: 'I can only meditate when I am walking. When I stop, I cease to think. My mind only works with my legs' (1782b: 382). Søren Kierkegaard, who was partial to lone walks through the streets of Copenhagen, states in a letter in 1847 to his niece: 'every day I walk myself into a state of wellbeing and walk away from every illness; I have walked myself into my best thoughts, and I know of no thought so burdensome that one cannot walk away from it' (Kierkegaard 1978: 241). Immanuel Kant is legendary for walking along the same street near to his house in Königsberg (now, Kaliningrad, Russia) at the exactly same time every day (supposedly 4.30 pm), and no fewer than eight times up and down the street on each occasion. So precise and regimented were his walks that the citizens are purported to have set their clocks to them; and so well known was his route that the street itself has been known since then as 'The Philosopher's Walk' [*Philosophengang*] (Caird 1889: 63).[9] Much of Martin Heidegger's ontological philosophy took shape while he was walking along the wooded pathways that meander through his Black Forest property, and within which, at Todtnauberg, one can still find his own veritable 'dwelling' hut (a cabin of three rooms), in which he lived and wrote (see Sharr 2006). Heidegger's work *Country Path Conversations* (1944/1945) invites us to consider the nature of thinking by presenting three fictional conversations between a scientist, a scholar, and a teacher, which in one way or other involve a walk along a path.[10]

Given the intimate connection between thinking and walking, it would be useful for our investigation to question whether different techniques or methods of walking encourage different kinds of thought processes—and, in particular, whether there is a type of walking that makes us more susceptible to creative thinking and to our unconscious use of the built environments that we encounter by walking. If we return briefly to our walking philosophers, we might well conjecture a correspondence between their different walking styles and the kinds of philosophical ideas they were led to ponder. We might suppose, for instance, that the rhythm of Kant's regimented daily strides, methodically up and down the same narrow street, led him to the careful, systematic prose of his philosophical works, whilst Heidegger's often meandering and convoluted prose was encouraged by his rambling jaunts through the Black Forest. Such a supposition implies that a familiar and prescribed route walked with a view to getting to Point A from Point B is more likely to meet the walker's expectations and yield fewer opportunities for surprise or reverie than the path taken by the wanderer. The wanderer's path is not predetermined; he or she creates it on a whim (or, we would say, unconsciously selects it), and does not always second-guess where it leads. We might further conjecture—as several scholars have—that the spontaneity of aimless wandering can bring to familiar surroundings an increased likelihood of surprise and of the disruption of focused thoughts, allowing greater opportunity for unconscious thinking. Walking without direction is, I suggest, more likely to disrupt the linear thought patterns or pathways of directed thinking and encourage thinking without direction. In this respect, the wanderer can be likened to a sleepwalker, who entertains 'dream-like' thoughts.

Reawakening architecture

There is a large collection of related ideas and traditions, broadly referred to as psychogeography, that explores practical ways to revitalise uninspiring built environments by emphasising the manner in which we move about them.[11] The term 'psychogeography' is itself applied in a multitude of ways and encompasses a range of disparate themes, theorists and practitioners, and writers and filmmakers, spanning centuries. Notable examples across the centuries are Xavier de Maistre's sedentary journey about his room in 1794; the visionary writings of William Blake (1757–1827) and the work of Thomas de Quincey (1785–1859); the romantic figures of the *flâneur* (drifter) on the nineteenth-century streets of Paris; theorists of 'Situationism' (1957–1968);[12] and the contemporary global youth movement known as Parkour or 'Freerunning'. Although 'psychogeography' means different things to different people, it has at its heart the event of walking (or running) within built environments that are in one way or other antagonistic and unreceptive to the needs of the pedestrian. Freewalking is deemed significant because, unlike travelling by car, for instance, it encourages people to go *off piste* and explore hidden and overlooked areas that deviate from the carefully prescribed street plans that the pedestrian is told to follow. In these cases, we find a type of walking that seeks to counter the authority imposed by conventional strategies of moving about the city, and prevailing norms of how architecture ought to function and be used, so that the hidden and surprising architectural life of the city can be experienced and awakened.

One could construe psychogeography as a demonstration of how bodily movements in relation to the built environment provoke dream-like thoughts, and thereby counter the feelings of banality, boredom, and passive submission that are otherwise associated with them. In so doing, it seeks to awaken us to the hidden pleasures of the built environment—to our cities, streets, houses, and places of work—and to the possibility of our subjective reworking of these places in such a way that we notice their unique features and use them to our own creative ends.

A journey about a room, pedestrian explorers, and the freedom to run through architecture

One of the earliest accounts of psychogeography, Xavier de Maistre's *A Journey Around My Room* (1790), suggests that the pleasure we derive from our journeys depends more on the manner in which we approach them than on the destinations themselves. De Maistre implicitly calls upon us to *notice* and to contemplate more closely those aspects of our environments that we ordinarily merely *see* and take for granted. De Maistre's precedes Horowitz's experiment by over 200 years, and is arguably a more impressive demonstration of *notitia*, for whilst Horowitz embarks on an exploration of the unique characteristics of her neighbourhood with travelling companions, de Maistre reduces the scope of his exploration to just one room, and to his own wandering gaze.[13]

Finding himself under house-arrest, de Maistre takes advantage of his enforced confinement to contemplate his rectangular room and the things in it, discovering them to be at once strange and familiar. His contemplation takes the form of a meditative journey, visiting parts of the room and the objects in it as if they were distant, uncharted places. The all-too-familiar places of his room become a place of evocative fantasy for him, and lead him to contemplate a string of associated ideas, chains of memories, stories, and anecdotes. His room measures 'thirty-six paces in circumference if you hug the wall' but, because the journey he undertakes is one of wandering without direction, it will, he says, 'measure much more than this, as I shall be crossing it frequently lengthwise, or else diagonally, without any rule or method' (1790: 7). We find that de Maistre begins to use the room and its furniture for his creative thinking, as his methods of wandering coincide with his non-direct thinking:

> I will even follow a zigzag path, and I will trace out every possible geometrical trajectory if need be. I don't like people who have their itineraries and ideas so clearly sorted out [...] There's no more attractive pleasure, in my view, than following one's ideas wherever they lead [...] without even trying to keep to any set route. And so, when I travel through my room, I rarely follow a straight line: I go from my table towards a picture hanging in a corner; from there I set out obliquely towards the door; but even though, when I begin, it really is my intention to go there, if I happen to meet my armchair en route, I don't think twice about it, and settle down in it without further ado.
>
> (de Maistre 1790: 7)

Using the features of his room to think through his non-directed thoughts is a deeply rewarding experience for de Maistre, as it allows him to elaborate his sense of self beyond the claustrophobic confines that he might otherwise experience with his enforced imprisonment, finding himself inscribed within the room itself, as a psychological extension of himself. He writes:

> Is there any more deeply satisfying pleasure than that of spreading out one's existence in this way [...] doubling, so to speak, one's being? Is it not the eternal, never-fulfilled desire of man to increase his powers and his faculties, to want to be where he is not, to recall the past and to live in the future?
>
> (1790: 14)

If we apply de Maistre's approach to our own familiar places, we might well discover, as Horowitz did, that the homes we live in and the streets and cities we frequent on a daily basis are no less captivating than those places we romanticise as ideal holiday locations. In that respect the architectural wonders of Rome or Giza, Cologne or Paris, become no more intriguing than the 1960s high-rise block of flats, or the matching terraced houses that line street after street, or indeed any building or architectural feature that has become invisible to us as part of our everyday routine. These seemingly mundane buildings are subsequently no less likely to set in motion day-dreams, reveries, and other creative imaginings.

De Maistre emphasises the limitations of approaching our environments with a mindset that presumes already to know what it will find. This can be avoided, he suggests, by moving about its terrain in an unsystematic way, with hesitations and sudden changes in direction, if and when desired; in other words, with a mindset that is directed by unconscious concerns: elaborating itself through bodily movement and associated thoughts.

This imaginative approach is demonstrated on a larger architectural scale in the work of philosopher Michel de Certeau, whose chapter 'Walking in the City' from his seminal work *The Practice of Everyday Life* (1980) is often cited as an influence on contemporary writings and practices of 'psychogeography'. De Certeau describes a man who has climbed to the top of the World Trade Center in New York City, from where he looks down to survey the city as a coherent whole. From his high vantage point the city is perceived visually as a coherent geometric grid—an image that suggests through its order and clarity that the city can be deciphered and its nature ascertained. To this man, who is lifted out of the city by his panoptic gaze, the depersonalised, logical system set out before him *is* the city; its totality is apprehended by him in the glance. But to the citizens who reside in the city there is no such comprehensive order to their environment. For them, no map could predict or prescribe the orientation of their footsteps. Rather, it is they themselves who create the city, in their own image. As de Certeau notes, individuals will 'make some parts of the city disappear and exaggerate others [...] fragmenting it, and diverting it from its immobile order' (1980: 102). It is the uniqueness of a person's own intertwined paths that give shape to spaces (1980: 93).

For de Certeau, our embodied experiences of walking in built environments by creating and recreating the city through our detours, shortcuts, and hesitations puncture the readable city surfaces that are seen by the man atop the tower. Although a rational mindset that surveys the scene abstractly from above and beyond lends clarity to the cityscape, it does not engage with it realistically. The rational vantage point imposes logical constraints onto experiences that otherwise defy rationalisation. Although the panoptic gaze finds the city 'legible', as Lynch maintains, it does so in such a way that it fails to notice the all-important hidden and surprising features that are characteristic of the city's fabric—features that can be noticed only at ground level, when walking. In so doing, the panoptic gaze fails to engage the important cues that orientate the subject within their environment, allowing them to participate in it.

De Certeau asserts that we engage with the built environment most effectively through our movements and our personal interactions with it. Our sporadic wanderings about our cities carve out paths that reveal the limitations of rational strategies and theoretical systems for capturing our subjective experiences of its architecture.

A final example goes further still in its attempt to subvert longstanding preconceptions about our bodily interactions with architecture and the extent to which we can move about it and thereby use it to our creative ends. The popular practice of Parkour, or Freerunning as it is also known, defies the intentions of the city planner to a greater extent than de Certeau's wandering pedestrian. If de Certeau's pedestrian circumvents the designated pathways of the city by recreating them according to their own subjective concerns, the Parkour runner proceeds as if there are no designated pathways whatsoever and no obstacles that cannot be surmounted. The only boundaries or constraints are those that are defined by the runner themselves. The pathways of the experienced Freerunner manifest themselves spontaneously and fluidly, often carving up the material fabric of the built environment, as if on a whim.

Parkour (derived from the French *parcours*, meaning a route or line, and the verb *parcourir*, to travel through, or to traverse) was founded in France in the late 1980s as a playful reinterpretation of the use, function, and form of architectural space, seeking to overcome the restrictions that such spaces normally impose. Practitioners of Parkour, known as '*traceurs*', leap, vault, and spring from—or, as their name suggests, 'trace' a path through—those material objects that ordinarily limit a person's movement. Objects such as walls, fences, curbs, railings, benches, street signs and roofs are no longer obstacles in one's path, and they no longer dictate their use and function or the direction of the path to be taken. Objects invite new possibilities for our movements and interactions, so that walls are walked up, handrails stood on, roofs run along, steps vaulted from, windows swung through, and so on. Parkour is thus a mode of movement that aims to be as fluid as possible, and it expresses a novel way of interacting with the built environment. In so doing it attempts to re-aestheticize architecture through unfamiliar bodily relationships with it and movements within it. This aesthetic reordering of architecture invests it with surprising and imaginative possibilities that seem absurd and nonsensical from conventional approaches that hold on to presuppositions about the purpose and function of architecture and its role in city life. The imagination of the Parkour runner reshapes objects and spaces, and by so doing challenges the conventional meanings assigned to them. Parkour therefore goes a step further, so to speak, than the wanderings of de Maistre and de Certeau's pedestrian, by radically reinventing pathways and redesigning architectural objects and the spaces between them according to the runner's own impulses.

Parkour is to some extent a reaction to the banalisation of much urban redevelopment in recent decades, seen most clearly perhaps in the design of designated play areas found in many a town and city. Although skateboard parks, basketball courts, and playgrounds are welcome communal sites that provide safe play areas for children, they tend to denote the segregation of playful activity, and to communicate the prohibitive message that the streets are not appropriate places for play. Playgrounds tend also to be overthought in their designs, dictating how one 'ought' to play. One must move *down* a slide, for instance, and move *to-and-fro* on a swing, and *round-and-round* on a roundabout; there is little room for imaginative use. Parkour reacts to the restrictions imposed on imaginative play by the social-spatial norms determined by city planners, by perceiving the fabric of entire cities as playgrounds for spontaneous play. As architectural theorists Christopher Rawlinson and Mirko Guaralda note:

> A dark foreboding alley becomes a place of laughter and excitement, an afterhours shopping centre car-park becomes a gymnasium and an afterhours school becomes a jungle to be explored. Parkour and other play activities never completely take over space, but rather borrow it for a time and then return it to normative uses.
>
> (Rawlinson and Guaralda 2011: 22)

Interestingly, Parkour in its early phases of development was referred to as *l'art du déplacement* ['the art of displacement'], a term that resonates with the Freudian dream-work of unconscious thinking in so far as the pathway of the traceur, like the paths of unconscious thought, comprises a network of activity with many options, each of which *displace* the established order of more linear pathways to allow for a subjective recreation of reality.[14]

Xavier de Maistre's journey around his room, de Certeau's pedestrian, and the Parkour runner illustrate how architecture can be reawakened so as to foster more imaginative and creative engagements with it. In each case, the subject *notices* the unique characteristics of their environments as opportunities for their own subjective expression, and the built environment becomes more responsive to the subject's unconscious concerns and imaginings. Architecture in these cases elicits surprise and curiosity, which cannot be achieved through a more deliberate and rationalised engagement with its material features—an engagement that is infused with the expectations and preconceptions of how the environment ought to function.

If we can encourage the architectural event by attending to the unique characteristics of our built environments, the designs of these environments can help by making these features more noticeable, so as to foster this kind of attention. In the final section of this book I draw together central themes from my argument to outline some of the strategies that architects and planners can adopt to design for the existential needs of all who come into contact with their buildings.

Designing for our existential needs

In this book I have considered the most salient aspects of our unconscious behaviours and relationships with architecture in order to explain how and why we are compelled to identify with specific elements and features of architectural design that are otherwise hidden from the conscious eye. In doing so I have established a framework with which to understand how to build more effectively for our human needs.

The character of our built environments is vital to our wellbeing because our personal identity is largely shaped by our unconscious identifications with it. We have seen that we are most satisfied and creative when architectural designs can be said to contain us, and to meet both our conscious and unconscious needs. Inevitably, it is our conscious needs that are most often targeted by architects and planners, in large part because of their lack of understanding of unconscious human behaviour and its impact on the relationships we have with the buildings and towns and cities they design. Problems inevitably arise when buildings seek principally to meet our material needs through their functionality or stylish design, but fail to inspire us or contain us in ways that are often difficult to measure.

We have seen that containment, or lack thereof, is gauged by two innate contrasting tendencies or impulses that we activate when we interact with our environments: to find ourselves merged with the environment and to find ourselves detached or cut loose from it. Identity is forged through the oscillation of these impulses, which are triggered as we negotiate our environments. If one or other impulse is impeded by the architectural designs we encounter, it can have a viscerally negative impact on us, inducing psychological difficulties, including spatial anxieties. Two fundamental anxieties can be discerned: a claustrophobic response to an environment that stifles the subject by enclosing them too tightly, and an agoraphobic response to a place that exposes and isolates the subject through lack of a distinctive structure and orientation. In highlighting these anxieties, I do not wish to claim that people in relatively good health are likely to experience acute, crippling panic in response to poorly designed architecture, but, rather, that these anxieties operate even when their effects are largely undetected or unrecognised. They can creep up on us unnoticed, and can continue to gnaw away at us unconsciously, contributing to a more general and pervading sense of unease and discomfort. As we have noted, spatial anxieties are often misunderstood and misdiagnosed as interpersonal problems, or as a result of stressful conditions at work. An architectural design that fails to contain us sufficiently will establish an existential malaise: a gap or distance between ourselves and our environment that prevents our participation in it, and incites instead symptoms of disembodiment, disorientation and alienation.[15]

The need for gaps and breaks

Ann Sussman and Justin B. Hollander, in their important work *Cognitive Architecture* (2015), arrive at conclusions that complement my own, claiming that we feel 'more at ease' when 'buildings create a room-like condition that surrounds' us on 'several sides'. The reason for this, they explain, is our innate biological tendency to 'gravitate to the sides of walls' as though 'pulled by a magnet'—a tendency that leads them to categorise humans as a 'wall-hugging' [*thigmotaxic*] species (2015: 10). This behaviour is well documented in urban studies, and is observed by, among others, Jane Jacobs in her influential investigation of pedestrians in American cities (1961: 452–3). What I wish to add to such investigations into our instinctual relationships with the built environment is a more comprehensive context that explains why they compel us in the way they do, and what end this compulsion serves. My investigation has suggested that a walled enclosure makes us feel 'at ease' not simply because, as Sussman and Hollander conclude, its edges provide us with a sense of orientation, helping us to navigate our surroundings, and direct our movements by telling us where to go. More importantly, I have argued, these feelings of being at ease denote the capacity of an architectural feature—in this case a walled enclosure—to *contain* us. Orientation is of course important to our containment, but, as I have argued, it is the capacity of architecture to orientate us in non-visible, existential ways that is of paramount significance. That is to say, it is not the provision of a material edge which directs our movement and tells us where to move that is significant here, but the fact that this architectural feature has provided the subject with a sense of containment. It provides an orientation not merely of direction, but of being; an orientation of identity, as one integrated and contained in place.

Sussman and Hollander go on to identify instances of good and bad architectural design according to its capacity to orientate us by means of movement and direction. The eighteenth-century Rue de Rivoli arcade in Paris is used to illustrate good design because 'it takes much of the uncertainty and guesswork out of walking in a large city. Everything seems so simple here [...] Orientation is easy; the layout directs you precisely where to go' (2015: 28). By contrast, the city of Columbia in Maryland, USA, is deemed highly problematic due to its emphasis on 'open landscapes' that 'provide little in the way of a street wall, making it difficult for people to figure out where they are and which way to head. Pedestrians and even newcomers traveling by car perennially feel lost in Columbia. The lack of street corners and grids became the city's Achilles' heel' (2015: 45).

The problems Sussman and Hollander attribute to poor architectural design resonate with the problematics of an agoraphobic architecture insofar as they leave a person feeling exposed and bewildered, lost and out of place. For Sussman and Hollander it would seem that an architecture that makes us feel 'at ease' is one that provides us with direction and directs our movement. However, if architectural design is properly to contain us, it must, as I have argued, also respond to our contrasting desire to cut ourselves loose from the bounded structures it imposes, and work to keep at bay corresponding anxieties of feeling too enclosed and restricted by its designs. Whereas Sussman and Hollander extol as a virtue the Rue de Rivoli's capacity to take away 'uncertainty and guesswork' by directing you 'precisely where to go', the insights of the psychogeographers undermine this position by questioning whether such investment in an architecture that predelineates our movement and direction is in fact so good for our wellbeing and subjective orientation.

I emphasise that a more appropriate architecture is one that provides orientation but without prescription of how one must direct oneself in relation to it. If we are to consider how to design a building in order to make a person feel 'more at ease', we can continue to think of an enclosure that surrounds us on several sides, and provides various edges; but it will be one that also has a variety of openings or breaks within its boundaries (akin to the box-like container with various openings that I postulated at the end of Chapter 4). Such breaks encourage a person to explore beyond the enclosure, granting them a greater sense of containment with the freedom to come and go as they wish. They may use its edges as a guide if they so wish, or they may break free of them. We can illustrate the difference between an enclosed space that surrounds us on several sides and the partial enclosure that incorporates breaks and openings with the contrasting urban scenes of Fig. 7.3 and Fig. 7.4.

Both the piazza and the street are flanked by buildings so as to establish an enclosed space. While the piazza incorporates a variety of side streets that interrupt its enclosing space at various angles, some curving away out of sight, the street has none, so that the pedestrian is compelled to walk in

Figure 7.4 Street, Lower Manhattan, New York City
© Bob Free

Figure 7.5 Piazza del Campo, Sienna, Italy

one straight path from one end of the street to the other. The piazza suggests additional security and containment by allowing us to leave, if we so wish, through its variety of exits; and by providing more options for our orientation within its space, it encourages us to pause and take stock of its character. As we noted, Jane Jacobs refers to such breaks and openings as 'visual interruptions', claiming them to be 'seductive' attributes to urban design in their suggestion of new vistas and scenes to explore (1961: 499). Far from seductive, the street, by contrast, invites anxiety, leaving us vulnerable to whatever we may encounter along it, with little opportunity for escape. The sense of alienation brought about by the rigidity of the street's enclosure extends beyond its visual components, and is compounded by the stifled sounds and unnatural wind tunnels caused by the proximity of its buildings, which can also trap unwanted smells, and block out natural light.

Ambiguous and contrasting features are evocative

Identity is fluid and cannot be locked into place. Good architectural design facilitates this development of self by providing a containing environment that encourages us to feel attached and securely grounded, furnishing us with an experience of our own structural integrity. But importantly, it also grants us the freedom to distract our attention from its more prominent features, encouraging us to explore with our gaze features that are obscure and concealed. A monotonous, prescriptive architecture will impede our subjective engagement with it, fail to encourage our imaginative perception of its features, and encourage instead a literal perception that registers its functional utility or its aesthetic appearance at a more superficial level. Buildings of this nature contribute to an environment that is sterile, predictable, unresponsive, and potentially oppressive. From my survey of the various 'architectural blueprints of psyche' with their spatial divisions of conscious and unconscious parts, together with my examination of the unconscious processes that inform our everyday interactions with architecture, I concluded that an architecture is evocative only if it captures the attentions of the conscious and unconscious aspects of mind alike, and responds to our contrasting needs to feel both attached and detached to our environments. An evocative architecture is therefore one that impresses upon us the complexities, ambiguities, and contradictions of its design, with its various tensions of contrasting spaces, materials, and solid forms. I mentioned the mannerist style as one that incorporates such creative play, and I described a variety of contrasting and contradictory features that encourage the ambiguity of designs, including the juxtaposition of voids and busy and ornate features; pristine geometric forms set against those that are fragmented, crumbling or ruined; new façades adorning old buildings; enclosed spaces punctured by unexpected openings; dark recesses and alcoves set apart from well-lit spaces; reflective glass-clad surfaces; the shock of the ugly merged with the beautiful and orderly. Given that the uncanny is an expression of tension disclosed by the double nature of a thing that is both familiar and unfamiliar, and also describes the nature of our experience of unconscious activity, the various tensions that are evoked by ambiguous and contradictory design features are likely to enhance its overall uncanny effect.

As we have seen, identity and creativity are founded on the tensions of antagonistic impulses. C.G. Jung notes that 'life is born only of the spark of opposites' (1917: par. 78), while Gaston Bachelard, speaking of the power of place, asserts that 'everything comes alive when contradictions accumulate' (1957: 3). Through the tensions of opposites the correspondence between psyche and place, or between 'intimate space and exterior space' as Bachelard puts it, is consolidated, with both aspects undergoing some sort of 'expansion' or enrichment as a result (1957: 201). And the philosopher Nietzsche, we saw, understands our greatest creative human achievements in terms of the tension that arises between contrasting instincts that he labels Apollonian and Dionysian, instincts that are discernible in both the creative character or mindset of people and aesthetic works, such as architecture.

Architectural designs that incorporate tensions through their ambiguous and contradictory features can capture the attention of the imagination, and set in motion its unconscious processes. As we saw in the application of Freud's method of 'dream-work' to architecture, designs can achieve their evocative power through the spatial misalignments and curious juxtapositions of their features—through, for instance, spatial displacements and the compression or condensation of multiple elements into one. When architecture puzzles us and thwarts our expectations of it, it can be said to encourage an imaginative, unconscious, 'dream-like' response in us.

Confusing designs, if carefully managed, are likely to enhance the evocative power of our buildings and cityscapes. Indeed, as Robert Venturi suggests, just a few tweaks to distort conventional features and designs is sufficient to capture our imagination:

> Cannot the architect and planner, by slight adjustments to the conventional elements of the townscape, existing or proposed, promote significant effects? By modifying or adding conventional elements to still other conventional elements they can, by a twist of context, gain a maximum effect through a minimum of means. They can make us see the same things in a different way.
>
> (Venturi 1966: 44)

It would seem that even Hillman—ardent critic of the skyscraper (and towers more generally)—finds some solace in the incorporation of small regions of distortion in otherwise bland and alienating architectural designs. He refers to the potential reinvigoration of skyscrapers by means of the inclusion of small openings to interrupt the building's expansive, unrelenting surfaces—such as the addition of various 'corners' and 'broken-up interiors' that encouraged 'intimacy' within a city and 'pauses' and breaks within routine (1998: 106). When the reflective shell of the skyscraper is broken, our senses are given opportunities to explore and graze upon a variety of textures and discernible shapes, rather than glide across the vast polished surfaces or repetitive patterns that appear to extend forever upwards and out of reach.

This is all well and good, but the incorporation of confusing features to encourage the likelihood of an uncanny experience is no easy matter. A subtle balance of surprise and expectation is required. Confusion must not be explicitly celebrated in such a way as to detract from our need for the building to contain and orientate us. As Nietzsche said of the Dionysian aesthetic impulse, on its own it is barbaric and dangerous; it shatters subjectivity, seeking the complete merger of the self with its environment. If we are to contain its chaotic nature and harness its creative energy, we require the order and composure of its aesthetic counterpart, the Apollonian.[16] Before we consider further the need for a creative balance of tension between contrasting design features, I wish to consider the role of light and shadow as important elements that can accentuate the contradictory features of a design and encourage our unconscious identification with it.

The interplay of shadow and light

The architectural blueprints of psyche that I have surveyed feature rooms of consciousness that are brightly lit—presumably with windows suitably placed to capture the natural light, and with fixtures installed to provide artificial light. The light makes things visible and discernible, and 'enlightens' all who use the room. The blueprints also feature rooms of the unconscious that are in stark contrast, clothed in shadow or completely dark so as to obscure the features hidden within, which remain mysterious and yet to be disclosed. The interplay of light and shadow and its accompanying sensuous experiences express in aesthetic terms the dynamic relationship between these two aspects of mind. This correspondence is alluded to in comments scattered throughout many other works that consider the aesthetic experiences of evocative architecture (or the architectural event, as I have understood it) as an event that begins as an uncanny experience and develops into one of either a sublime or numinous nature. Anthony Vidler, for example, in *The Architectural Uncanny* (1992) assigns a chapter to 'dark space', where darkness or shadow is associated with the affective presence of the unknown. There Vidler cites remarks of Roger Caillois (1938) on the power of darkness, and its capacity to 'touch the individual directly'. Darkness, Caillois claims, is not the mere absence of light; it 'envelops' and 'penetrates' a person, and 'even passes through him'. Caillos concludes that '"the ego is *permeable* for darkness while it is not so for light"' (cited in Vidler 1992: 175).[17] Edmund Burke in his treatise on the sublime (1757) asserts that the more striking the contrast of light and dark in an architectural design, the more powerful its psychological affect:

> You ought to pass from the greatest light, to as much darkness as is consistent with the uses of architecture. At night the contrary rule will hold, but for the same reason; and the more highly a room is then illuminated, the grander will the passion be.
>
> (Burke 1757: 81)

And, speaking of the power of architecture to convey the numinous, Rudolf Otto (1917) maintains that the building perceived in half-light expresses the numinous most effectively, and in such a way that its dimly lit features captivate the 'soul':

> Darkness must be such as is enhanced and made all the more perceptible by contrast with some last vestige of brightness, which it is, as it were, on the point of extinguishing; hence the 'mystical' effect begins with semi-darkness [...] The semi-darkness that glimmers in vaulted halls [...] strangely quickened and stirred by the mysterious place of half-lights, has always spoken eloquently to the soul, and the builders of temples, mosques, and churches have made full use of it.
>
> (Otto 1917: 68)

Our sense of self is influenced by the effects of shadow and light on architecture. Jung is perhaps best known for his personification of the personal unconscious as 'the shadow'—a shadowy double, akin to Freud's uncanny double (or Doppelgänger), which accompanies our conscious personas at all times as our body's closest witness. This figure is one we must accept if we are to remain in good mental health.[18] The shadow offers us an alternative perspective on the body's role as an intimate guide to the quality of architectural design, one that enables us to engage with the more ambiguous features of a design, including its spatial uncertainties and uncanny sense of otherness. John Ruskin similarly explains how architecture achieves its affective 'power' when it is able to 'express a kind of human sympathy' with us: which is to say, an 'equivalent expression for the trouble and wrath of life, for its sorrow and its mystery'. Architecture does so, he asserts, 'only by depth or diffusion of gloom, by the frown upon its front, and the shadow of its recess'. Moreover, he asserts, 'I do not believe that ever any building was truly great, unless it had mighty masses, vigorous and deep, of shadow mingled with its surface' (Ruskin 1849: III: §13).

One might think that Ruskin had a particularly 'gloomy' view of human life; but the important point we wish to focus on here is that these shadowy spaces are thought to encourage our unconscious identification with architecture in a number of ways. They confuse us, and lead us to uncertainty and to imagination. Within shadows we become more easily merged with our environments, as boundaries between things lose their distinctive character. As architect Juhani Pallasmaa asserts, 'deep shadows and darkness are essential, because they dim the sharpness of vision, make depth and distance ambiguous, and invite unconscious peripheral vision and tactile fantasy' (1996: 46). In other words, darkness evokes a curiosity in us and invites us to explore the hidden features of a building clothed in shadow in the only way available: indirectly, though our imagination. In so doing, the dark building calls upon our own hidden features, which become intimately involved and disclosed in the process. 'How much more mysterious and inviting is the street of an old town with its alternating realms of darkness and light than are the brightly and evenly lit streets of today!' exclaims Pallasmaa (1996: 46).

Architects and planners, by carefully manipulating the effects of light and shadow within their features, have the opportunity to accentuate the complexities of their designs in subtle ways. By doing so they can invite those who use them for more ordinary, practical purposes also to notice their unique characteristics, and use them unconsciously for the creative elaboration of themselves. As Fred Botting notes, 'mysterious doors and hidden passageways encourage desire as well as trepidation', and, ultimately, 'a wish to know' (2013: 6). Homogeneous bright light, by contrast, 'paralyses the imagination' (Pallasmaa 1996: 46), and makes one 'suffer every single day you look at it [...] coming right down on your skull like a KGB man putting a light on you, straight down on you—shadowless, ruthless, cruel' (Hillman and Ventura 1993: 4–5). Bright light without contrasting shadow privileges certainty and information; it encourages us to scan the foreground environment in order to notice only that which satisfies our immediate needs, and leaves us fundamentally unsatisfied, desiring more.[19]

Incorporating the radical within the conventional

Without the interplay of contradictions in architectural design, curiosity and surprise are more difficult to arouse, and will probably result in buildings that simply meet our expectations, rather than challenging them; and as a result, go largely unnoticed. Likewise, too great an emphasis on contradictions and contrasting features will leave us confused, disoriented, or alarmed. Designing with a view to containing a person by providing them with sufficient orientation while at the same time inducing in them curiosity and surprise is difficult, and made all the more so by the fact that the desired effect depends in part on the subjective predisposition of the person who uses it. To that end, it is much easier to provide guidelines to prevent some of the more common pitfalls that are encountered in architectural designs, especially those that seek explicitly to arouse curiosity and surprise in those who come to use them.

A problematic architecture is one that fails to engage the aesthetic sensibilities of both aspects of mind, or accentuates one to the detriment of the other, leaving a person vulnerable to the corresponding spatial anxieties that occur when either is unchecked and allowed free rein. In this chapter I have focused on the more common problem of buildings that are designed to accommodate our practical needs and thereby to appease the measured demands of ego-consciousness, but that fail to respond to our non-rational sensibilities and unconscious needs. This problem is embodied by those banal, conventional designs that lack imagination but nevertheless fulfil their functional role. A repercussion of this lack, we noted, is their vulnerability to attacks from people, who seek unconsciously to re-aestheticise them by transforming them into unique, bespoke designs, with decorations of vandalism, such as graffiti or physical damage.

We saw that the most evocative images—those that stir the unconscious most vigorously—are the twisted, distorted, and idiosyncratic forms that are often attributed to a 'tortured psychology' (Yates 1966: 112), or to an aesthetics of 'pathology' (Hillman 1997: 203). The unconscious expresses itself and exerts influence on our behaviour most forcibly in reaction to the various barriers of resistance and defence put in place by the rationalisations of the ego, which seeks to keep hidden and repressed whatever it deems unfavourable. The unconscious is made manifest by those twisted, distorted images and forms, which usurp the ego's desire for convention, order, self-containment, and control. Many contemporary architects have recognised, sometimes explicitly, the need to incorporate unconscious aesthetics into their architectural designs, Rem Koolhaas and Robert Venturi being two of the more recognisable and influential. However, all too often we find that the methods employed by architects in the management of the unconscious are problematic—seeking, for instance, to manipulate it and fix it in place, an approach that inevitably results in a loss or dilution of its dynamic effects and evocative power.

Koolhaas and the problematic surrealist approach

I noted that art historian Arnold Hauser singles out mannerist architecture as the style that recognises most explicitly the importance of maintaining opposites in creative tension. To recall, the very 'essence' of the mannerist style, he claims, 'lies in this tension, this union of apparently irreconcilable opposites', in 'conflicting stylistic elements'; the 'purest and most striking expression' of the mannerist style is expressed 'in paradox'(1965: 12). Hauser describes this paradox in terms similar to the dynamic interaction between the conscious and unconscious, and the contrasting impulses we have in relation to our environments. Thus, mannerist architecture, he states, is dependent on the tensions between 'rationalism and irrationalism' (1965: 12), and between a 'sense of restriction and unfreedom in spite of all its desire for release' (1965: 280). Mannerist architecture, he continues, embodies a desire for 'flight into chaos in spite of all its need of protection against it; the tendency to depth, the advance into space, the effort to break out into the open combined with the sudden sense of isolation from the environment' (1965: 280).

Following Hauser, Venturi, writing in 2004, describes mannerism as 'an architecture appropriate for now'. It is, he argues, an architecture that 'acknowledges order rather than original expression but breaks the conventional order to accommodate complexity and contradiction and thereby engages ambiguity—engages ambiguity unambiguously' (2004: 74). Venturi wishes to incorporate the 'boring' and 'ordinary' alongside the 'eclectic' and 'dissonant' to establish the ambiguous tensions he seeks (2004: 76). What he doesn't aspire to is an architecture that accentuates complexities to an extreme without the banal and conventional to stabilise them, without which architecture becomes a 'wilful', 'excessive', and 'ideological' spectacle (2004: 77).

Koolhaas's work is likewise regarded as a celebration of opposite extremes that embodies the needs of ego and unconscious alike. Architect Charles Jencks describes Koolhaas's work as adopting a curious position between and at the extremities of 'differentiation, radical eclecticism, and collage, on the one hand, and the pressures for standardization and generic structures, on the other' (Jenks 2002: 180–5). The Office of Metropolitan Architecture, established by Koolhaas with colleagues in 1975, was intended among other things as a 'laboratory of the collective unconscious' to 'restore mythical, symbolic, literary, oneiric, critical and popular functions to the architecture of urban centres' (Koolhaas and Mau 1995: 926).[20] So far, so good. However, problems arise when we look more closely at the method Koolhaas cites in his early work as one he himself employs to reimagine and rework modernist architecture. The method, known as the 'Paranoid-Critical Method', originates with the surrealist artist, Salvador Dalí,[21] and is extolled by Koolhaas, who devotes a entire section to its discussion in his celebrated work *Delirious New York* (1978: 235–82). The method is, however, not without significant flaws in its handling of the unconscious, and has unrealistic expectations of the extent to which the unconscious can be manipulated to deliver desired results.

With his Paranoid-Critical Method, Dalí sought to advance the objectives of the Surrealist Movement, which up until that point (the early 1930s) had been intent simply on exposing the workings of the unconscious. Dalí, by contrast, endeavoured to exploit the unconscious, by recreating its various 'delirious' connections and associations in rationalised, conscious form. In so doing, Dalí, and Koolhaas following his lead, sought to re-establish the often lost continuity between the imaginary and the rational, the practical and the visionary, the conscious and the unconscious. The method itself, as the name suggests, involves two consecutive operations. Koolhaas delineates them as follows:

> 1. the synthetic reproduction of the paranoiac's way of seeing the world in a new light—with its rich harvest of unsuspected correspondences, analogies and patterns; and
> 2. the compression of these gaseous speculations to a critical point where they achieve the density of fact.
>
> (Koolhaas 1978: 238)

It is an approach analogous to Freud's 'dream-work'. Here, the spatial alignments of displacement and condensation that underpin Freud's method are utilised within Dalí's artworks and Koolhaas's architecture to compress incompatible images into one. The result is a 'systematic confusion' of 'delirious' imagery that seeks to re-aestheticise what Koolhaas refers to as the 'worn, consumed contents of the world' by distorting them and inscribing them with new and revitalised meanings, while retaining the familiarity of their form (Koolhaas 1978: 235, 241).

Koolhaas argues that a range of late twentieth-century buildings exemplify the implementation of the Paranoid-Critical Method in their design, and he highlights London Bridge in Lake Havasu City, Arizona, as perhaps the 'most blatant' example (Fig. 7.5). The bridge, originally constructed in the 1830s and spanning the River Thames in London, was dismantled in 1967 and relocated to Arizona, where it was rebuilt, stone by stone, across the artificial lake of Havasu in order to attract tourists and potential residents to the area. Although bestowed with new meanings and also solving the problem of a 'Reality Shortage at Lake Havasu', the bridge incorporates original 'fragments of London life', with, as Koolhaas notes, 'the red phone booths, the double-decker buses, [and] the guards', all of which adds 'authenticity' (1978: 240). This example illustrates equally the Freudian dream-work, with the spatial displacement of the image of the bridge, moved from its original context, and the condensation of meanings: those that applied to the bridge in its original context spanning the River Thames merged with those that apply to it as the bridge that now spans Havasu Lake. Condensation in this case is similar to

Venturi's notion of the 'vestigial element' of architecture, which, he says, 'is the result of a more or less ambiguous combination of the old meaning, called up by associations, with a new meaning created by the modified or new function, structural or programmatic, and the new context' (1966: 38).

The essential difference between Freud's dream-work and the Paranoid-Critical Method, however, is the latter's emphasis on the manipulation of the unconscious so as to 'force', 'rationalise', 'fabricate', and 'exploit' it in order to achieve its 'density of fact', as Koolhaas puts it. Such manipulation is akin, Koolhaas remarks, to 'banging a piece into a jigsaw puzzle so that it sticks, if not fits' (1978: 241). This naïve and misguided approach to the unconscious, as Freud saw it, led Freud to refer to the Surrealists as 'absolute cranks' or fools.[22] According to Freud, the unconscious cannot be exploited in this way: if it were, unconscious meanings would be reduced to conscious terms, and thereby lost in translation. Koolhaas suggests that unconscious meanings can be 'grafted' onto the world through architecture, where they then act in society, often unnoticed, like a spy working undercover to bring about that society's destruction (1978: 241). From a psychoanalytic perspective, however, what we discover if we follow this Surrealist method isn't the unconscious at work, but an abstract rendition of it: a conscious construct that parades as

Figure 7.6 London Bridge, Lake Havasu, Arizona

unconscious fantasy, and thus one significantly diluted in its power of affect. Surrealist architecture *represents* the unconscious, and in this respect is little different from the architectural metaphors or blueprints of psyche that I surveyed in Chapter 2. But the message that is intended by this Surrealist architectural metaphor is misplaced (rather than displaced, as their designers claim), and points towards a more widespread issue that I have sought to address throughout this book in relation to our under-appreciation of the utility of architectural metaphors more generally. That is to say, scholars are largely concerned with the abstract, figurative details of these metaphors—as Freud himself remarked in his criticism of the concerns of the Surrealists—and overlook their value as commentaries on the various ways in which we identify with our built environments and use architectural features to elaborate ourselves. The important point here is that the power of architecture lies not in its capacity to *represent* the unconscious, but to *evoke* it. Architecture is an event. If the unconscious is stripped from this personal dynamic context and reduced to abstract features or mere signage, architecture becomes less a profound 'event', and more a superficial 'type' or 'style'.

Koolhaas extols Dalí's method of utilising objects in 'the external world' to convey in an image the workings of the unconscious with, as Dalí puts it, 'the troubling particularity' of making the reality of this image 'valid for others' (1930: 10). But, as we have seen, the event of architecture is an experience that arises out of the individual's personal participation in architecture; it is an event fashioned in their own image, and not that of the architect or artist, or one established by consensus. Surrealist buildings represent the unconscious, whereby their therapeutic role is diminished. They lead not to creative imagining, but to a fixed representation of how such imaginings should be. As Freud laments, it is difficult to ascertain what surrealist designs may have to say to anybody at all (see Breton 1932: 152[23]).

Buildings that are designed in order to flout the conventions and expectations of our ego-sensibilities can be just as problematic as the banal and predictable buildings that such designs react against. One of the dangers of designing in such a way as to be a simple reaction against the failings of outmoded conventions, is that a new architectural 'convention', 'type', or 'style' is simply created as a replacement—one that is susceptible to being as disappointing as the architecture it sought to overcome. Postmodern and deconstructivist architecture that seeks to reconfigure modernist conventions with their disorienting mishmash of forms often fall into this trap, resulting in superficial effects that mock our sensibilities rather than transforming them with new, refreshing ways of thinking. Such buildings, I have maintained, appear as a parody of themselves: crass rather than genuinely intriguing. Evocative architectural designs do not replicate conventional designs so that we barely notice them; nor are they so radical that we fail to engage with them. Such extremes, I contend, invite negative responses in those who use these buildings, born out of the need to compensate for their extremeness and to seek out what they are perceived to lack. Conventional architecture attracts the desire for its radical refacement through subversive acts of 'vandalism',[24] and idiosyncratic architecture is often snubbed for its want of a reality-check, to ground it within more familiar and intimate configurations. A balance is therefore required, with designs that are able to resist the temptation to showcase the aesthetic concerns of either the unconscious or consciousness.

Ultimately, what we require are places that sneak up on us unannounced—buildings that contain us, and thereby provide us with the containment we require in order to experience ourselves as sufficiently free to explore the uncertainties of ourselves and our environments without restraint.

Notes

1 Harold Searles concludes that the ability to project aspects of oneself into the built environment with relative ease is the preserve of children, some eastern traditions, and schizophrenics (1960: 19–20). In terms of schizophrenia, he writes: that

> we know that some psychotic patients will sit or lie, for days on end, as much like stone statues [...] I have worked with one schizophrenic patient who expressed to me the unmistakable conviction that she had been 'a statue myself, over and over'. She said this in the course of asserting her definite belief that certain well known statues which she had visited in nearby Washington were really people, 'put into concrete,' and she protested to me that if only the doctors here 'would go around stripping statues,' freeing the persons entombed within them, we would then be doing good.
>
> (Searles 1960: 98)

However, Searles was keen to point out the health benefits of this ability:

> the so-called mentally ill may in fact be more closely in touch with these lost connections between self and environment than any of us realize. It seems to me that, in our culture, a conscious ignoring of the psychological importance of the non-human environment exists simultaneously with a (largely unconscious) overdependence upon that environment. I believe that the actual importance of that environment to the individual is so great that he dare not recognize it. Unconsciously it is felt, I believe, to be not only an intensely important conglomeration of things outside the self, but also a large and integral part of the self.
>
> (1960: 395)

2 Indeed, we might well question whether we have any agency in the situation at all, for, as Bollas intimates, we can be 'pushed to thought by objects' as often as 'we seek objects to use [...] as forms of thinking' (2009: 92–3).

3 The modern mind, Jung says, is 'caught in the toils of egohood', so that we trust ourselves only with that which we can quantify and explain (Jung 1954c: par. 396; cf. Jung 1961a: pars. 581, 582).

4 As one commentator on Hillman describes it, *notitia* involves a 'careful attention that is sustained, patient, subtly attuned to images and metaphors, tracking both hidden meanings and surface presentations' (Watkins 2008: 419).

5 Venturi illustrates his point with the example of Nicholas Hawksmoor's St George's in Bloomsbury, London (built 1716–1731), where 'the contradictory axes inside become alternatingly dominant or recessive as the observer moves within them, so that the same space changes meaning' (1966: 32).

6 Following his account of walking in a city, Bollas concludes that by walking 'we are engaged in a type of dreaming'; 'each gaze that falls upon an object of interest may yield a moment's reverie', and these 'constitute an important feature of our psychic lives' (2009: 63).

7 Heidegger, in *What Is Called Thinking*?, refers to walking more metaphorically:

> The way of thinking cannot be traced from somewhere to somewhere like a well worn rut, nor does it all exist as such in any place. Only when we walk it, and in no other fashion, only, that is, by thoughtful questioning, are we on the move on the way.
>
> (1951–1952: 168)

Heidegger was, of course, not speaking theoretically. He did, in fact, undertake much of his later work while walking the *Holzwege* (wooded paths) that meandered through his Schwarzwald property.

8 See Conway (1998:49); Ingold (2011: 17, 46).

9 The nineteenth-century philosopher Edward Caird quotes the humorous description of Kant by Heinrich Heine (a German journalist and poet, and contemporary of Kant):

> He lived an abstract, mechanical, old-bachelor existence in a quiet, remote street of Königsberg, an old city at the northeastern boundary of Germany. I do not believe that the great cathedral clock of that city accomplished its day's work in a less passionate and more regular way than its countryman Immanuel Kant. Rising from bed, coffee-drinking, writing, lecturing, eating, walking, everything had its fixed time: and the neighbours knew that it must be exactly half-past four when they saw Professor Kant in his grey coat with his cane in his hand step out of his house door, and move towards the little lime-tree avenue, which is called after him the Philosopher's Walk. Eight times he walked up and down that walk at every season of the year, and when the weather was bad or the grey clouds threatened rain, his servant, old Lampe, was seen anxiously following him with a large umbrella under his arm, like an image of Providence [...] But the good people saw nothing in him but a professor of philosophy, and when he passed at the appointed hour, they gave him friendly greetings and set their watches.
>
> (Caird 1889: 63–4)

10 Bret W. Davies, an English translator of Heidegger, emphasises in his Foreword to Heidegger's *Country Path*, the entwined nature of walking and talking:

> these conversations by no means consist of small talk on strolls through a park. As 'country path conversations,' they veer off the pavement of our accustomed ways of speaking and at times venture into a thicket; their ponderous yet radical manner of speaking frequently transgresses the limits of our familiar horizons and goes several strides beyond our established 'clearings' of intelligibility.
>
> (Davies 2010: xx)

11 For a particularly lucid and accessible account of this term and some of the many theories that underpin it, see Merlin Coverley (2010).

12 Guy Debord sought to turn psychogeography into a rigorous scientific discipline that brings psychology and geography together, defining it as the study of 'the precise laws and specific effects of the geographical environment, consciously organized or not, on the emotions and behaviour of individuals' (1955). For Debord, the skilled psychogeographer is able to identify and engage with his emotions by aimlessly wandering about the city. The results are then plotted carefully on a map, thereby establishing a new cartography of the city that disregards the prescribed zones of attraction that city planners intend tourists to frequent. In 1957 Debord published his revised map of Paris, entitled *The Naked City*. The users of the map are encouraged to follow their own path through it, following a number of arrows which link different segments of the city according to the emotional context the user wishes to ascribe to them. See Sadler (1999); Tom McDonough (2004: 241–65).

13 Albert Camus presents a similar account of an exploration of a single room in his famous novella *L'Etranger* (1942). There, Meursault, the protagonist, passes time in prison by trying to remember every item in his room, gradually amassing more and more details. He says:

> the more I thought about it the more things I dug out of my memory that I hadn't noticed before or that I'd forgotten about. I realized then that a man who'd only lived for a day could easily live for a hundred years in a prison. He'd have enough memories not to get bored.
>
> (Camus 1942: 77)

14 The philosophy of Gilles Deleuze and Félix Guattari, especially their work *A Thousand Plateaus* (1980) with its ideas of the 'striation' of urban space, is often cited in scholarly discussions of Parkour. The striation of space has affinities with the authority of the city street 'grid' plan that enables the city to be read, navigated, and made intelligible (in the manner that de Certeau's man atop the tower relates to the city he views below), and also establishes the means of control of citizens through its orientation of their movement. According to Deleuze and Guatttari, striated space establishes 'fixed paths in well-defined directions, which restrict speed, regulate circulation, relativize movement, and measure in detail the relative movements of subjects and objects' (Deleuze and Guattari 1980: 386). The art of Parkour seeks to undermine striated spaces, by overcoming their restrictions as smoothly and efficiently as possible. The aim is, in the words of David Belle, to be 'fluid like water' (cited in Geyh 2006). Parkour is thus an attempt to outwit the logic of the city and to transform the built environment into what Deleuze and Guattari refer to as 'smooth space', 'a field without conduits or channels', where subjects are free to express themselves through their own inhibited movements.

15 Jane Jacobs in her influential study of American cities asserts that city planners and architectural designers 'operate on the premise that city people seek the sight of emptiness, obvious order and quiet. [But] nothing could be less true' (1961: 47). For pedestrians gravitate to where they can 'watch activity and other people'. Jacobs discusses the importance of placing buildings around a park in the interest

of 'enclosing' the space, and making 'a definitive shape out of the space so that it appears as an important *event* in the city scene, rather than a no-account left-over' (1961: 138; emphasis mine).

16 I noted in Chapter 3 that Nietzsche refers to architecture as an example of the Apollonian instinct in its pure form, on the grounds that architecture presents itself clearly and distinctly in the solidity of its form (while music, by contrast, exemplifies the Dionysian). Nietzsche here is speaking of architecture in abstract terms. If we are to speak of an evocative architecture, I would argue that it is one that embodies and negotiates the creative tension between the Apollonian and Dionysian: with, as Nietzsche says of creativity, as much Dionysian energy as Apollonian consciousness can handle. Such a building is, I am arguing, one that introduces distortion into its conventional design. It could be a building in a state of ruin, or any number of variations on its design that thwart our expectations.

17 Caillois is here quoting psychiatrist Eugène Minkowski.

18 Jung, for instance, asserts that if a 'person wants to be cured [of neurosis] it is necessary to find a way in which his conscious personality and his shadow can live together' (Jung 1938: par. 132).

19 One could argue that to encourage darkened spaces within architectural design is to encourage the corresponding repressed and unconscious material of the perceiver's mind. Whilst Ruskin regards darkness as indicative of a troubled, sorrowful, even wrathful mind, the repressed contents that are brought to light in the architectural event are, as I have argued, positively enriching to the personality as a whole, and beneficial, too, to our appreciation of the built environments we inhabit. It is perhaps more appropriate to construe the connection as a therapeutic *negotiation* with the sorrows, troubles, and wrath that were too challenging for conscious thought alone. From out of undifferentiated spaces of shadow, the imagination brings forth shapes that are invested with the unconscious desire for self-containment and separation from the environment; but when juxtaposed with features that are lit and sharply defined, the subject is directed and finds itself grounded and in proximity to the environment.

20 See also Koolhaas (1976: 34).

21 Just as Hillman's term 'pathology' subverts the conventional use of the term, extending its definition beyond a problematic condition that calls for a cure to refer to a creative way of perceiving the unique characteristics of the world, Dalí's use of 'paranoia' extends beyond its conventional definition as problematic persecution mania to a more creative approach to the world that is underpinned by a distorted perception of it.

22 Letter to Stefan Zweig, July 20, 1938 (cited in Ernst L. Freud, 1961: 449).

23 In a letter to the Surrealist André Breton, Freud states: 'I am not able to clarify for myself what surrealism is and what it wants' (26 December 1932, in Breton 1932: 152). In his comments on Dalí's paintings, Freud notes:

> It is not the unconscious I look for in your pictures, but the conscious, whereas in the works of old masters, which are full of hidden mystery, I look for the unconscious. In your pictures what is mysterious and hidden is expressed directly[;] it is in fact the theme of the pictures.
>
> (cited in Ades 1982: 74)

24 Jane Jacobs alludes to an impulse to make homogeneous buildings 'look special (in spite of not *being* special)' by establishing a superficial appearance of distinction, through the addition, for instance, of different colours or textures. This impulse results, she says, in 'a chaos of shouted, but superficial, differences' that may be 'eye-catching' for a brief moment, but are 'meaningless' (1961: 292–4). See Plate 1 for examples of this.

Bibliography

Abercrombie, Stanley (1996) *Architecture as Art: An Esthetic Analysis*, New York, Cincinnati, Toronto, London, and Melbourne: Van Nostrand Reinhold.

Abramovitz, Anita (1979) *People and Spaces*, New York: Viking Press.

Adams, Parveen (1996) *The Emptiness of the Image: Psychoanalysis and Sexual Differences*, London and New York: Routledge.

Ades, Dawn (1982) *Dalí*, London: Thames and Hudson.

Adorno, Theodor (1970/1984) *Aesthetic Theory*, eds Gretel Adorno and Rolf Tiedemaan, trans. C. Lenhardt, London: Routledge & Kegan Paul.

Adorno, Theodor and Horkheimer, Max (1946/1972) *Dialectic of Enlightenment*, trans. J. Cumming, New York: Continuum.

Alexander, Christopher, Ishikawa, Sara, and Silverstein, Murray (1977) *A Pattern Language: Towns, Buildings, Construction*, Center for Environmental Structure, Berkeley, CA, New York, and Oxford: Oxford University Press.

Anon. (1994) *Rhetorica ad Herennium*, ed. and trans. Harry Caplan, Loeb Classical Library, Cambridge, MA: Harvard University Press.

Anzieu, Didier (1974) 'Le moi-peau' / 'The Skin Ego', *Nouvelle revue de psychanalyse*, 9: 195–208.

Anzieu, Didier (1985/1989) *The Skin Ego*, trans. Chris Turner, New Haven: Yale University Press.

Anzieu, Didier (1986) *Une peau pour les pensées : entretiens de Didier Anzieu avec Gilbert Tarrab sur la psychologie et la psychanalyse / A Skin for Thought: Interviews with Gilbert Tarrab on Psychology and Psychoanalysis*, Paris: Clancier-Guénaud.

Anzieu, Didier (1990) *Psychic Envelopes*, trans. D. Briggs, London: Karnac.

Anzieu, Didier (1996) *Créer-Détruire: Le travail psychique créateur / Create-Destroy: The Creative Psychic Work* (new edition, 2012), Paris: Dunod.

Bachelard, Gaston (1957/1994) *The Poetics of Space*, trans. Maria Jolas, 9th edition, Boston: Beacon Press.

Balint, Michael (1959/1987) *Thrills and Regressions*, Maresfield Library, New Edition, London: Karnac Books.

Ballantyne, Andrew (2002) *Architecture: A Very Short Introduction*, Oxford: Oxford University Press.

Balmond, Cecil and Smith, J. (2002) *Informal*, Munich: Prestel Verlag.

Barbara, Anna and Perliss, Anthony (2006) *Invisible Architecture: Experiencing Places Through the Sense of Smell*, Milan: Skira.

Barrie, Thomas (2010) 'Carl Jung's House in Bollingen: Architecture as a Medium of Transformation', *The Sacred In-Between: The Mediating Roles of Architecture*, Abingdon and New York: Routledge.

Battista, Alberti (1485/1988) *On the Art of Building*, 10 vols., trans. Joseph Rykwert, Neil Leach, and Robert Tavernor, Cambridge, MA: MIT Press.

Benjamin, Walter (1978) 'On the Mimetic Faculty', trans. E. Jephcott, in ed. P. Demetz, *Reflections*, New York: Schocken.

Bennet, E.A. (1966/1983) *What Jung Really Said*, New York: Schocken Books.

Bennet, E.A. (1985) *Meetings with Jung: Conversations Recorded During the Years 1946–1961*, Einsiedeln: Daimon Verlag.

Benton, Tim (1987) 'The Sacred and the Search for Myths', in eds M. Reaburn and V. Wilson, *Le Corbusier: Architect of the Century*, London: Courtauld Institute of Art: 238–54.

Bick, Esther (1968) 'The Experience of the Skin in Early Object Relations', *The International Journal of Psychoanalysis*, 49(2–3): 484–6.

Bion, Wilfred R. (1962/1989) *Learning from Experience*, London: Heinemann.

Blum, H.P. (1995) 'Freud Correspondence', *Journal of the American Psychoanalytic Association*, 43: 869–73.

Bollas, Christopher (1978) 'The Aesthetic Moment and the Search for Transformation', *Annual of Psychoanalysis*: 385–94.

Bollas, Christopher (1987) *The Shadow of the Object: Psychoanalysis of the Unthought Known*, London: Free Association Books.

Bollas, Christopher (1989) *Forces of Destiny: Psychoanalysis and the Human Idiom*, London: Free Association Books.

Bollas, Christopher (1992) *Being a Character: Psychoanalysis and Self Experience*, London and New York: Routledge.

Bollas, Christopher (2000) 'Architecture and the Unconscious', *International Forum of Psychoanalysis*, 9: 28–42. Also in The Evocative Object World, London and New York: Routledge: 47–78.

Bollas, Christopher (2007/2013) *The Freudian Moment*, 2nd edition, London: Karnac Books.

Bollas, Christopher (2009) *The Evocative Object World*, London and New York: Routledge.

Borch-Jacobsen, Mikkel (1991) *The Absolute Master*, Palo Alto, CA: Stanford University Press.

Botting, Fred (2013) *Gothic*, The New Critical Idiom series, London and New York: Routledge.

Bouchard, F. (1995) 'Sigmund Freud and Romain Rolland: Correspondence 1923–1936', *Journal of the American Psychoanalytic Association*, 43: 883–7.

Breton, André (1932/1997) *Communicating Vessels*, trans. Mary Ann Caws, French Modernist Library, new edition, Lincoln NE: University of Nebraska Press.

Breuer, Josef (1893) 'Theoretical', in eds J. Breuer and S. Freud, *Studies of Hysteria*, eds J. Strachey and A. Freud, *The Standard Edition of the Complete Psychological Works of Sigmund Freud*, vol. 2 (1893–1895/2001), London: Vintage: 183–251.

Buchanan, Peter (2012) 'The Big Rethink', Architecture Review, https://www.architectural-review.com/archive/campaigns/the-big-rethink/the-big-rethink-part-1towards-a-complete-architecture/8624049.article (accessed 11/2016).

Burke, Edmund (1757/2008) *A Philosophical Enquiry into the Origin of our Ideas of the Sublime and the Beautiful*, ed. Adam Philips, Oxford World Classics, Oxford: Oxford University Press.

Caird, Edward (1889/2000) *The Critical Philosophy of Immanuel Kant*, Vol. 2, New York: Macmillan.

Calatrava, Santiago (2002) *Conversations with Students*, Cambridge, MA: MIT Press.

Campbell, D.T. (1960) 'Blind Variation and Selective Retention in Creative Thought as in Other Knowledge Processes', *Psychological Review*, 67: 380–400.

Carruthers, Mary (1998/2000) *The Craft of Thought: Meditation, Rhetoric, and the Making of Images, 400–1200*, Cambridge Studies in Medieval Literature, Cambridge: Cambridge University Press.

Camus, Albert (1942/2000) *L'Etranger / The Outsider*, trans. Joseph Laredo, London: Penguin Classics.

Chalup, Stephan K., Hong, Kenny, and Ostwald, Michael J. (2010) 'Simulating Pareidolia of Faces for Architectural Image Analysis', *International Journal of Computer Information Systems and Industrial Management Applications*, 2: 262–78.

Cicero, M. Tullius (1902) *De Oratore*, ed. A.S. Wilkins, Oxford Classical Texts, Oxford: Clarendon Press.

Claparède, Édouard (1908) 'Quelques mots sur la définition de l'hystérie', *Archives de psychologie*, VII, Geneva.

Claxton, Guy (1998) *Hare Brain, Tortoise Mind: Why Intelligence Increases When You Think Less*, new edition, New York: Fourth Estate.

Clayton, Susan D. and Opotow, Susan (eds) (2003) *Identity and the Natural Environment: The Psychological Significance of Nature*, Cambridge, MA: MIT.

Clinebell, John (1996) *Ecotherapy: Healing Ourselves, Healing the Earth*, London and New York: Routledge.

Conway, Daniel W. (1998) 'Answering the Call of the Wild: Walking with Bugbee and Thoreau', *The Personalist Forum*, 14(1): 49–64.

Cook, J. and Klotz, H. (1973) *Conversations with Architects*, New York: Praeger.

Cooper, Clare (1974) 'The House as Symbol of the Self', in eds J. Lang, C. Burnette, W. Moleski, and D. Vachon, *Designing for Human Behavior: Architecture and the Behavioral Sciences*, Community Development Series, New York: Dowden, Hutchinson & Ross: 130–46.

Cooper-White, Pamela (2014) 'A Tale of Two Houses: Küsnacht and Bollingen', part 1, Jung Society of Atlanta, at: www.jungatlanta.com/articles/summer14-two-houses.pdf (accessed 11/2017).

Coverley, M. (2010) *Psychogeography*, Harpenden: Pocket Essentials.

Dalí, Salvador (1930) 'L'Ane pourri', in *Le Surréalisme au Service de la Révolution*, No. 1, Paris: Editions des Cahiers: 9–12.

Davies, Bret W. (2010) 'Translator's Foreword', in Heidegger, Martin (1944/1945/2010) *Conversations on a Country Path*, Bloomington: Indiana University Press.

Davis, Whitney (1995) *Drawing the Dream of the Wolves: Homosexuality, Interpretation, and Freud's Wolf Man*, Theories of Representation and Difference, Bloomington: Indiana University Press.

Davis, Whitney (1996) *Replications: Archaeology, Art, History, Psychoanalysis*, Pennsylvania: Pennsylvania State University Press.

Deamer, Peggy (2004) 'Adrian Stokes: The Architecture of Phantasy and the Phantasy of Architecture', in eds Jerome A. Winer, James William Anderson, and Elizabeth A. Danze, *Psychoanalysis and Architecture, The Annuals of Psychoanalysis*, 33, New York: Institute for Psychoanalysis Chicago, Mental Health Resources: 125–38.

de Botton, Alain (2002) *The Art of Travel*: London: Hamish Hamilton/Penguin Books.

Debord, Guy Louis (1955/2007) 'Introduction to a Critique of Urban Geography', in ed. Ken Knabb *Situationist International Anthology*, Berkeley, CA: Bureau of Public Secrets.

de Certeau, Michel (1980/1984) 'Walking in the City', in *The Practice of Everyday Life*, Berkeley and Los Angeles: University of California Press: 91–110.

Deleuze, Gilles, and Guattari, Félix (1980/2003) *A Thousand Plateaus: Capitalism and Schizophrenia*, trans. Brian Massumi, London and New York: Continuum.

de Maistre, Xavier (1790/2013) *A Journey Around My Room*, trans. Andrew Brown, London: Alma Classics.

Descartes, René (1637/1999) 'Discourse on the Method of Rightly Conducting One's Reason and of Seeking Truth in the Sciences', in *The Philosophical Writings of Descartes*, Vol. 1, trans. John Cottingham, Robert Stoothoff, and Dugald Murdoch, Cambridge: Cambridge University Press: 109–76.

Descartes, René (1641/1996) *Meditations on First Philosophy*, trans. John Cottingham, revised edition, Cambridge: Cambridge University Press.

Donald, James (1999) *Imagining the Modern City*, London: The Athlone Press.

Evernden, Neil (1978) 'Beyond Ecology: Self, Place and the Pathetic Fallacy', *The North American Review*, 263(4): 16–20.

Filarete (Antonio di Pietro Averlino) (c.1464/1965) *Filarete's Treatise on Architecture: Being the Treatise by Antonio di Pietro Averlino, Known as Filarete*, trans. John Spencer, 2 vols., New Haven: Yale University Press.

Fisher, A. (2002) *Radical Ecopsychology: Psychology in the Service of Life*, Albany: SUNY Press.

Flannery, J.G. (1980) 'Freud's Acropolis Revisited', *International Review of Psycho-Analysis*, 7: 347–52.

Francesco di Giorgio, Martini (c.1478–1490/1967) *Trattato di architettura, Ingegneria e Arte Militare*, 2 vols., eds Corrado Maltese and Livia Maltese Degrassi, Edizioni il Polifilo: Milan.

Freud, Ernst L. (1961) *Letters of Sigmund Freud*, trans. T. Stern and J. Stern, New York: Basic Books.

Freud, Sigmund (1896/2001) 'Heredity and the Aetiology of the Neuroses', in eds J. Strachey and A. Freud, The Standard Edition of the Complete Psychological Works of Sigmund Freud, vol. 3, London: Vintage: 141–58.

Freud, Sigmund (1897/2001) 'Draft L. [Notes I]' / 'Draft M. [Notes II]' [May 2, 1897], Pre-Psycho-Analytic Publications and Unpublished Drafts, in eds J. Strachey and A. Freud, *The Standard Edition of the Complete Psychological Works of Sigmund Freud*, vol. 1, London: Vintage: 248–51.

Freud, Sigmund (1899/1985) 'Letter to Fliess: August 6, 1899', in trans. and ed. Jeffrey Moussaieff Masson, *The Complete Letters of Sigmund Freud to Wilhelm Fliess, 1887–1904*, Cambridge, MA: Harvard University Press.

Freud, Sigmund (1900/2001) The Interpretation of Dreams', in eds J. Strachey and A. Freud, *The Standard Edition of the Complete Psychological Works of Sigmund Freud*, vols 4 and 5, London: Vintage.

Freud, Sigmund (1905/2001) 'Jokes and their Relation to the Unconscious', in eds J. Strachey and A. Freud, *The Standard Edition of the Complete Psychological Works of Sigmund Freud*, vol. 8, London: Vintage.

Freud, Sigmund (1910/2001) 'Five Lectures on Psychoanalysis', in eds J. Strachey and A. Freud, *The Standard Edition of the Complete Psychological Works of Sigmund Freud*, vol. 11, London: Vintage: 3–55.

Freud, Sigmund (1913/2001) 'On Beginning the Treatment' (Further Recommendations on the Technique of Psychoanalysis I), in eds J. Strachey and A. Freud, *The Standard Edition of the Complete Psychological Works of Sigmund Freud*, vol. 12: 121–44.

Freud, Sigmund (1914/2001) 'On Narcissism: An Introduction', in eds J. Strachey and A. Freud, *The Standard Edition of the Complete Psychological Works of Sigmund Freud*, vol. 14, London: Vintage: 67–104.

Freud, Sigmund (1915a/2001) 'Thoughts for the Times on War and Death', in eds J. Strachey and A. Freud, *The Standard Edition of the Complete Psychological Works of Sigmund Freud*, vol. 14, London: Vintage: 275–300.

Freud, Sigmund (1915b/2001) 'Instincts and their Vicissitudes', in eds J. Strachey and A. Freud, *The Standard Edition of the Complete Psychological Works of Sigmund Freud*, vol. 14, London: Vintage: 109–40.

Freud, Sigmund (1917a/2001) 'Resistance and Repression', *Introductory Lectures on Psychoanalysis (1916–17)*, in eds J. Strachey and A. Freud, *The Standard Edition of the Complete Psychological Works of Sigmund Freud*, vol. 16, London: Vintage: 286–302.

Freud, Sigmund (1917b/2001) 'A Difficulty in the Path of Psychoanalysis', in eds J. Strachey and A. Freud, *The Standard Edition of the Complete Psychological Works of Sigmund Freud*, vol. 17, London: Vintage: 135–44.

Freud, Sigmund (1919/2001) 'The Uncanny', in eds J. Strachey and A. Freud, *The Standard Edition of the Complete Psychological Works of Sigmund Freud*, vol. 16, London: Vintage: 217–52.

Freud, Sigmund (1921/2001) 'Group Psychology and the Analysis of the Ego', in eds J. Strachey and A. Freud, *The Standard Edition of the Complete Psychological Works of Sigmund Freud*, vol. 18, London: Vintage: 69–144.

Freud, Sigmund (1923/2001) 'The Ego and the Id', in eds J. Strachey and A. Freud, *The Standard Edition of the Complete Psychological Works of Sigmund Freud*, vol. 19, London: Vintage: 12–68.

Freud, Sigmund (1930/2001) 'Civilization and Its Discontents', in eds J. Strachey and A. Freud, *The Standard Edition of the Complete Psychological Works of Sigmund Freud*, vol. 21, London: Vintage: 64–148.

Freud, Sigmund (1936/2001) 'A Disturbance of Memory on the Acropolis', in eds J. Strachey and A. Freud, *The Standard Edition of the Complete Psychological Works of Sigmund Freud*, vol. 22, London: Vintage: 239–50.

Freud, Sigmund (1937/2001) 'Constructions in Analysis', in eds J. Strachey and A. Freud, *The Standard Edition of the Complete Psychological Works of Sigmund Freud (1937–1939)*, vol. 23, London: Vintage: 257–69.

Freud, Sigmund (1940/2001) 'Medusa's Head', in eds J. Strachey and A. Freud, *The Standard Edition of the Complete Psychological Works of Sigmund Freud*, vol. 18, London: Vintage: 273–4.

Freud, Sigmund and Jung, C.G. (1974) *The Freud/Jung Letters: The Correspondence Between Sigmund Freud and C.G. Jung*, ed. William McGuire, trans. Ralph Manheim and R.F.C. Hull, Bollingen Series, New Jersey: Princeton University Press.

Frieden, Ken (1990) *Freud's Dream of Interpretation*, Albany, NY: State University of New York Press.

Gadamer, Hans-Georg (1960/2004) *Truth and Method*, Continuum Impacts series, London and New York: Continuum.

Gagnebin, M. (1994) *Pour Une Esthétique Psychanalytique: L'artiste, stratège de l'inconscient / For a Psychoanalytic Aesthetics: The Artist, Strategist of the Unconscious*, Paris: Paris-Sorbonne University Press.

Geyh, Paula (2006) 'Urban Free Flow: A Poetics of Parkour', *M/C Journal: A Journal of Media and Culture*, 9(3), at: http://journal.media-culture.org.au/0607/06-geyh.php (accessed 10/2017).

Giegerich, Wolfgang (2004) 'The End of Meaning and the Birth of Man: An Essay about the State Reached in the History of Consciousness and an Analysis of C.G. Jung's Psychology Project', *Journal of Jungian Theory and Practice*, 6(1): 1–65.

Gledhill, Martin (2014) *The Tower: Myth and Fiction*, Masters Dissertation, Centre for Psychoanalytic Studies, University of Essex.

Goodman, Nelson (1977) 'When Is Art?' in eds David Perkins and Barbara Leondar, *The Arts and Cognition*, Baltimore, MD: Johns Hopkins University Press: 11–19.

Graafland, Arie (1996) *Architectural Bodies*, ed. Michael Speaks, Rotterdam: 010.

Grotstein, James (1981) *Splitting and Projective Identification*, New York: Jason Aronson.

Grotstein, James (1987) 'An Object Relations Perspective on Resistance in Narcissistic Patients', *Techniques of Working with Resistance*, New York: Jason Aronson: 317–39.

Guillaumin J. (1995) 'Sigmund Freud et Romain Rolland, correspondence 1923-1936', *International Journal of Psychoanalysis*, 76: 1056–60.

Hadjikhani, N., Kveraga, K., Naik, P., and Ahlfors, S.P. (2009) 'Early (N170) Activation of Face-Specific Cortex by Face-Like Objects', *Neuroreport*, 20(4): 403–7.

Hakala, J.T. (2012) *The Art of Scientific Discovery: Creativity, Giftedness, and the Nobel Laureates*, trans. Lissa Hughes and Glyn Hughes, Finland: Ideo Oy.

Hall, James A. (1983) *Jungian Dream Interpretation: A Handbook of Theory and Practice*, Studies in Jungian Psychology by Jungian Analysts series, Toronto: Inner City Books.

Harrison, I.B. (1966) 'A Reconsideration of Freud's "A Disturbance of Memory on the Acropolis" in Relation to Identity Disturbance', *Journal of the American Psychoanalytic Association*, 14: 518–27.

Hart, Vaughan (1994) 'Carl Jung's Alchemical Tower at Bollingen', *Res Anthropology and Aesthetics*, 25: 26–50.

Hauke, Christopher (2000) *Jung and the Postmodern: The Interpretation of Realities*, London and New York: Routledge.

Hauser, Arnold (1965) *Mannerism: The Crisis of the Renaissance and the Origin Modern Art*, 2 vols, Cambridge, MA: Harvard University Press.

Heidegger, Martin (1935/1953) *Introduction to Metaphysics: The Fundamental Questions*, trans. Gregory Fried and Richard Polt, second edition, New Haven and London: Yale University Press.

Heidegger, Martin (1944/1945/2010) *Country Path Conversations*, trans. Bret W. Davies, Bloomington: Indiana University Press.

Heidegger, Martin (1951/2001) 'Building, Dwelling, Thinking' in *Poetry, Language, Thought*, trans. Albert Hofstadter, New York: HarperCollins.

Heidegger, Martin (1951–1952/1968) *What is Called Thinking?* trans. J. G. Gray, New York: Harper & Row.

Hillman, James (1978/2006) 'City and Soul', in ed. Robert J. Lever, *City & Soul*, Uniform edition, New York: Spring: 20–6.

Hillman, James (1982/1992) '*Anima Mundi*: Return of the Soul to the World', in *The Thought of the Heart and Soul of the World*, 5th edition, Dallas TX: Spring: 89–130.

Hillman, James (1986) 'Interiors in the Design of the City: Ceilings', in eds Robert Sardello and Gail Thomas, *Stirrings of Culture: Essays from the Dallas Institute*, Dallas, TX: Dallas Institute Publications: 78–84.

Hillman, James (1991/2006) 'The Repression of the Beauty', in ed. Robert J. Leaver, *City & Soul*, Uniform edition, vol. 2, Connecticut: Spring: 172–86.

Hillman, James (1993a) 'TOWER', typed notes in numbered sections from Box Number: Hillman 185A, Santa Barbara, CA, The James Hillman Collection, Opus Archives.

Hillman, James (1993b) 'DOORS', typed notes in numbered sections from Box Number: Hillman 185A, Santa Barbara, CA, The James Hillman Collection, Opus Archives.

Hillman, James (1994) *Insearch: Psychology and Religion*, Dallas, TX: Spring.

Hillman, James (1995a) 'A Psyche the Size of the Earth: A Psychological Foreword', in eds Theodore Roszak, Mary E. Gomes, Allen D. Kanner, *Ecopsychology: Restoring the Earth/ Healing the Mind*, Berkeley: University of California Press: xvii–xxiii.

Hillman, James (1995b/2006) 'Segregation of Beauty', in ed. Robert J. Leaver, *City & Soul*, Uniform edition, vol. 2, Connecticut: Spring: 187–206.

Hillman, James (1995c/2006) 'Natural Beauty without Nature', in ed. Robert J. Leaver, *City & Soul*, Uniform edition, vol. 2, Connecticut: Spring: 155–71.

Hillman, James (1996) *The Soul's Code*, New York: Random House.

Hillman, James (1997/2006) 'The Cost of the Ugly', in ed. Robert Leaver, *City & Soul*, Putnam, CT: Spring: 194–206.

Hillman, James (1998) *A Blue Fire: Selected Writings by James Hillman*, ed. Thomas Moore, New York: Harper Perennial.

Hillman, James (2006) *City & Soul*, Uniform edition, vol. 2, Putnam, CT: Spring: 194–206.

Hillman, James and Ventura, Michael (1993) *We've Had a Hundred Years of Psychotherapy and the World's Getting Worse*, San Francisco: Harper.

Horowitz, Alexandra (2013) *On Looking: Eleven Walks with Expert Eyes*, New York: Simon & Schuster.

Hough, M. and Mayhew, P. (1985) *Taking Account of Crime: Key Findings from the Second British Crime Survey*. London: HMSO.

Huskinson, Lucy (2004) *Nietzsche and Jung: The Whole Self in the Union of Opposites*, London and New York: Routledge.

Huskinson, Lucy (2013) 'Housing Complexes: Redesigning the House of Psyche in light of a Curious Mistranslation of C.G. Jung Appropriated by Gaston Bachelard', *International Journal of Jungian Studies*, 5(1): 64–80.

Husserl, Edmund (1931/1981) 'The World of the Living Present and the Constitution of the Surrounding World External to the Organism', in eds Peter McCormach and Frederick Elliston, *Husserl Shorter Works*, Indiana: Notre Dame Press.

Ingold, Tim (2011) *Being Alive: Essays on Movement, Knowledge, and Description*, London and New York: Routledge.

Kierkegaard, Søren (1978) *Kierkegaard's Letters and Documents*, trans. Henrik Rosenmeier, New Jersey: Princeton University Press.

Jacobs, Jane (1961/1993) *The Death and Life of Great American Cities*, New York: The Modern Library.

Jencks, Charles (2002) *The New Paradigm in Architecture: The Language of Post-Modernism*, New Haven and London: Yale University Press.

Jones, Ernest (1955) *Life and Works*, vol. 2. New York: Basic Books.

Jones, Lindsay (2000) *The Hermeneutics of Sacred Architecture: Monumental Occasions, Reflections on the Eventfulness of Religious Architecture*, vol. 1: *Experience, Interpretation, Comparison*, Religion of the World series, Cambridge, MA: Harvard University Press.

Jung, Andreas (2009) *House of C.G. Jung: The History and Restoration of the Residence of Emma and Carl Gustav Jung-Rauschenbach*, Asheville, NC: Chrion Publishers.

Jung, C.G. (1902) 'On the Psychology and Pathology of So-valled Occult Phenomena in Psychiatric Studies', in eds Herbert Read, Michael Fordham, Gerhard Adler, *C.G. Jung: The Collected Works*, vol. 1, *Psychiatric Studies*, Bollingen Series, New Jersey: Princeton University Press: 3–88.

Jung, C.G. (1911–12/1952/1990) 'Two Kinds of Thinking', in eds Herbert Read, Michael Fordham, Gerhard Adler, William McGuire, trans. R.F.C. Hull, *C.G. Jung: The Collected Works*, vol. 5, *Symbols of Transformation*, New Jersey: Princeton University Press: 7–33.

Jung, C.G. (1917/1926/1943/1966) 'On the Psychology of the Unconscious', in eds and trans. Gerhard Adler and R.F.C. Hull, *C.G. Jung: The Collected Works*, vol. 7, *Two Essays in Analytical Psychology*, Bollingen Series, New Jersey: Princeton University Press: 1–122.

Jung, C.G. (1921/1992) 'Psychological Types', in eds Michael Fordham and Gerhard Adler, *C.G. Jung: The Collected Works*, vol. 6, *Psychological Types*, trans. R.F.C. Hull, London and New York: Routledge.

Jung, C.G. (1925/1991) *Analytical Psychology: Notes of the Seminar Given in 1925*, Bollingen series, ed. William McGuire, trans. R.F.C. Hull, New Jersey: Princeton University Press.

Jung, C.G. (1927/1970) 'Mind and Earth', in eds Herbert Read, Michael Fordham, and Gerhard Adler, *C.G. Jung: The Collected Works*, vol. 10, Civilization in Transition, trans. R.F.C. Hull, second edition, London and New York: Routledge: 29–49.

Jung, C.G. (1928a/1935/1966) 'The Relations Between the Ego and the Unconscious', in eds and trans. Gerhard Adler and R.F.C. Hull, *C.G. Jung: The Collected Works*, vol. 7, Two Essays in Analytical Psychology, Bollingen Series, New Jersey: Princeton University Press: 123–244.

Jung, C.G. (1928b/1994) *Dream Analysis: Part 1: Notes of the Seminar Given in 1928–30*, London and New York: Routledge.

Jung, C.G. (1934–1939/1989) *Nietzsche's Zarathustra: Notes of a Seminar Given in 1934–1939*, 2 vols, ed. J.L. Jarrett, London: Routledge.

Jung, C.G. (1935/1976) 'The Tavistock Lectures', in eds Gerhard Adler and R.F.C. Hull, *C.G. Jung: The Collected Works*, vol. 18, *The Symbolic Life: Miscellaneous Writings*, trans. Gerhard Adler and R.F.C. Hull, Bollingen Series, New Jersey: Princeton University Press: 5–184.

Jung, C.G. (1936/1980) 'Psychology and Alchemy', in eds Gerhard Adler and R.F.C. Hull, *C.G. Jung: The Collected Works*, vol. 12, *Psychology and Alchemy*, trans R.F.C. Hull, Bollingen Series, New Jersey: Princeton University Press.

Jung, C.G. (1938/1940/1991) 'Psychology and Religion' (The Terry Lectures), in eds Michael Fordham and Gerhard Adler, *C.G. Jung: The Collected Works*, vol. 11, *Psychology and Religion: West and East*, trans. R.F.C. Hull, Bollingen Series, New Jersey: Princeton University Press: 1–168.

Jung, C.G. (1942/1948/1991) 'A Psychological Approach to the Dogma of the Trinity', in eds Michael Fordham and Gerhard Adler, *C.G. Jung: The Collected Works*, vol. 11, *Psychology and Religion: West and East*, trans. R.F.C. Hull, Bollingen Series, New Jersey: Princeton University Press: 169–295.

Jung, C.G. (1945/1954/1983) 'The Philosophical Tree', in eds and trans. Gerhard Adler and R.F.C. Hull, *C.G. Jung: The Collected Works*, vol. 13, *Alchemical Studies*, Bollingen Series, New Jersey: Princeton University Press: 304–482.

Jung, C.G. (1946) 'Analytical Psychology and Education', in eds and trans. Gerhard Adler and R.F.C. Hull, *C.G. Jung: The Collected Works*, vol. 17, *The Development of Personality*, Bollingen Series, New Jersey: Princeton University Press: 63–132.

Jung, C.G. (1947/1954/1960) 'On the Nature of the Psyche', in eds Herbert Read, Gerhard Adler and R.F.C. Hull, *C.G. Jung: The Collected Works*, vol. 8, *The Structure and Dynamics of the Psyche*, trans. R.F.C. Hull, Bollingen Series, New Jersey: Princeton University Press: 343–442.

Jung, C.G. (1951) 'The Psychological Aspects of the Kore', in eds Gerhard Adler and R.F.C. Hull, *C.G. Jung: The Collected Works*, vol. 9 (Part 1), *Archetypes and the Collected Unconscious*, trans. Gerhard Adler and R.F.C. Hull, Bollingen Series, New Jersey: Princeton University Press: 182–206.

Jung, C.G. (1952a/1991) 'Foreword to [R.J.Zwi] Werblowsky's *Lucifer and Prometheus*', in eds Michael Fordham and Gerhard Adler, *C.G. Jung: The Collected Works*, vol. 11, *Psychology and Religion: West and East*, trans. R.F.C. Hull, Bollingen Series, New Jersey: Princeton University Press: 311–15.

Jung, C.G. (1952b/1991) 'Foreword to White's "God and the Unconscious"', in eds Michael Fordham and Gerhard Adler, *C.G. Jung: The Collected Works*, vol. 11, *Psychology and Religion: West and East*, trans. R.F.C. Hull, Bollingen Series, New Jersey: Princeton University Press: 449–67.

Jung, C.G. (1954a) 'Archetypes of the Collected Unconscious', in eds Gerhard Adler and R.F.C. Hull, *C.G. Jung: The Collected Works*, vol. 9 (Part 1), *Archetypes and the Collected Unconscious*, trans. Gerhard Adler and R.F.C. Hull, Bollingen Series, New Jersey: Princeton University Press: 3–41.

Jung, C.G. (1954b/1966) 'On the Psychology of the Unconscious', in eds and trans. Gerhard Adler and R.F.C. Hull, *C.G. Jung: The Collected Works*, vol. 7, *Two Essays in Analytical Psychology*, Bollingen Series, New Jersey: Princeton University Press: 9–122.

Jung, C.G. (1954c/1983) 'The Philosophical Tree', in eds Herbert Read, Michael Fordham, Gerhard Adler and William McGuire, *C.G. Jung: The Collected*

Works, vol. 13, *Alchemical Studies*, trans. R.F.C. Hull, Bollingen Series, New Jersey: Princeton University Press: 251–350.

Jung, C.G. (1955/1987) *Jung Speaking: Interviews and Encounters*, eds William McGuire and R.F.C. Hull, Bollingen Series, New Jersey: Princeton Universtiy Press.

Jung, C.G. (1958/1970) 'Flying Saucers: A Modern Myth of Things Seen in the Skies', in eds Herbert Read, Michael Fordham, and Gerhard Adler, *C.G. Jung: The Collected Works*, vol. 10, *Civilization in Transition*, trans. R.F.C. Hull, second edition, London and New York: Routledge: 307–436.

Jung, C.G. (1959/1970) 'Good and Evil in Analytical Psychology', in eds Herbert Read, Michael Fordham, and Gerhard Adler, *C.G. Jung: The Collected Works*, vol. 10, *Civilization in Transition*, trans. R.F.C. Hull, second edition, London and New York: Routledge: 858–884.

Jung, C.G. (1961a/1976) 'Symbols and the Interpretation of Dreams', in eds Herbert Read, Michael Fordham, Gerhard Adler and William McGuire, *C.G. Jung: The Collected Works*, vol. 18, *The Symbolic Life: Miscellaneous Writings*, trans. R.F.C. Hull, Bollingen Series, New Jersey: Princeton University Press: 185–264.

Jung, C.G. (1961b/1995) *Memories, Dreams, Reflections*, recorded and edited Aniela Jaffé, trans. R. Winston and C. Winston, London: Fontana.

Jung, C.G. (1964) 'Approaching the Unconscious', in eds C.G. Jung and M.-L. von Franz, *Man and his Symbols*, London: Aldus:18–103.

Jung, C.G. (2009) *The Red Book: Liber Novus*. A replica of the red leather-bound folio crafted by Jung between 1915 and 1930, recounting experiences between 1913 and 1916. Philemon, trans. Martin Kyburz, John Peck, and Sonu Shamdasani, New York: W.W. Norton and Company.

Kahn, Louis (1991) 'I love Beginnings', in ed. Alessandra Latour, *Louis I Kahn: Writings, Lectures, Interviews*, New York: Rizzoli International Publishers.

Kant, Immanuel (1764/2011) *Observations on the Feeling of the Beautiful [and Sublime and Other Writings]*, eds Patrick Firerson and Paul Guyer, Cambridge Texts in the History of Philosophy, trans. Paul Guyer, Cambridge: Cambridge University Press.

Kant, Immanuel (1781/1787/1999) *Critique of Pure Reason*, eds and trans. Paul Guyer and Allen W. Wood, The Cambridge Edition of the Works of Immanuel Kant, Cambridge: Cambridge University Press.

Kant, Immanuel (1790/2000) *Critique of the Power of Judgement*, ed. Paul Guyer, *The Cambridge Edition of the Works of Immanuel Kant*, trans. Paul Guyer and Eric Matthews, Cambridge: Cambridge University Press.

Kidel, Mark (1993) *Architecture of the Imagination*, BBC Television series in 5 episodes of 30 minutes each, aired BBC2 July 1993, DVD 1994, Opus Archives, Santa Barbara, CA.

Klein, M. (1946/1991) 'Notes on Some Schizoid Mechanisms', in ed. Juliet Mitchell, *The Selected Melanie Klein*, London: Penguin: 175–200.

Klotz, Heinrich (1984/1988) *The History of Postmodern Architecture*, trans. Radka Donnell, London and Cambridge MA: MIT Press.

Koolhaas, Rem (1976) 'O.M.A.', in *Lotus International*, 11: 34–42.

Koolhaas, Rem (1978/1994) *Delirious New York: A Retroactive Manifesto for Manhattan*, new edition, New York: Monacelli Press.

Koolhaas, Rem and Mau, Bruce (1995), ed. Jennifer Sigler, *S, M, L, XL: O.M.A.*, New York: Monacelli Press, 1998.

Lacan, Jacques (1949/2006) 'The Mirror Stage as Formative of the Function of the *I* Function as Revealed in Psychoanalytic Experience', in *Ecrits: The First Complete Edition in English*, trans. Bruce Fink, New York and London: W.W. Noton: 75–81.

Lacan, Jacques (1953) 'Some Reflections on the Ego', *International Journal of Psychoanalysis*, 34: 15–16.

Lacan, Jacques (1954/1988) *Freud's Papers on Technique 1953–4: The Seminar of Jacques Lacan, Book I*, ed. Jacques-Alain Miller, trans. John Forrester, New York: Norton.

Lafrance, Marc (2013) 'From the Skin Ego to the Psychic Envelope: An Introduction to the Work of Didier Anzieu', in eds Sheila L. Cavanagh, Angela Failler, Rachel Alpha Johnston Hurst, *Skin, Culture, and Psychoanalysis*, Basingstoke: Palgrave: 16–44.

Langer, Susanne (1941/2007) *Philosophy in a New Key: A Study in the Symbolism of Reason, Rite, and Art*, 3rd revised ed., Cambridge, MA: Harvard University Press.

Larson, Judith and Savage, Mark (2004) 'Mystical Emergence: An architectural journey through Jung's Tower', www.iaap.org/congress/barcelona (accessed 5/2009).

Leach, Neil (2005a) 'Vitruvius Crucifixus: Architecture, Mimesis, and the Death Instinct', in eds George Dodds and Robert Tavernor, *Body and Building: Essays on the Changing Relation of body and Architecture*, Cambridge, MA: MIT Press: 210–25.

Leach, Neil (2005b) *Camouflage*, Cambridge, MA: MIT Press.

Leach, Neil (2007) 'Topophilia/Topophobia: The Role of the Environment in the Formation of Identity', in eds Xing Ruan and Paul Hogben, *Topophilia and Topophobia: Reflections on Twentieth-Century Human Habitat*, London and New York: Routledge: 31–43.

Le Corbusier (1948/2004) *Le Modulor: A Harmonious Measure to the Human Scale, Universally Applicable to Architecture and Mechanics*, devised in 1948, first published in 2 vols in 1954 and 1958, Basel and Boston: Birkhäuser.

Lefebvre, Henri (1974/1991) *The Production of Space*, trans. Donald Nicholson-Smith, Oxford and Cambridge, MA: Wiley-Blackwell.

Lowenfeld, Viktor and Brittain, Lambert (1987) *Creative and Mental Growth*, 8th Edition, Upper Saddle River, NJ: Prentice Hall.

Luria, A.R. (1968) *The Mind of a Mnemonist*, trans. Lynn Solotaroff, Cambridge, MA: Harvard University Press.

Lym, Glenn Robert (1980) *A Psychology of Building: How we Shape and Experience our Structured Spaces*, Englewood Cliffs, NJ: Prentice Hall.

Lynch, Kevin (1960) *Image of the City*, Harvard-MIT Joint Center for Urban Studies, Cambridge, MA: MIT Press.

MacCannell, Juliet (2005) 'Freud Space', in eds Jerome A. Winer, James William Anderson, and Elizabeth A. Danze, *Psychoanalysis and Architecture*, The Annuals of Psychoanalysis, Vol. 33, Institute for Psychoanalysis Chicago, New York: Mental Health Resources: 93–107.

Maclagan, David (2001) *Psychological Aesthetics: Painting, Feeling and Making Sense*, London: Jessica Kingsley Publishers.

Maguire, M. (1980) 'The Impact of Burglary Upon Victims', *The British Journal of Criminology*, 20 (3): 261–275.

Mahon, Eugene (2005) 'Dreams of Architecture and the Architecture of Dreams', *Annual of Psychoanalysis*, 33: 25–37.

Mallgrave, Harry Francis (2010) *The Architect's Brain: Neuroscience, Creativity, and Architecture*, Massachusetts and London: Willey-Blackwell.

Masson, J.M. and Masson, T.C. (1978) 'Buried Memories on the Acropolis: Freud's response to Mysticism and Anti-Semitism', *International Journal of Psychoanalysis*, 59: 199–208.

McDonough, Tom (2004) 'The Naked City', in *Guy Debord and the Situationist International: Texts and Documents*, Cambridge, MA: MIT Press: 241–65.

McGrath, W.J. (1986) *Freud's Discovery of Psychoanalysis: The Politics of Hysteria*, Ithaca, NY: Cornell University Press.

Meltzer, Donald (1975/2008) *Explorations in Autism: A Psychoanalytic Study*, London: Karnac.

Merleau-Ponty, M. (1945/1996) *Phenomenology of Perception*, trans. Colin Smith, London and New York: Routledge.

Merleau-Ponty, M. (1964/1969) *The Visible and the Invisible*, ed. Claude Lefort, trans. Alphonso Lingis, Evanston, IL: Northwestern University Press.

Moore, Richard A. (1980) 'Alchemical and Mythical Reference Themes in the Poem of the Right Angle, 1945–1965', *Oppositions*, 19/20: 111–39.

Mugerauer, Robert (1995) *Interpreting Environments: Tradition, Deconstruction, Hermeneutics*, Austin: University of Texas Press.

Myers, Steve (2009) 'The Cryptomnesic Origins of Jung's Dream of the Multi-Storeyed House', *Journal of Analytical Psychology*, 54(4): 513–31.

Nicholsen, Shierry Weber (2002) *The Love of Nature and the End of the World*, Cambridge, MA: MIT Press.

Niemeyer, Oscar (2000) *The Curves of Time: The Memoirs of Oscar Niemeyer*, London: Phaidon.

Nietzsche, Friedrich (1872/1967) *The Birth of Tragedy From the Spirit of Music*, trans. W. Kaufmann, New York: Vintage.

Ogden, Thomas (1989) *The Primitive Edge of Experience*, New York: Jason Aronson.

O'Keefe, J. and Nadal, L. (1978) *The Hippocampus as a Cognitive Map*, Oxford: Oxford University Press.

Ostrihanska, Z. and Wojcik, D. (1993) 'Burglaries as Seen by the Victims', *International Review of Victimology*, 2(3): 217–26.

Otto, Rudolf (1917/1958) *The Idea of the Holy: An Inquiry into the Non-Rational Factors in the Idea of the Divine and its Relation to the Rational*, trans. John W. Harvey, Oxford: Oxford University Press.

Pallasmaa, Juhani (2000) 'Stairways of the Mind', *International Forum of Psychoanalysis*, 9: 7–18.

Pallasmaa, Juhani (1996/2005) *The Eyes of Skin: Architecture and the Senses*, London and New Jersey: John Wiley.

Phillips, Adam (2013) Interview for BBC Radio 4 programme, *The Uncanny*, 28 minutes, broadcast 28 June 2012/16 Sept. 2013.

Pile, Steve (2005) *Real Cities: Modernity, Space and the Phantasmagorias of City Life*, London and New York: Sage Publications.

Plato (1997) *Cratylus*, trans. C.D.C. Reeve, in ed. John M. Cooper, *Plato: The Complete Works*, Indianapolis, IN: Hackett.

Plato (2013) *Republic*, ed. and trans. Chris Emlyn-Jones and William Preddy, in two vols, Loeb Classical Library, Cambridge, MA: Harvard University Press.

Poincaré, Henri (1908/1913) *The Foundations of Science, Science and Hypothesis: The Value of Science and Method*, trans. George Bruce Halsted, New York and Garrison: The Science Press.

Potolsky, Matthew (2006) *Mimesis: The New Critical Idiom*, London and New York: Routledge.

Quintilian, M. Fabius (1970) *Institutio Oratoria*, ed. M. Winterbottom, 2 vols., Oxford Classical Texts, Oxford: Clarendon Press.

Rappolt, M. (2008) *Gehry Draws*, Cambridge MA: MIT Press.

Rawlinson, C. and Guaralda, M. (2011) 'Play in the City: Parkour and Architecture', in The First International Postgraduate Conference on Engineering, Designing and Developing the Built Environment for Sustainable Wellbeing, 27–29 April, Brisbane: Queensland University of Technology.

Redfearn, J.W.T. (1982) 'When are Things Persons and Persons Things?' *Journal of Analytical Psychology*, 27: 215–37.

Reik, Theodor (1948/1983) *Listening with the Third Ear*, New York: Farrar Straus and Giroux.

Rendell, Jane (2012) 'The Architecture of Psychoanalysis: Constructions and Associations', in eds O. Knellessen and H. Mooshammer, *Bauarten von Sexualität, Körper, Phantasmen: Architektur und Psychoanalyse / Ways of Building Sexuality, Bodies, Phantasms: Architecture and Psychoanalysis*, Zurich: Scheidegger and Spiess. See also: www.janerendell.co.uk/chapters/the-architecture-of-psychoanalysis-constructions-and-associations (accessed 9/2016).

Resina, Joan (2003) 'Ana Ozores's Nerves', *Hispanic Review*, 71(2): 229–52.

Richards, Simon (2003) *Le Corbusier and the Concept of Self*, New Haven: Yale University Press.

Rilke, Rainer Maria (1910/1992) *The Notebooks of Malte Laurids Brigge*, trans. Herter Norton, New York and London: WW Norton.

Ritter, S.M. and Dijksterhuis, A. (2014) 'Creativity—The Unconscious Foundations of the Incubation Period', *Frontiers in Human Neuroscience*, at http://doi.org/10.3389/fnhum.2014.00215

Robert, Francois and Robert, Jean (2000) *Faces*, San Francisco: Chronicle Books.

Rodman, F. Robert (2005) 'Architecture and the True Self', in eds Jerome A. Winer, James William Anderson, and Elizabeth A. Danze, *Psychoanalysis and Architecture*, The Annuals of Psychoanalysis, 33, Institute for Psychoanalysis Chicago, New York: Mental Health Resources: 57–66.

Rose, Gilbert J. (1980/1986) *The Power of Form: A Psychoanalytic Approach to Aesthetic Form*, Madison, CT: International Universities Press.

Rossi, Aldo (1981/2010) *A Scientific Autobiography*, Cambridge, MA: MIT Press.

Roszak, Theodore (2002) *Voice of the Earth: An Exploration of Ecopsychology*, new edition, Boston: Phanes Press.

Roszak, Theodore, Gomes, Mary E., and Kanner, Allen D. (eds) (2002) *Ecopsychology: Restoring the Earth/Healing the Mind*, Berkeley: University of California Press.

Rousseau, Jean-Jacques (1782a/2011) *Reveries of a Solitary Walker*, trans. Russell Goulbourne, Oxford World Classics, Oxford: Oxford University Press.

Rousseau, Jean-Jacques (1782b/1953) *Confessions*, trans. J. Cohen, London: Penguin Classics.

Ruan, Xing and Hogben, Paul (eds) (2007) 'Topo-philia and -phobia', in eds Xing Ruan and Paul Hogben, *Topophilia and Topophobia: Reflections on Twentieth-Century Human Habitat*, London and New York: Routledge: 12–21.

Ruskin, John (1849/2000) *The Seven Lamps of Architecture*, New York: Dover Publications.

Rust, Mary-Jayne (2006) 'Creating Psychotherapy for a Sustainable Future', *Psychotherapy and Politics International*, 2(2): 157–70.

Rykwert, Joseph (1972) *On Adam's House in Paradise: The Idea of the Primitive Hut in Architectural History*, Museum of Modern Art, Cambridge, MA: MIT Press.

Rykwert, Joseph (1996) *The Dancing Column: On Order in Architecture*, Cambridge, MA: MIT Press.

Saari, Carolyn (2002) *The Environment: Its Role in Psychosocial Functioning and Psychotherapy*, New York: Columbia University Press.

Sadler, Simon (1999) *The Situationist City*, new edition, Cambridge, MA: MIT Press.

Saint Teresa of Jesus (Ávila) (1577/1944) *The Interior Castle: or The Mansions* (trans. *A Discalced Carmelite*, Catholic Publishing), South Ascot, Bath: The Pitman Press.

Samuel, Flora (2002) 'Animus, Anima and the Architecture of Le Corbusier', *Harvest Journal for Jungian Studies*, 48(2): 42–60.

Samuels, Andrew (1989) *The Plural Psyche: Personality, Morality and the Father*, London and New York: Routledge.

Sanders, Joel (1996) *Stud: Architectures of Masculinity*, New York: Princeton Architectural Press.

Sardello, Robert J. (1986) 'A Note on Old and New Buildings', in eds Robert Sardello and Gail Thomas, *Stirrings of Culture: Essays From the Dallas Institute*, Dallas TX: The Dallas Institute: 71–4.

Sawyer, K.R., John-Steiner, V., Moran, S., Sternberg, R.J., Feldman, D.H., Gardner, H., Nakamura, J., Csikszentmihalyi, M. (2003) *Creativity and Development*, Oxford: Oxford University Press.

Scherner, Karl Albert (1861) *Das Leben des Traumes*, Berlin: Verlag von Heinrich Schindler.

Schwaller de Lubicz, R.A. (1949/1981) *The Temple in Man: Sacred Architecture and the Perfect Man*, trans. Robert Lawlor and Deborah Lawlor, illustrated by Lucie Lamy, Vermont: Inner Traditions.

Scruton, Roger (1979) *Aesthetics of Architecture*, London: Methuen.

Seamon, David (2000) 'Concretizing Heidegger's Notion of Dwelling: The Contributions of Thomas Thiis-Evensen and Christopher Alexander', in ed. Eduard Führ, *Building and Dwelling*, Munich and New York: Waxmann: 189–202.

Searles, Harold (1960) *The Nonhuman Environment in Normal Development and in Schizophrenia*, Madison, CT: International Universities Press.

Shapland, Joanna and Hall, Matthew (2007) 'What Do We Know About the Effects of Crime on Victims?' *International Review of Victimology*, 14: 175–217.

Sharr, Adam (2006) *Heidegger's Hut*, Cambridge, MA: MIT Press.

Shover, N. (1991) 'Burglary', *Crime and Justice*, 14: 73–113.

Simmel, Georg (1909/1994) 'Brücke und Tür' / 'Bridge and Door', trans. Mark Ritter, *Theory, Culture & Society*, February 1994, 11(1): 5–10.

Simmons, Laurence (2006) *Freud's Italian Journey* (Psychoanalysis and Culture), Amsterdam and New York: Rodopi.

Simonton, D.K. (1988) *Scientific Genius: A Psychology of Science*, Cambridge: Cambridge University Press.

Slochower, H. (1970) 'Freud's déjà vu on the Acropolis: A Symbolic Relic of "mater nuda"', *Psychoanalytic Quarterly*, 39: 90–102.

Slochower, H. (1971) 'Freud's Gradiva: Mater Nuda Rediviva: A Wish-Fulfilment of the "Memory" on the Acropolis', *Psychoanalytic Quarterly*, 40: 646–62.

Smith, Edward L. (1985/2001) *The Body in Psychotherapy*, Jefferson NC: McFarland.

Sonnenberg, Stephen M. (2005) 'What Can Psychoanalysis Learn from an Enhanced Awareness of Architecture and Design?', in eds Jerome A. Winer, James William Anderson, and Elizabeth A. Danze, *Psychoanalysis and Architecture*, The Annuals of Psychoanalysis, 33, New York: Institute for Psychoanalysis Chicago, Mental Health Resources: 39–56.

Stärcke, August (1921) 'The Castration Complex', *International Journal of Psychoanalysis*, 2: 179–201.

Steiner, George (1991) *Real Presences*, Chicago: University of Chicago Press.

Stokes, Adrian (1951a/1978) *The Critical Writings of Adrian Stokes*, II, London: Thames and Hudson.

Stokes, Adrian (1951b) *Smooth and Rough*, London: Faber and Faber.

Stokes, Adrian (1965/2001) *The Invitation of Art*, London and New York: Routledge.

Stokes, Adrian (1972) *The Image of Form: Selected Writings of Adrian Stokes*, ed. Richard Wollheim, New York: Harper and Row.

Sugarman, S. (1998) *Freud on the Acropolis: Reflections on a Paradoxical Response to the Real*, Boulder CO: Westview.

Sussman, Ann and Hollander, Justin B. (2015) *Cognitive Architecture: Designing for How We Respond to the Built Environment*, London and New York: Routledge.

Thiis-Evensen, Thomas (1990) *Archetypes in Architecture*, Oslo: Scandinavian University Press.

Tschumi, Bernard (1996) *Architecture and Disjunction*, Cambridge, MA: MIT Press.

Tuan, Yi-Fu (1974) *Topophilia: A Study of Environmental Perception, Attitudes, and Values*, Englewood Cliffs, NJ: Prentice-Hall.

Tuan, Yi-Fu (1977/2001) *Space and Place*, Minneapolis: University of Minnesota Press.

Tuan, Yi-Fu (2007) 'Time, Space, and Architecture: Some Philosophical Musings', in eds Xing Ruan and Paul Hogben, *Topophilia and Topophobia: Reflections on Twentieth-Century Human Habitat*, London and New York: Routledge: 22–30.

Ulnik, Jorge (2008) *Skin in Psychoanalysis*, London: Karnac.

Venturi, Robert (1966) *Complexity and Contradiction in Architecture*, New York: The Museum of Modern Art.

Venturi, Robert (2004) *Architecture as Signs and Systems: For a Mannerist Time*, The William E. Massey Sr. Lectures in the History of American Civilization, Cambridge, MA: Belknap Press.

Vidler, Anthony (1992) *The Architectural Uncanny: Essays in the Modern Unhomely*, Cambridge, MA: MIT Press.

Vitruvius (Marcus Vitruvius Pollio) (1486/1999) *Ten Books on Architecture*, trans. Ingrid D. Rowland, commentary and illustrations by Thomas Noble Howe, Cambridge: Cambridge University Press.

Wallas, Graham (1926/2014) *The Art of Thought*, Tunbridge Wells: Solis Press.

Walter, E.V. (1988) *Placeways: A Theory of the Human Environment*, Chapel Hill and London: University of North Carolina Press.

Watkins, Mary (2008/2012) '"Breaking the Vessels": Archetypal Psychology and the Restoration of Culture, Community, and Ecology', in ed. Stanton Marlan, *Archetypal Psychologies: Reflections in Honor of James Hillman*, Studies in Archetypal Psychology series, Louisiana: Spring: 415–39.

Werman, D.S. (1977) 'Sigmund Freud and Romain Rolland', *International Review of Psycho-Analysis*, 4: 225–42.

Whitehead, Christiania (2003) *Castles of the Mind: A Study of Medieval Architectural Allegory*, Religion and Culture in the Middle Ages series, Cardiff: Wales University Press.

Wigley, Mark (1993) *The Architecture of Deconstruction: Derrida's Haunt*, Cambridge, MA: MIT Press.

Winnicott, D.W. (1960) 'The Theory of the Parent–Infant Relationship', *International Journal of Psychoanalysis*, 41: 585–95.

Winnicott, D.W. (1965) 'The Maturational Processes and the Facilitating Environment: Studies in the Theory of Emotional Development', *The International Psycho-Analytical Library*, London: The Hogarth Press and the Institute of Psycho-Analysis: 1–276.

Winnicott, D.W. (1967) 'The Location of Cultural Experience', *International Journal of Psychoanalysis*, vol. 48 (3): 368–372.

Winnicott, D.W. (1971) *Playing and Reality*, Routledge Classics, London and New York: Routledge.

Woodman, Ellis (2010) 'Strata Tower Wins 2010 Carbuncle Cup', Building Design, www.bdonline.co.uk/strata-tower-wins-2010-carbuncle-cup/5004110.article

Worringer (1911/1964) *Form Problems of the Gothic*, trans. Herbert Read, New York: Schocken Books.

Wortis, Joseph (1954) *Fragments of an Analysis with Freud*, New York: Simon and Schuster.

Yates, Frances A. (1966/1992) *The Art of Memory*, new edition, London: Pimlico.

Zevi (1948/1993) *Architecture as Space: How to Look at Architecture*, 2nd revised edition, Cambridge, MA: Da Capo Press.

Ziolkowski, Theodore (1999) *The View from the Tower: Origins of an Antimodernist Image*, Princeton, NJ: Princeton University Press.

Index